IMAGES
of America

EAST CHICAGO

On the Cover: A group of Inland Steel Company workers wave for the camera in this 1942 photograph. (Courtesy of the Calumet Regional Archives, Indiana University.)

IMAGES
of America

EAST CHICAGO

Jane and Evan Ammeson
with an Introduction by Andy Prieboy

ARCADIA
PUBLISHING

ISBN 978-1-4671-1500-1

Published by Arcadia Publishing
Charleston, South Carolina

Printed in the United States of America

Library of Congress Control Number: 2015942101

For all general information, please contact Arcadia Publishing:
Telephone 843-853-2070
Fax 843-853-0044
E-mail sales@arcadiapublishing.com
For customer service and orders:
Toll-Free 1-888-313-2665

Visit us on the Internet at www.arcadiapublishing.com

We dedicate this book in memory of Dan and Lorraine Simon, our parents and grandparents and true East Chicago residents. And also to Nia Ammeson and Aden Kamala, beloved members of our family.

Contents

ACKNOWLEDGMENTS

One of the wonderful things about working on a book like this is getting to renew friendships and meet new people who also treasure the town where I grew up and where my son, Charles Evan Ammeson, often visited and works hard to preserve its history. This seems particularly true in East Chicago, which despite its many challenges and changes, still holds a great place in people's hearts.

We would like to thank many people and organizations. They include Mary Ben Young, who, at 96, remembered so much about Indiana Harbor history and its Romanian culture. Coincidentally, she and her parents lived above my grandparents' dairy for several years when she was quite young (the photograph is included in this book). Of course, there is Arch McKinley, an invaluable chronicler of East Chicago history; Steve McShane at the Indiana University Northwest Calumet Regional Archives; Debra Powers, East Chicago Room, East Chicago Public Library; Lake County Public Library, Daniese Sprague; Violet Strimbu; and Steve Shook, who has a marvelous photographic collection and is generous in sharing it. Also, there is Andrew Prieboy, an Indiana Harbor fanatic like me who, though we had never met in the time we grew up in Indiana Harbor, bonded with me decades later over our shared past. Andy lives in Malibu, California, and is a professional musician. Though his world is in many ways vastly different from the streets of Indiana Harbor, he has never lost his passion for the city and the icons from its past.

Other wonderful memory keepers include the Honorable Lorenzo Arredondo, who introduced me to his sister Juanita Sanchez and brother Ray Arredondo. Ray, with his wife, Trish, wrote *Maria's Journey*, a fantastic book about his mother that in so many ways chronicles not only a family but also East Chicago itself. I appreciate the support of Carole Wilson Yeager and her sister Leona Buchan, Anna Manolios Williams, Steve Spicer, and the Facebook community of East Chicago—particularly the fans and contributors of the "You Know You're from East Chicago Harbor If . . ." page.

—Jane Simon Ammeson

INTRODUCTION

In 1887, a clique of cigar-chomping tycoons transformed the pristine wetlands of northwest Indiana into a smoking, clanging, shrieking industrial Oz called East Chicago. Jane Simon Ammeson's *East Chicago* tells the pictorial history of the city, its industry, and the people who did the dirty work and made the best of it. Though the idea of a super-city at the base of Lake Michigan had long inflamed imaginations, the land lay largely dormant. Corrugated with rolling dunes, deep swamps, and tangled forests, the area was listed as an impassible morass on a mid-19th-century topographical map. That all changed in 1887.

At that point, the tycoons bought land, had a rail line built to the future site of Standard Steel, and a town was planned. The workers came, a canal was mapped out, and the story begins. Within four decades, there would be over 50 factories, two main districts, two illustrious harbors, and thousands of people from around the world busy at work.

The fortunes of East Chicago would rise and fall with the needs of the nation. Civic expansion followed the wealth created by World Wars I and II. In the 1920s, East Chicago celebrated its success with public pools and the planting of thousands of trees. By the 1950s, in the wake of World War II, urban renewal attempted to replace the grim and grimy with a new industrial utopia. However, by the 1970s the boom was over, despite optimistic plans and good intentions. Sadly, no grand new city emerged. Sheer determination might have carried East Chicago through the Great Depression, but the original city, "The 20th Century Wonder," would struggle to survive the collapse of American industry in the 1980s.

The story of East Chicago is the story of 20th-century America told in miniature.

The East Chicago I knew was a fortress of steel mills, oil refineries, chemical plants, and lead mills—in essence, a walled city whose interior was a clamorous, often claustrophobic, environment. Different languages, races, nationalities, accents, foods, faiths, music, and cultures were all a part of daily life.

Growing up in the Harbor, as I did in the 1960s, the great American dream seemed indestructible. We knew that Inland Steel—or one of many factories—would always have a job for us. We believed that union wages and benefits, college education for the kids, and a new house in Prairie Park were facts of life. My neighbors, like my classmates, were international and diverse: Romanians, Jews, African Americans, Croatians, Serbians, Poles, Mexicans, Germans, Greeks, Lithuanians, Italians, and more. Some, like me, were second-generation American, some first-generation, and some had just arrived. Every block seemed to have a church or temple, and Main Street hummed while Four Corners throbbed. Mills worked at full capacity, and cars were big, thirsty, and flashy. When shifts ended, traffic inched up and down Euclid Avenue and the two-lane blacktop version of Cline Avenue. The air was acrid and sooty, a harsh chemical scent mixing with the cold, fishy breath of the lake.

And music! The endless trains clacked, the mill whistles wailed, and forges thumped while the Washington Park jukebox belted James Brown all summer long. At the weddings and festivals, there were Mexican bands, soul bands, Polish bands, Greek bands, and Croatian and Serbian bands. And the people all did their special dances, sang their treasured songs, and served their glorious traditional dishes.

I am very grateful for my upbringing in East Chicago and the Harbor. When I left in 1973 to make my way in the world, I felt like a childhood spent there had blessed me with a deeper understanding of humanity in all its many delightful manifestations. No matter where I went on this planet, I was already at home.

Jane Simon Ammeson and I grew up a few blocks apart. Her father taught my mother and father at Washington High School. Though she lived a house or so away from those wild-ass friends of mine, somehow we never met. At this writing, we have still to meet in person. Ours is a friendship based on words and images about East Chicago.

A posting I encountered online had me debating East Chicago trivia with Jane. This led to friendly e-mail correspondence, where we exchange pictures and information of our hometown's past. As it turns out, she and I—oblivious to one another—explored the same wild patch of prairies and swamps—a remnant of the original wetlands—behind Franklin School. She once complained that she and her girlfriends would build cunning, complex forts among the cottonwoods only to find them destroyed the next time she visited. I explained, "That was just tradition out there. You'd build a fort and someone else would wreck it. They wrecked mine. I wrecked theirs. It was just the rules of the prairies."

So, I want to congratulate Jane Simon Ammeson on the publication of this, her latest book. And Jane, sorry I wrecked your fort.

—Andy Prieboy
Malibu, California

One

Beginnings

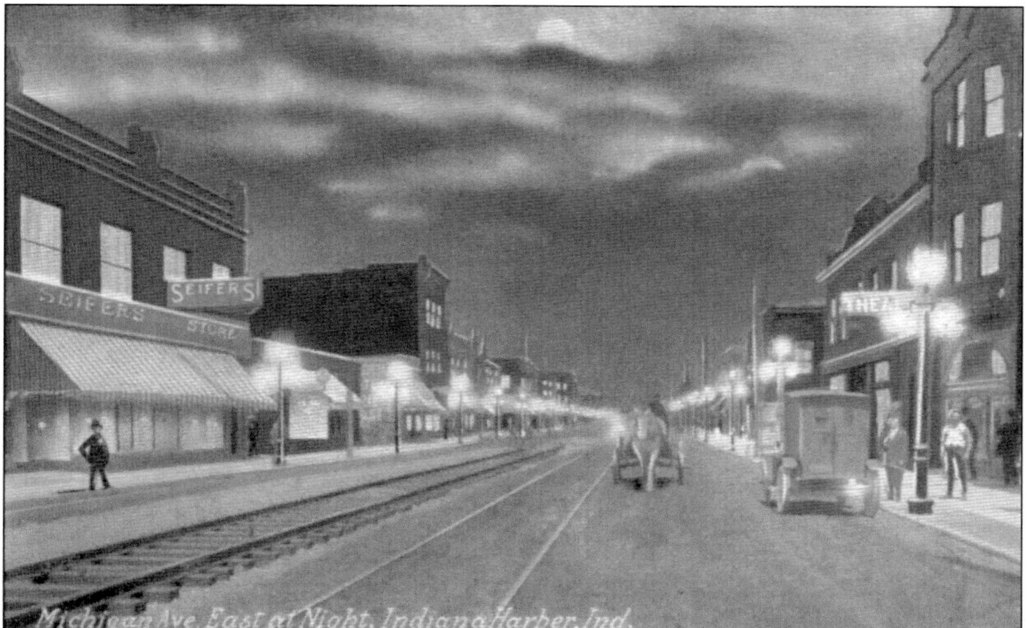

Scenes of East Chicago, romantic in an urban industrial way, inspired locals to quote Henry Wadsworth Longfellow in describing the newly emerging city: "And far in the hazy distance / Of that lovely night in June, / The blaze of the flaming furnace / Gleamed redder than the moon." (Courtesy of the Simon family.)

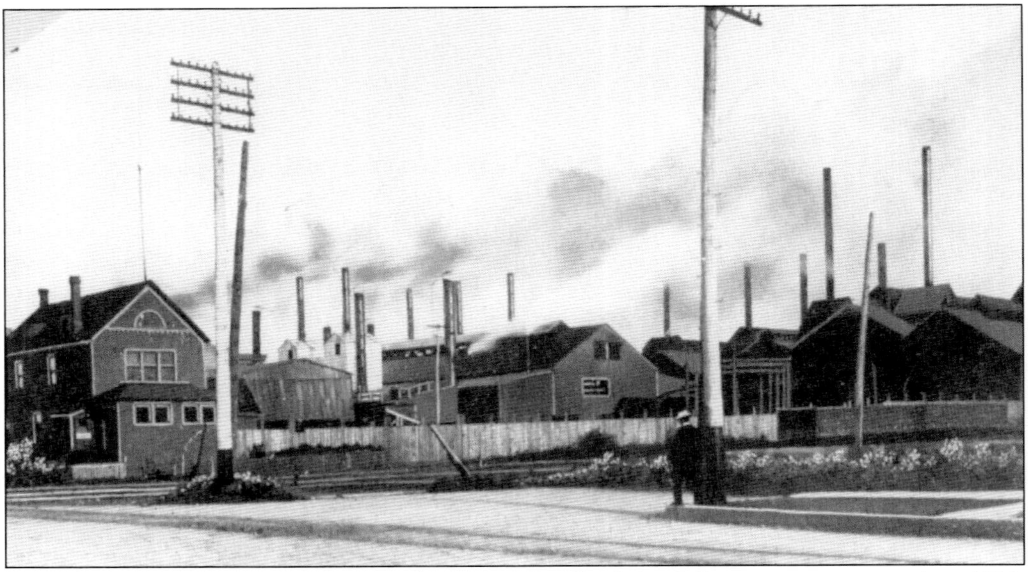

Inland Iron Works, the precursor to the gigantic Inland Steel Company, is pictured in 1888. What would be called the "Workshop of the World" began on inhospitable land—swales, dunes, and marshes. But the city's closeness to Chicago and the visions of British financiers and local promoters turned the area into an industrial magnet. (Courtesy of the Calumet Regional Archives, Indiana University.)

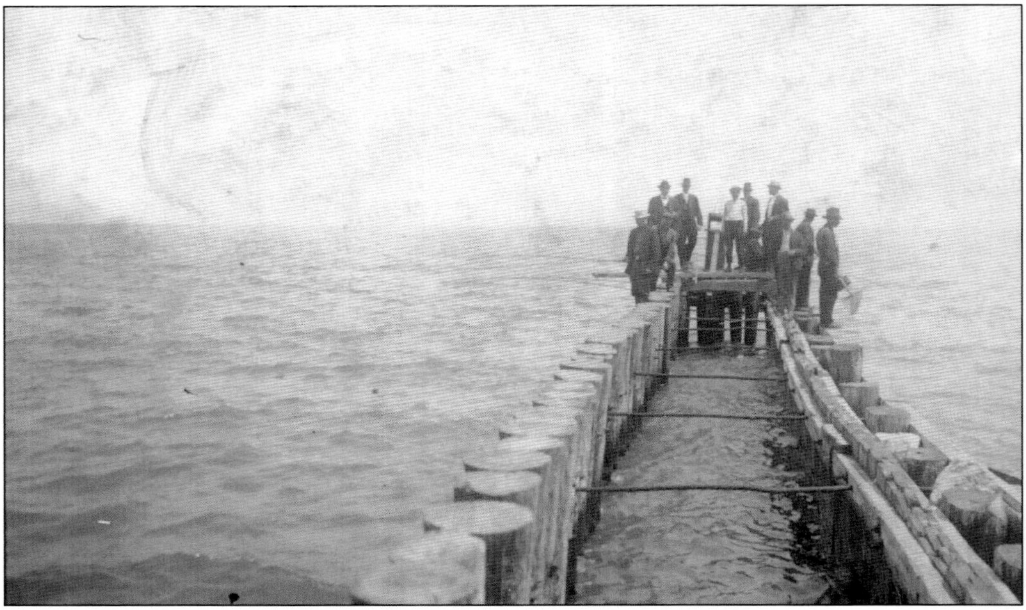

Dominick Mutter, the first settler in Indiana Harbor, established a 120-acre farm in 1857. Six years later, Jacob Forsyth bought Mutter's property, building a sawmill, trading post, and housing for his workers. It was named Casella (also spelled Cassello in some old records) after Ella Case, the wife of railroad president George Case. In 1871, just a day after the Great Chicago Fire, Casella burned down. (Courtesy of Andrew Prieboy.)

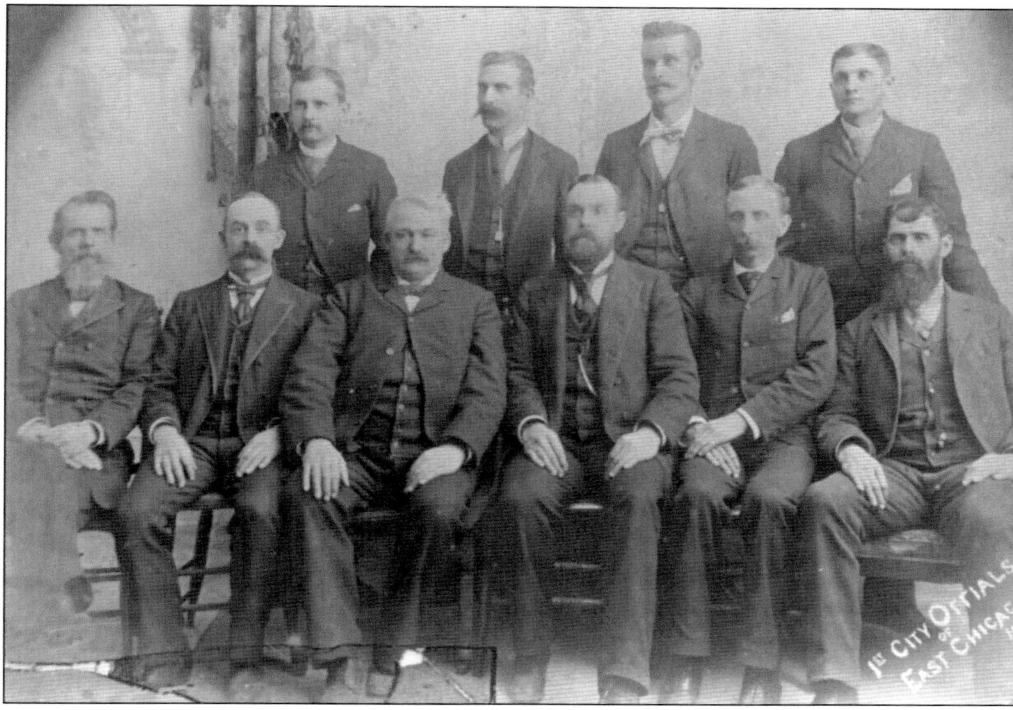

East Chicago became a city on March 14, 1893, when voters elected their first officers and councilmen. From left to right are (first row) Byron Cheney, justice of the peace; John M. White, alderman; Robert Ross, alderman; William H. Penman, mayor; Louis T. Loucks, alderman; and Jule C. Pepin, alderman; (second row) Edwin S. Gilbert, clerk; Frank W. Clinton, treasurer; Neil Patterson, police chief; and E.S. Yaste, alderman. (Courtesy of the Calumet Regional Archives, Indiana University.)

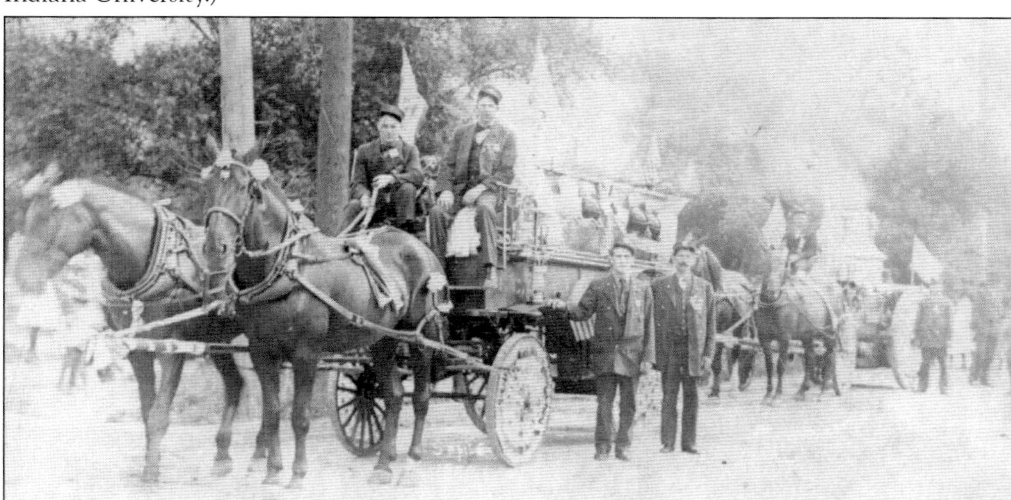

The fire department had to borrow horses from Maxwell's livery stable whenever a fire alarm went off. It frequently took around 30 minutes to get the machinery ready and moving. In the time of wood buildings, that frequently meant an edifice was gone before the firemen (all men back then) arrived. (Courtesy of the Calumet Regional Archives, Indiana University.)

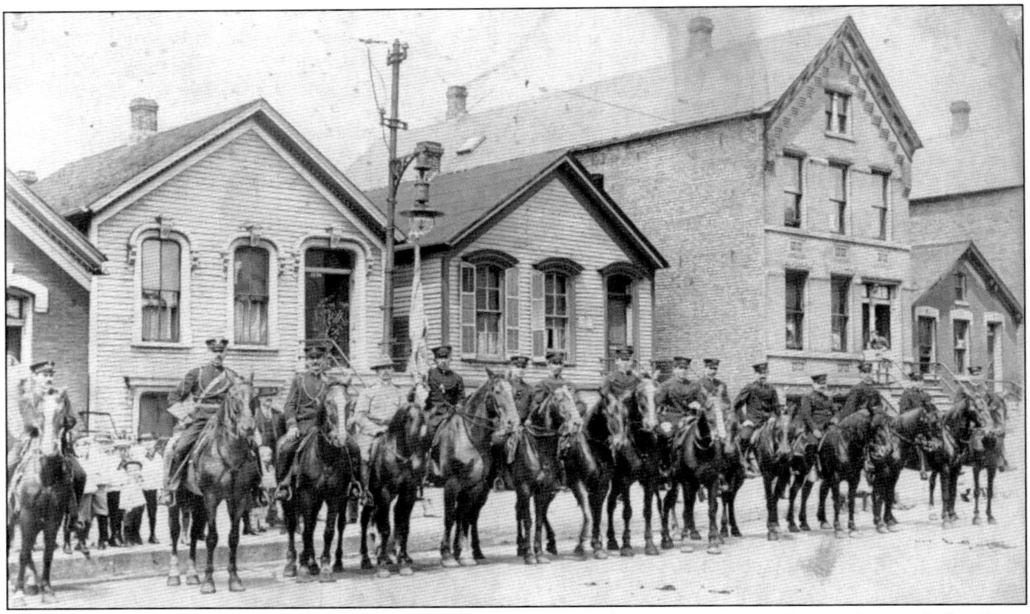

Though the source for this photograph identifies it as showing mounted members of the East Chicago Police Department, they may have been part of a cavalry unit based in Indiana. In 1890, East Chicago had about 1,255 citizens; by 1900, that number had increased to 3,441. With such a large influx of workers, many without the constraints of their families, a policeman's job was a busy one. (Courtesy of the East Chicago Public Library.)

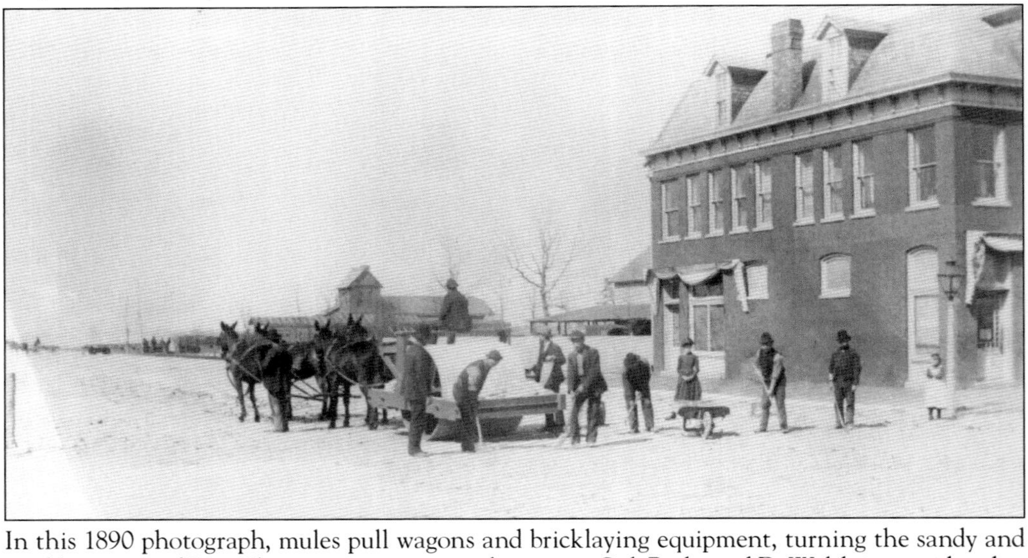

In this 1890 photograph, mules pull wagons and bricklaying equipment, turning the sandy and muddy terrain of East Chicago into streets and avenues. Col. Redmond D. Walsh is considered to be the "Father of East Chicago," erecting many of its first buildings. To create streets, he bought 27 mules from Jacob Forsyth, but when he decided the animals were not worth the $10 he paid for them, Walsh sued Forsyth, and the two fought a long court battle. Eventually, Forsyth was ordered to pay Walsh $600. At right is the first building constructed in East Chicago. Located at the corner of Forsyth and Chicago Avenues, it was the home of George Neer, whose wife was the first woman to live in the new city. (Courtesy of the Calumet Regional Archives, Indiana University.)

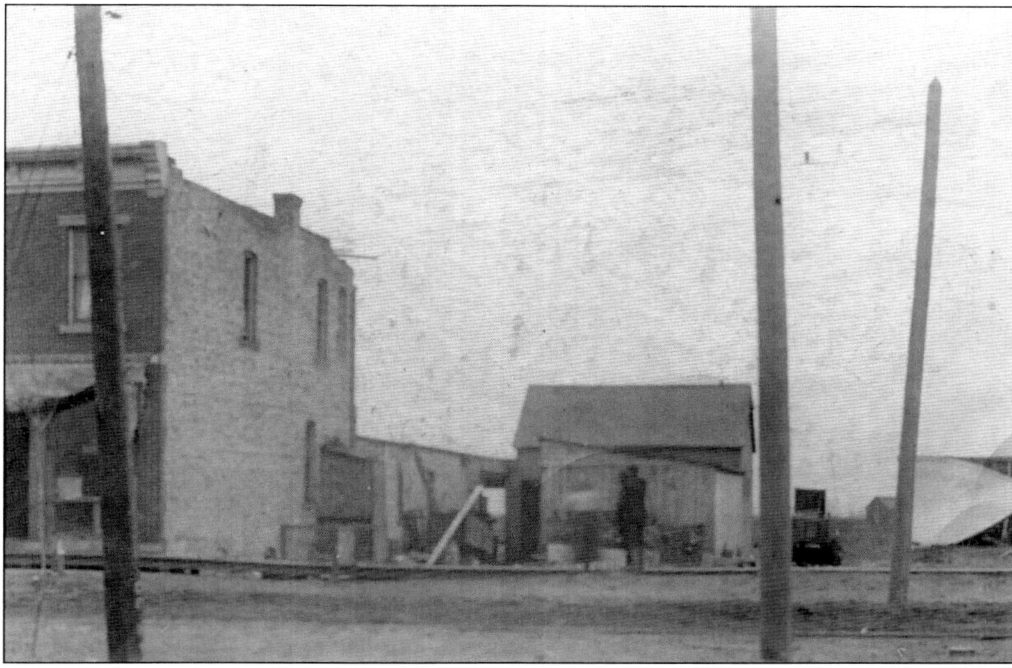

In 1889, Andrew Wickey opened the Famous Manufacturing Company, supplying electricity to the town of East Chicago, which was not incorporated as a city until 1893. (Courtesy of the Calumet Regional Archives, Indiana University.)

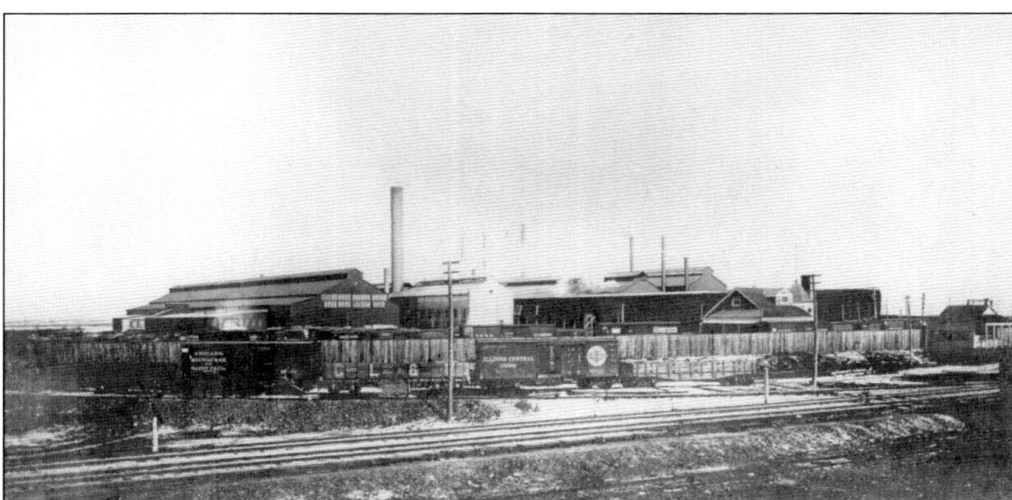

On March 26, 1901, Albert DeWolfe Erskine offered the Block family, owners of Inland Steel, 50 acres of free land at Poplar Point if they agreed to construct a steel mill that would cost around $1 million. Their acceptance depended upon Erskine guaranteeing both a harbor and belt railroad be built to service their plant. (Courtesy of the Calumet Regional Archives, Indiana University.)

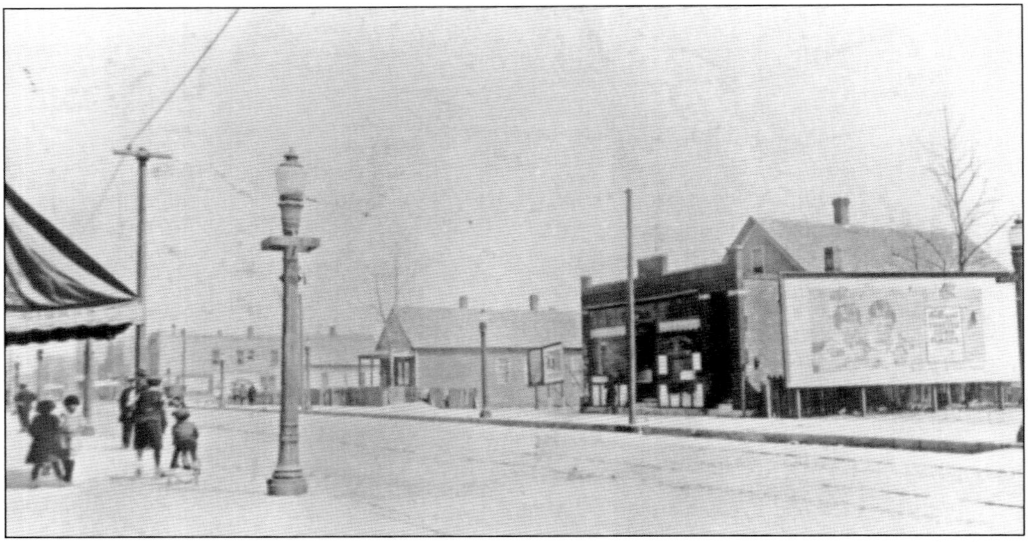

This early Indiana Harbor photograph looks northeast at the corner of 139th and Cedar (later Main) Streets. Board sidewalks, as seen here, made it easier to get around the city. Otherwise, the dirt streets were dusty in dry weather and muddy when wet. (Courtesy of the East Chicago Public Library.)

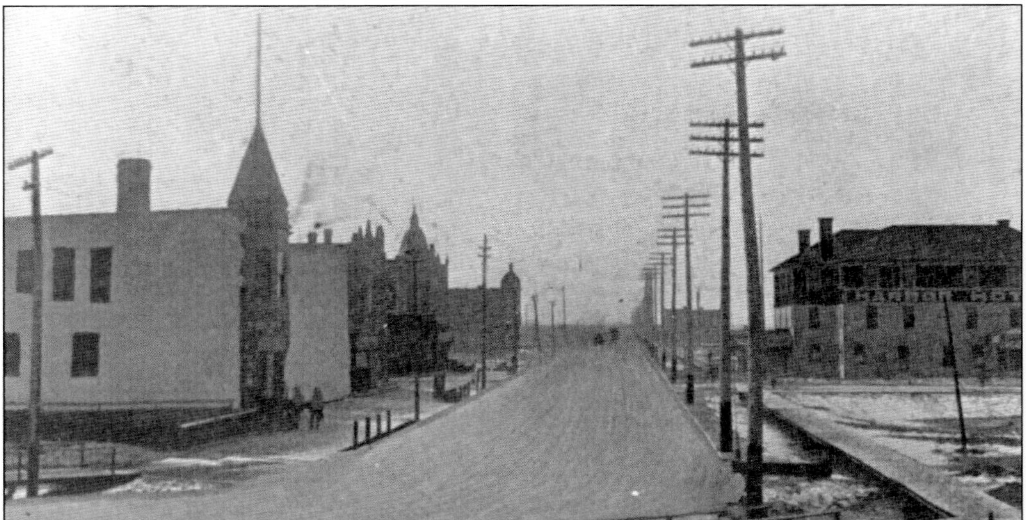

The Harbor Hotel is on the right in this photograph taken at the corner of Michigan and Commonwealth Avenues south of the Baltimore and Ohio railroad tracks in 1903. When Captain Friedrich opened the hotel, it had 66 boarders on opening night, despite the fact it was only partially finished and there were no beds. Friedrich had $4,000 worth of furniture on its way, but because of the swampy and stumpy terrain, delivery was slow. (Courtesy of the East Chicago Public Library.)

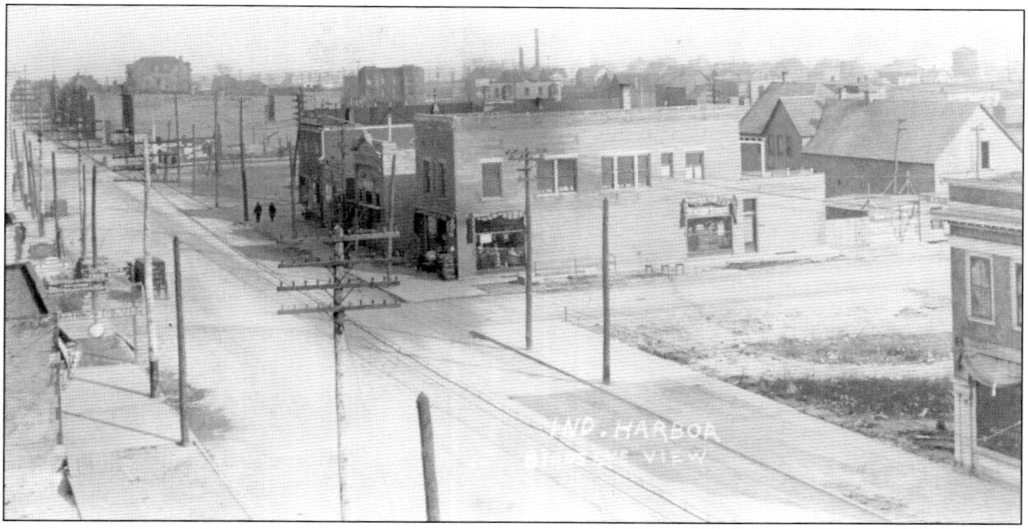

Built in 1901 and located at 3415 Michigan Avenue, the two-story Barker's Fair Store (center right) was Indiana Harbor's first store, opening before Inland Steel was built. It sold a mélange of merchandise, including home furnishings, sundries, baby buggies, stoves, pots and pans, and about everything else needed for a developing city. (Courtesy of the East Chicago Public Library.)

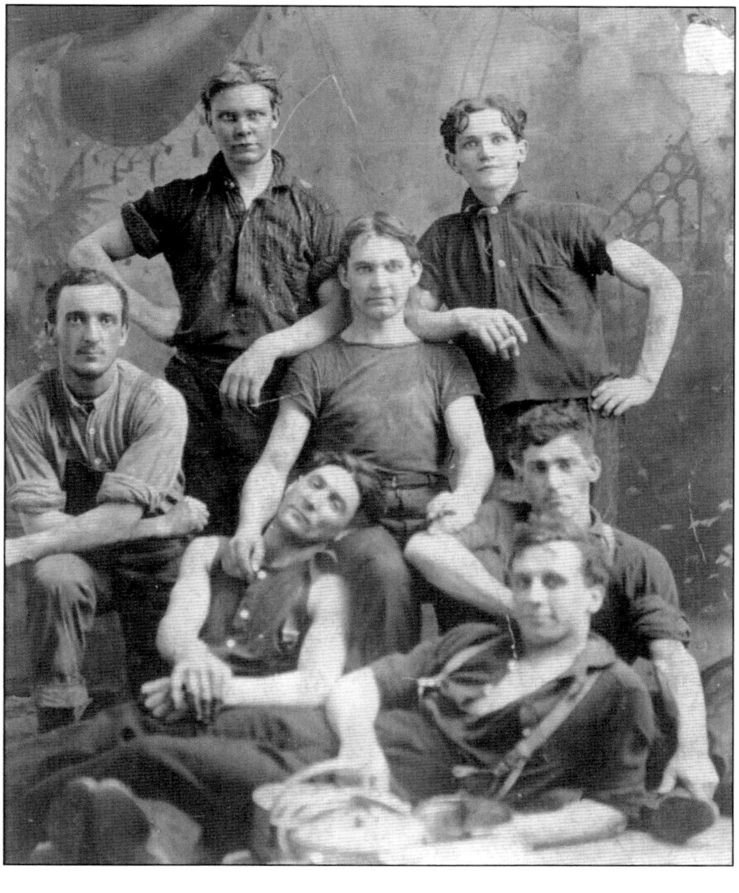

These sheet workers from Muncie, shown here in a 1902 photograph, were members of the Amalgamated Association of Iron and Steel Workers. They were summoned to East Chicago on special trains at the request of R.J. Beatty, a heavy investor in the mills and Inland's first general manager as well as a board member. (Courtesy of Archibald McKinlay.)

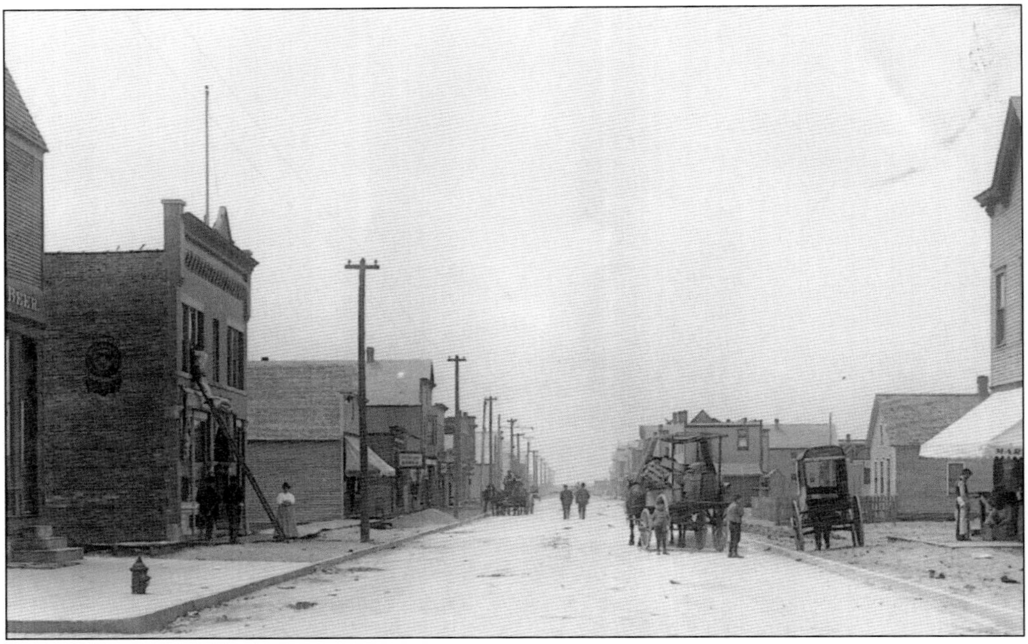

This view of Cedar Street looking south shows boomtown building, yet dirt streets were so tough to navigate that grocers would deliver provisions to the end of a street and then transfer the goods to wheelbarrows, which they then took to their destinations. (Courtesy of the Calumet Regional Archives, Indiana University.)

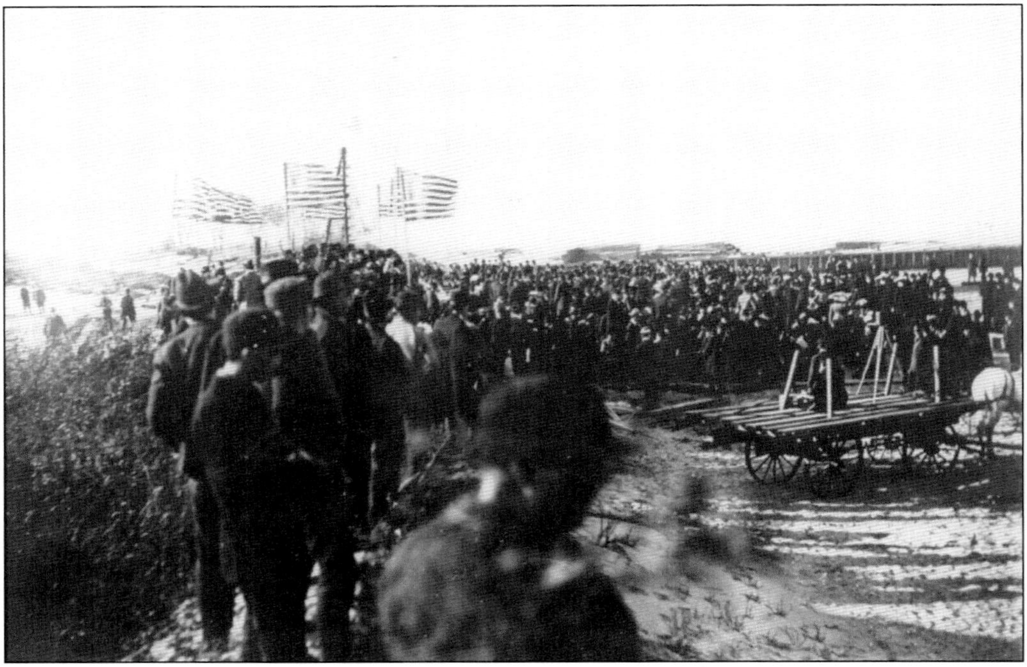

The dedication of the Indiana Harbor and Ship Canal, which within two years was expected to be completed with seven miles of dockage, factories, and elevators lining its banks, was celebrated as Canal Day. (Courtesy of the Calumet Regional Archives, Indiana University.)

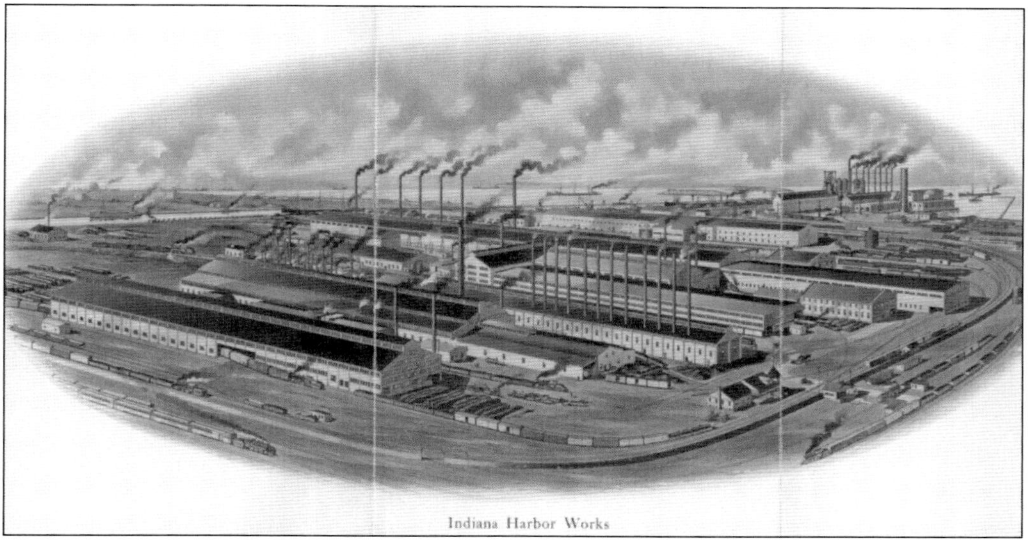

This is an artist's depiction of Inland Steel. The first investor from Indiana to buy land in the Calumet region was George W. Clark, who planned to build a pier at Indiana Harbor (then called Poplar Point). After his death in 1868, his sister Caroline M. Forsyth sold the land to the East Chicago Improvement Corporation. (Courtesy of the Calumet Regional Archives, Indiana University.)

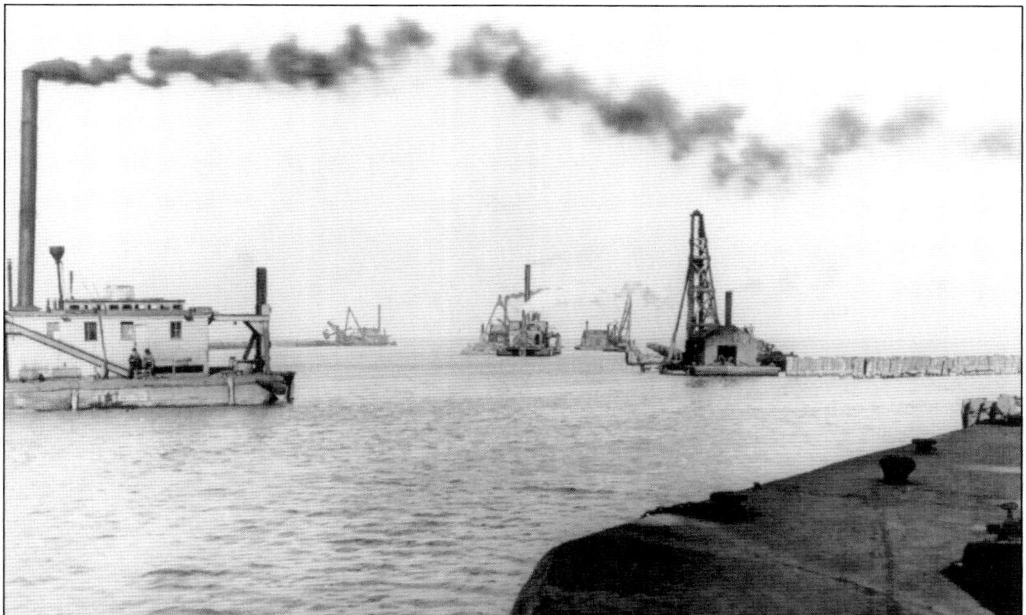

The Indiana Harbor and Ship Canal, an artificial waterway on the southwest shore of Lake Michigan, was developed to connect the Grand Calumet River to Lake Michigan and ensure that goods and materials could get to and from the steel mills. (Courtesy of the Calumet Regional Archives, Indiana University.)

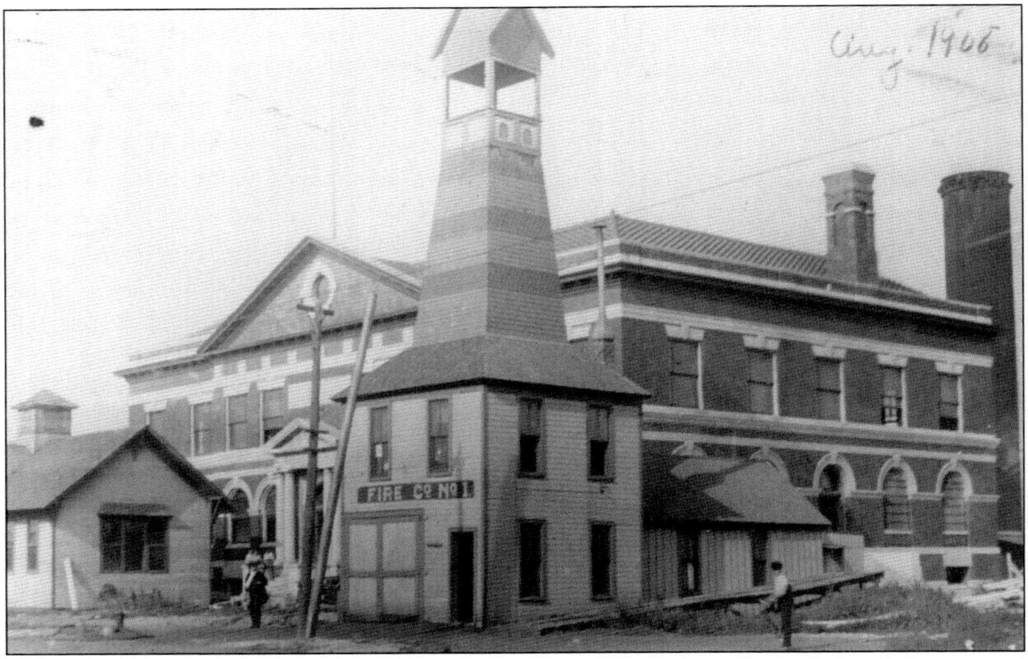

East Chicago City Hall, as seen in this 1909 photograph, is the addition behind the original firehouse. The building on the left is the first East Chicago schoolhouse. At far right is the city water tower. (Courtesy of the Calumet Regional Archives, Indiana University.)

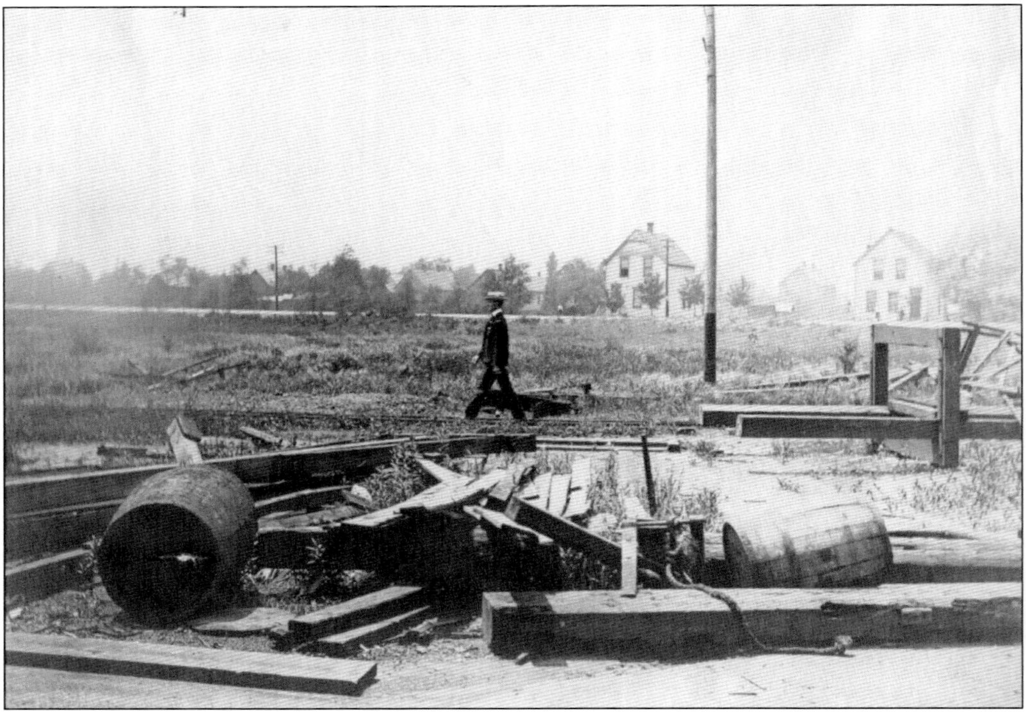

Because of swales, marshes, and sand, residents often walked along railroad beds to get to their destinations. (Courtesy of the East Chicago Public Library.)

Two

STEEL!

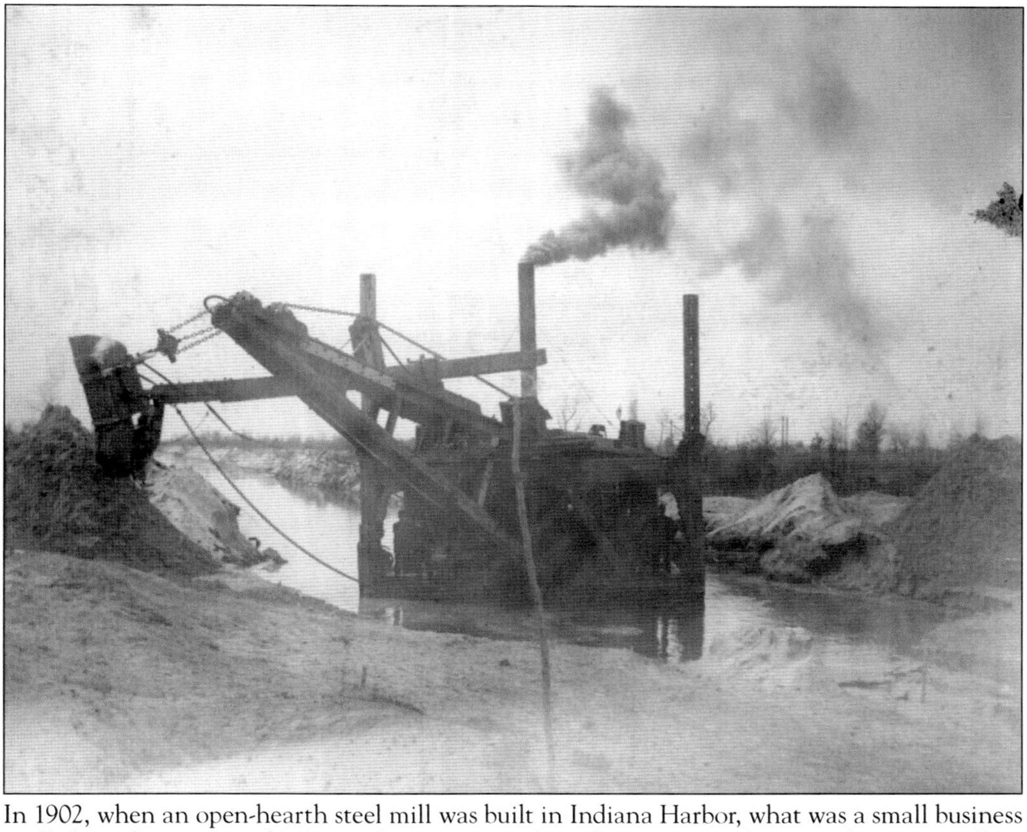

In 1902, when an open-hearth steel mill was built in Indiana Harbor, what was a small business swelled, employing around 2,600 workers in 1910 and supplying an annual output of over one million tons seven years later. (Courtesy of the Calumet Regional Archives, Indiana University.)

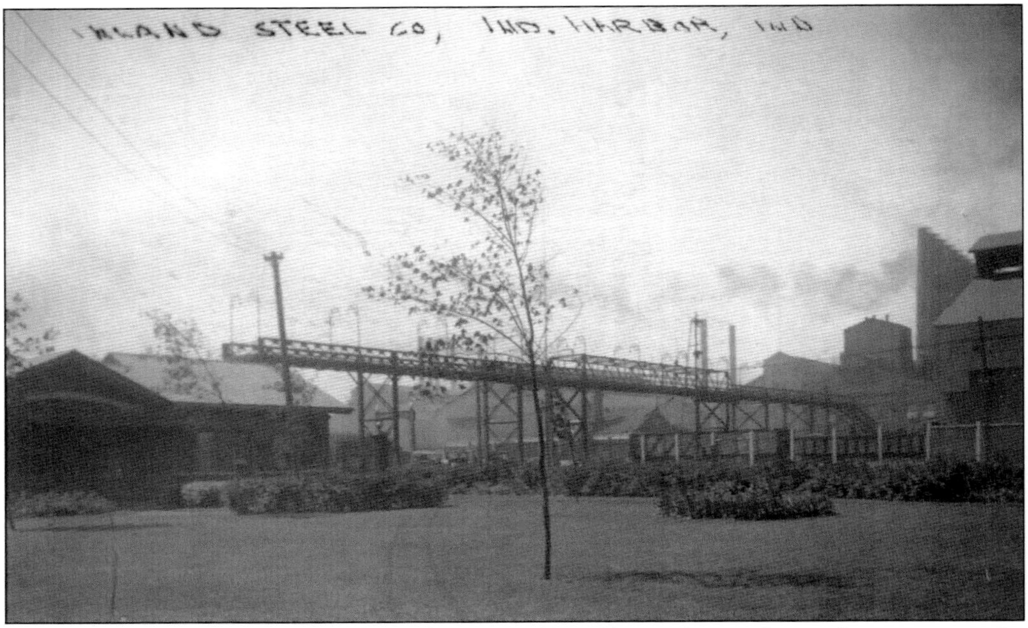

By the end of the first decade of the 20th century, East Chicago's growth was the greatest in the United States. In the seven years preceding 1918, the city had 100 percent growth. (Courtesy of the Calumet Regional Archives, Indiana University.)

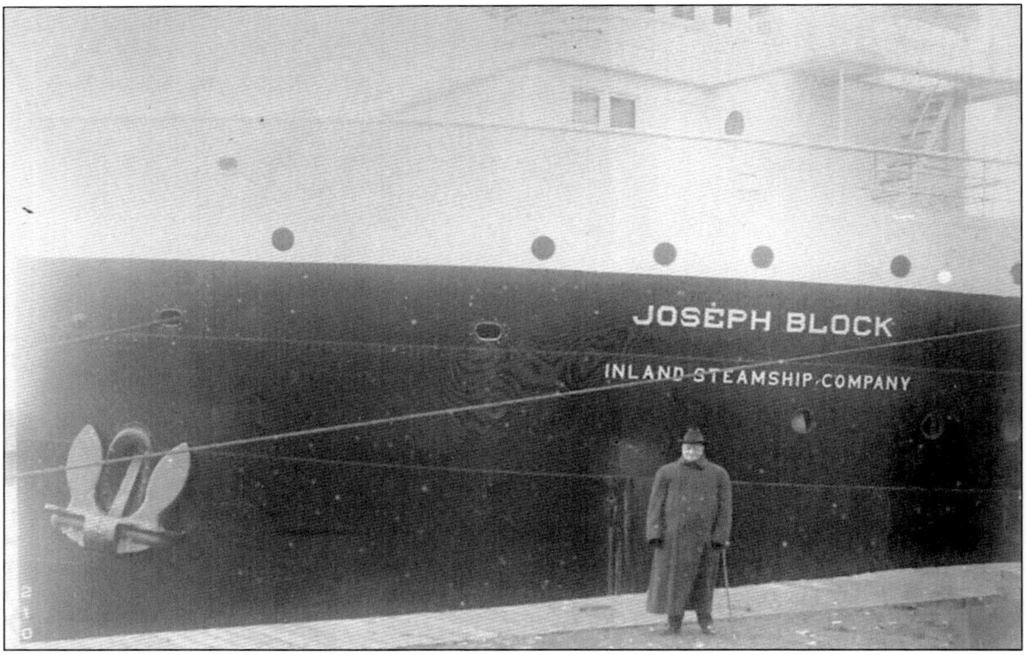

Joseph Block and his son Phillip were two of the founders of Inland Steel. In the 1920s, Inland made about two percent of all the steel produced in the United States, and its workforce grew to about 7,000 people. Block is pictured in front of the *Joseph Block* in 1912. "Inland Steamship Company" is displayed on the vessel, a subsidiary of Inland Steel, which was liquidated in 1936. (Courtesy of the Calumet Regional Archives, Indiana University.)

Philip D. Block Sr. purchased the physical assets of the bankrupt East Chicago Iron and Steel Company for $50,000 in 1897. Block, vice president of Inland Steel in nearby Chicago Heights, started a subsidiary called the Inland Iron and Forge Company a month later. According to historian Arch McKinlay, not only did the rolling mill become the city's largest employer, it also was the financial basis for Inland Steel. (Courtesy of the Calumet Regional Archives, Indiana University.)

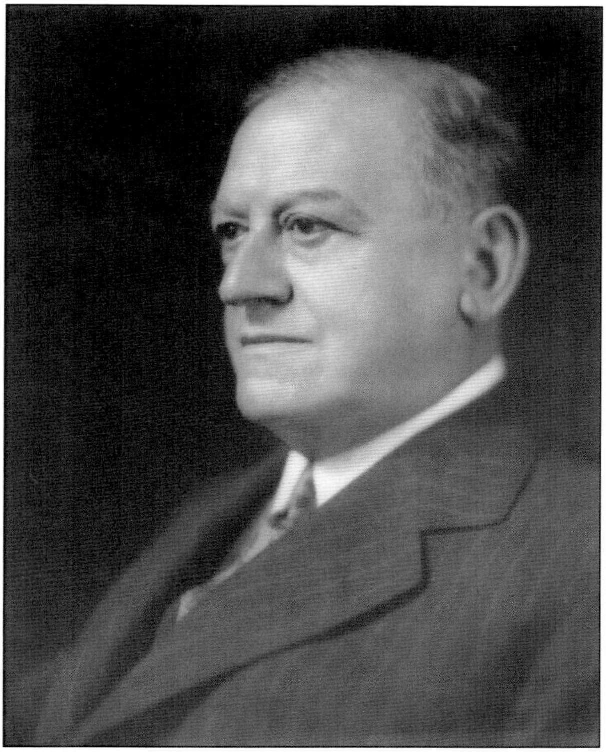

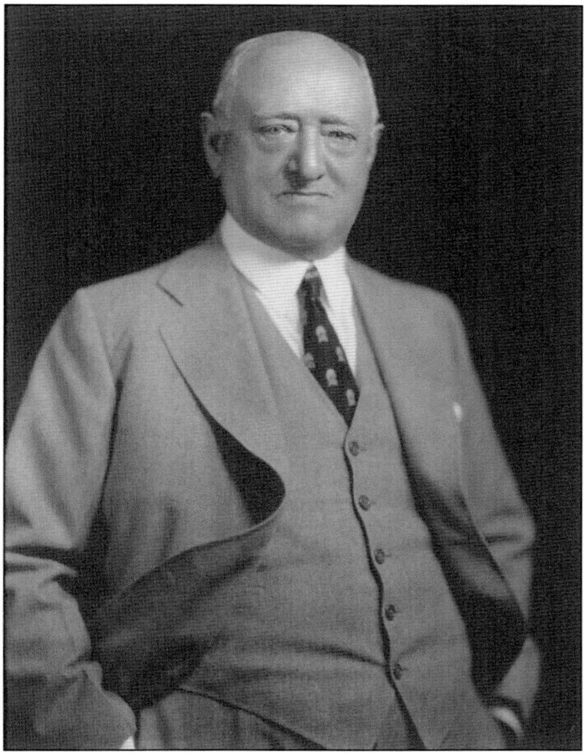

Leopold Block was working in Pittsburgh when his father, Joseph, asked him to run Inland Iron and Forge Company. With his business acumen, he was able to make the rolling mill extremely profitable, and through a series of transactions, sold stock on the New York Curb Exchange for around $500,000, which he used to build a new open-hearth plant in Indiana Harbor. (Courtesy of the Calumet Regional Archives, Indiana University.)

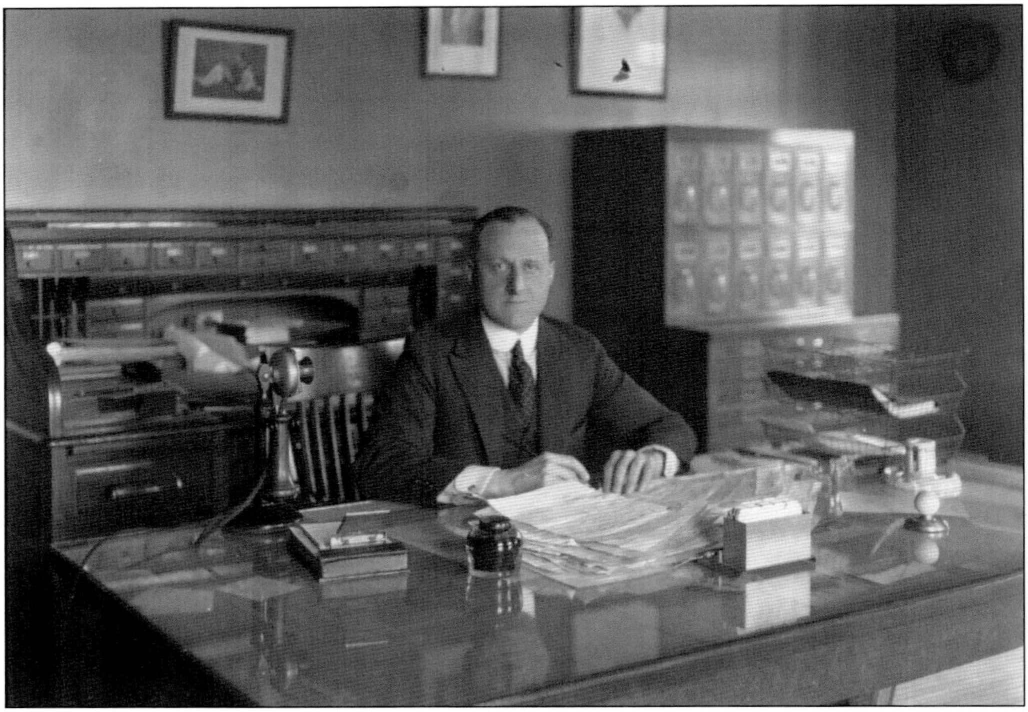

Emanuel Block, who joined Inland Steel in 1901, became vice president and director. He was one of three brothers holding high positions in the company. The others were Philip D. Block Jr. and Leopold Block. (Courtesy of the Calumet Regional Archives, Indiana University.)

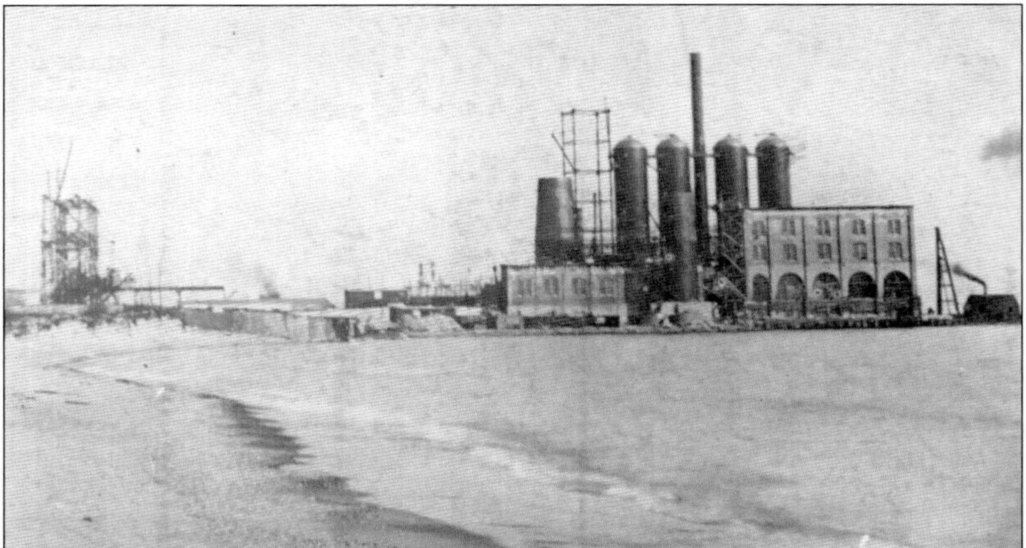

Emanuel J. Block, ("E.J." or "Jimmie"), was the younger brother of L.E. Block and P.D. Block. E.J. joined Inland Steel in 1901, became the purchasing agent in 1908, and was a director by 1910. In 1920, he served as vice president in charge of purchasing. (Courtesy of the Calumet Regional Archives, Indiana University.)

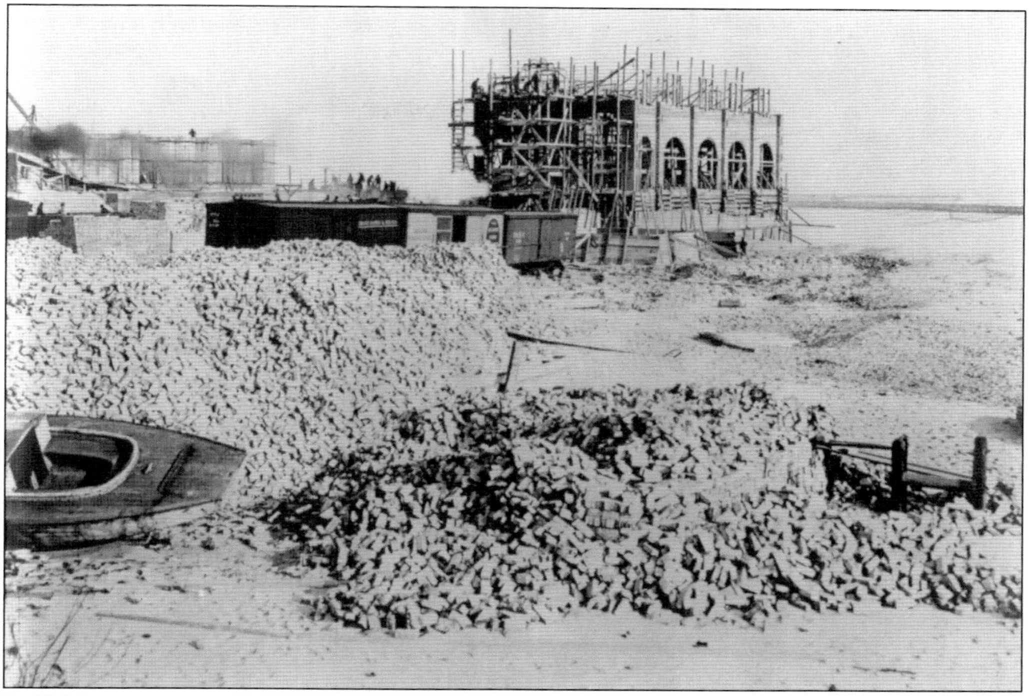

In 1906, construction began on blast furnace Madeline No. 1. The photograph above shows the progress made on the engine house in the throes of the build. The photograph below documents the completion of the furnace on September 2, 1907. (Both, courtesy of the Calumet Regional Archives, Indiana University.)

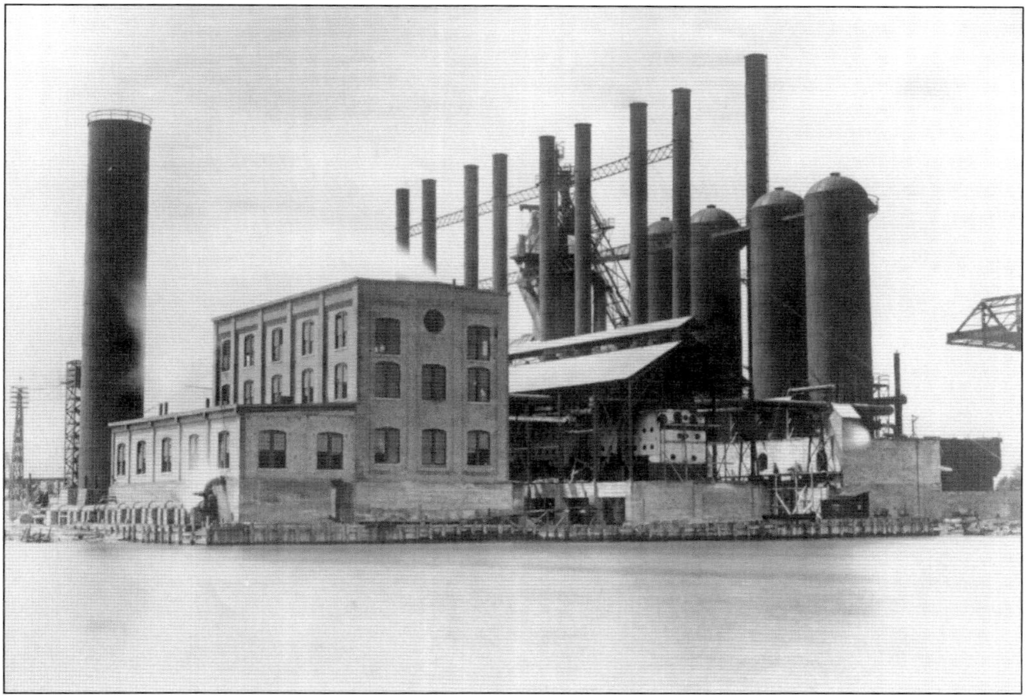

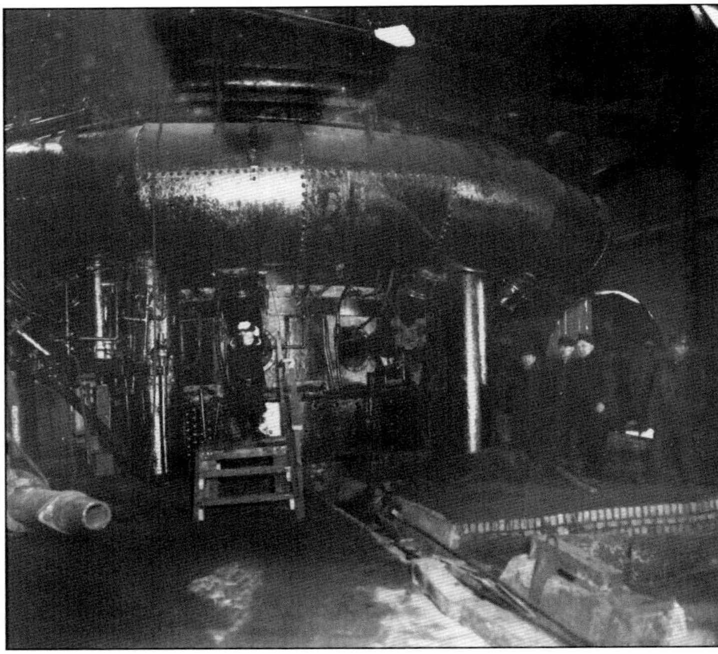

In 1907, Five-year-old Madeline Block lights the Madeline No. 1, the first steel blast furnace for Inland Steel of Indiana Harbor Works. All subsequent Inland furnaces were also named for her. (Courtesy of the Calumet Regional Archives, Indiana University.)

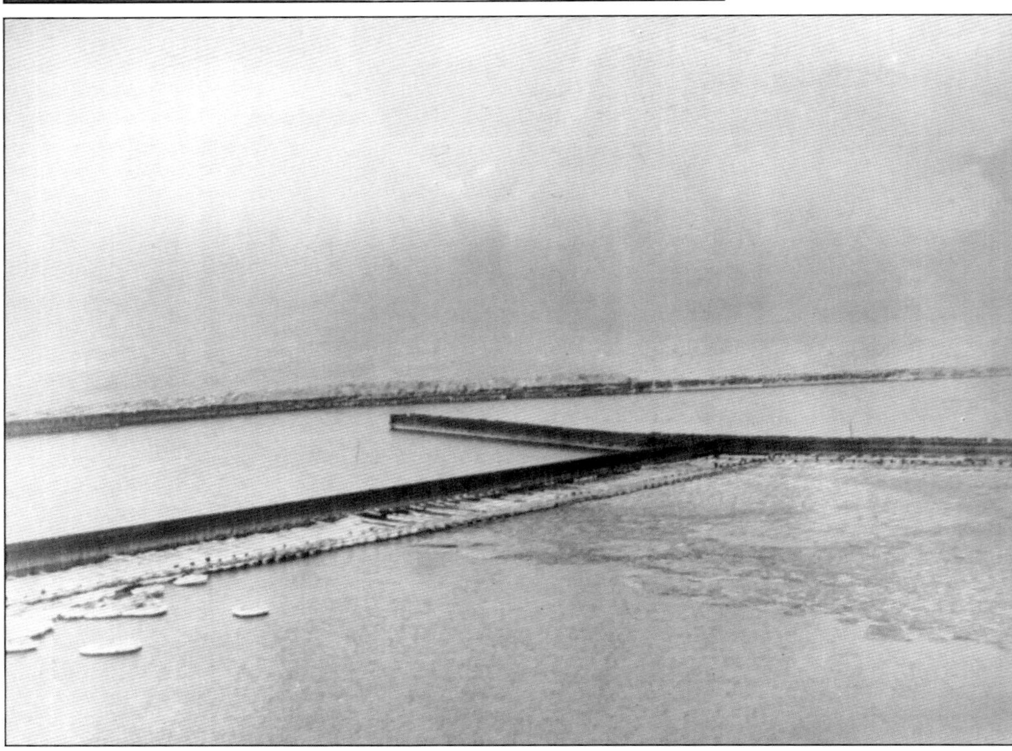

By opening up the waterways connecting Lake Michigan and the Great Calumet River, as shown in this January 1908 view of the harbor entrance, goods could easily be shipped to and from East Chicago, making it a major port on the Great Lakes. (Courtesy of the Calumet Regional Archives, Indiana University.)

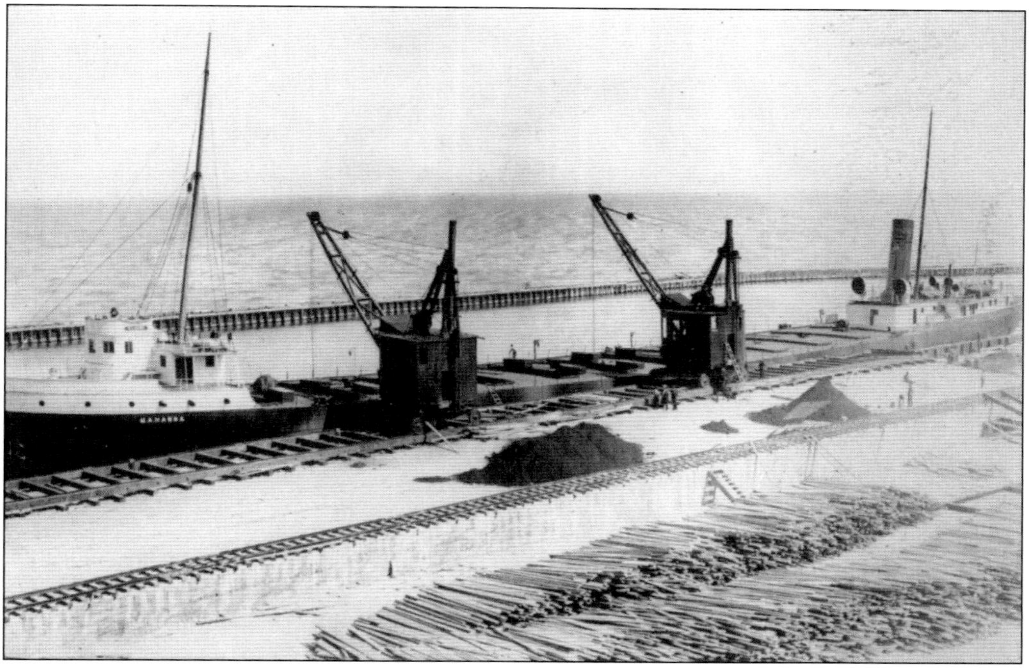

Ore boats, such as the M.A. *Hanna* pictured arriving at the Inland Steel docks on July 29, 1907, brought materials in to be used to create tons of steel. (Courtesy of the Calumet Regional Archives, Indiana University.)

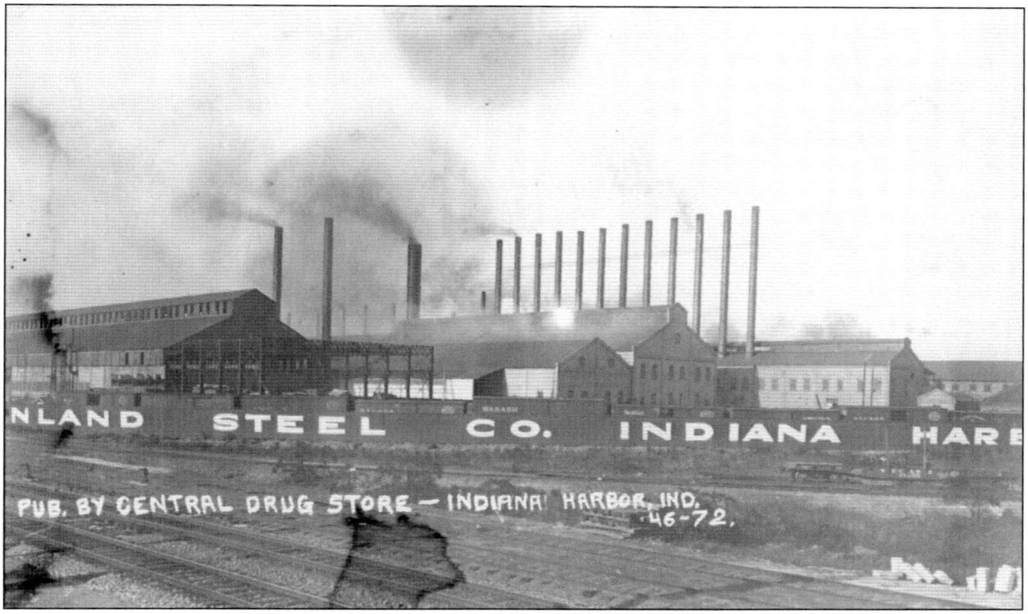

Located on the southwest shore of Lake Michigan, East Chicago was 19 miles from the center of Chicago's business district and in the northwest section of Lake County, the heart of the great Calumet manufacturing district. The "Twin City" (East Chicago–Indian Harbor) was surrounded on the east, south, and west sides by the cities of Gary, Hammond, and Whiting. (Courtesy of the Calumet Regional Archives, Indiana University.)

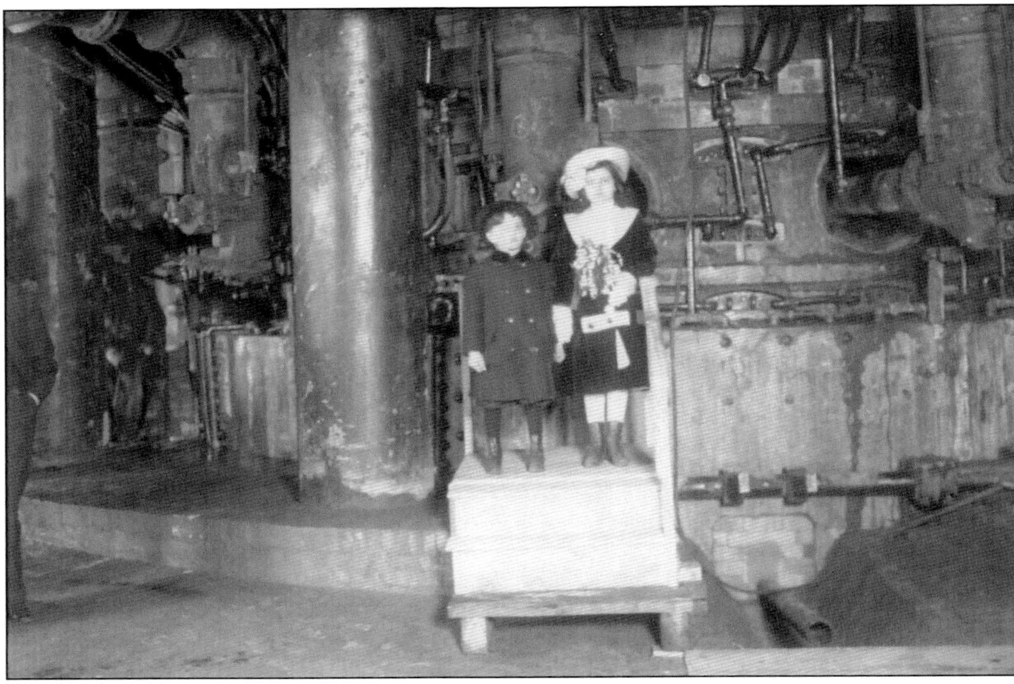

Madeline Block and her brother Philip D. Block Jr. stand ready to light the Madeline No. 2 blast furnace for Inland Steel of Indiana Harbor Works in 1912. (Courtesy of the Calumet Regional Archives, Indiana University.)

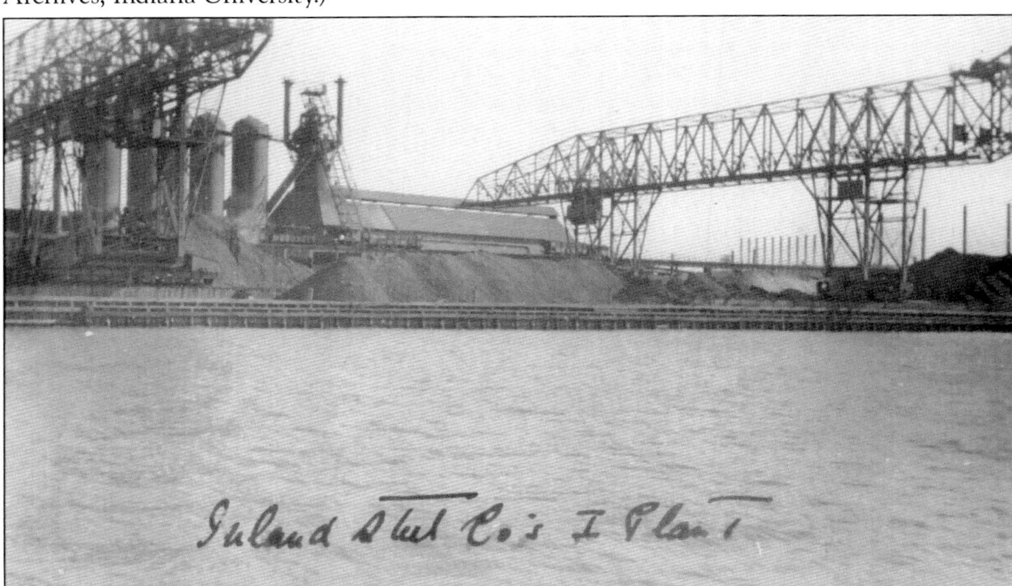

The steel mills stretched along the beachfront, the perfect location for shipping materials such as ore, iron, and steel up through the Great Lakes and—depending how far they were going—to the Mississippi River or the St. Lawrence Seaway. This photograph of Inland Steel's No. 1 Plant shows the beginning of this great steel dynasty. (Courtesy of the Calumet Regional Archives, Indiana University.)

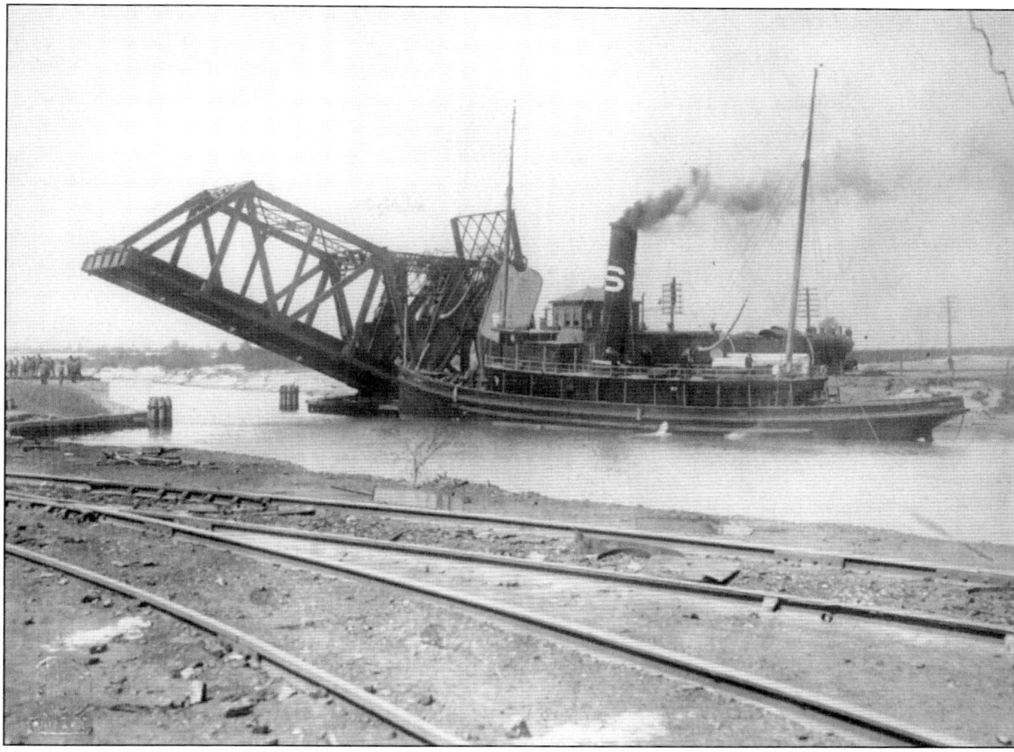

Pictured is the first commercial boat to sail the Indiana Harbor and Ship Canal in 1912. The canal simultaneously functions as a harbor, running 1.4 miles before reaching the Indiana Harbor, which opens into Lake Michigan. (Courtesy of the Calumet Regional Archives, Indiana University.)

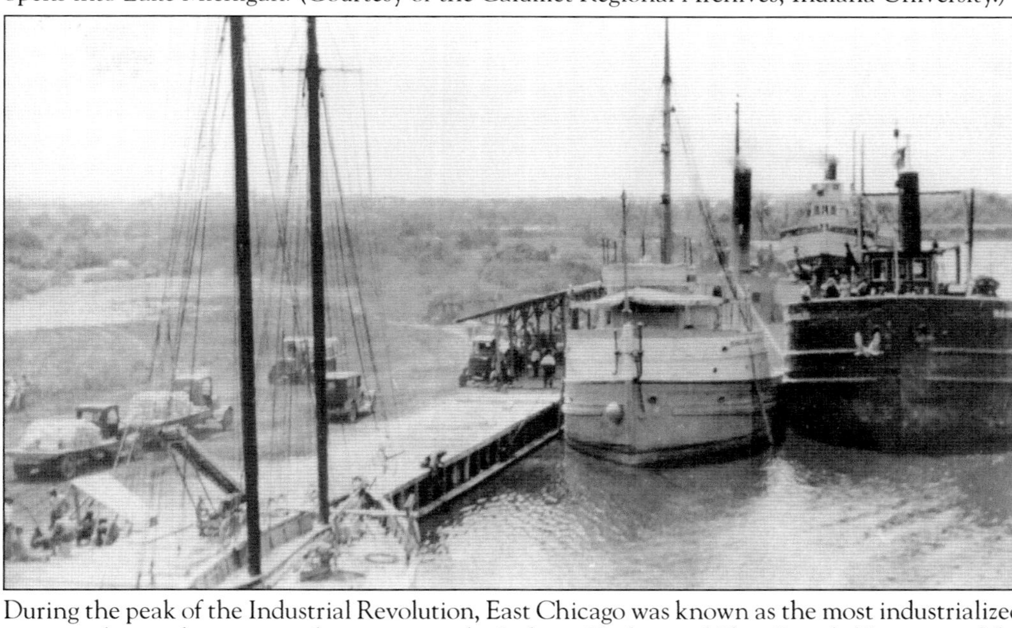

During the peak of the Industrial Revolution, East Chicago was known as the most industrialized municipality in the country, due in part to the Indiana Harbor and Ship Canal. (Courtesy of the Calumet Regional Archives, Indiana University.)

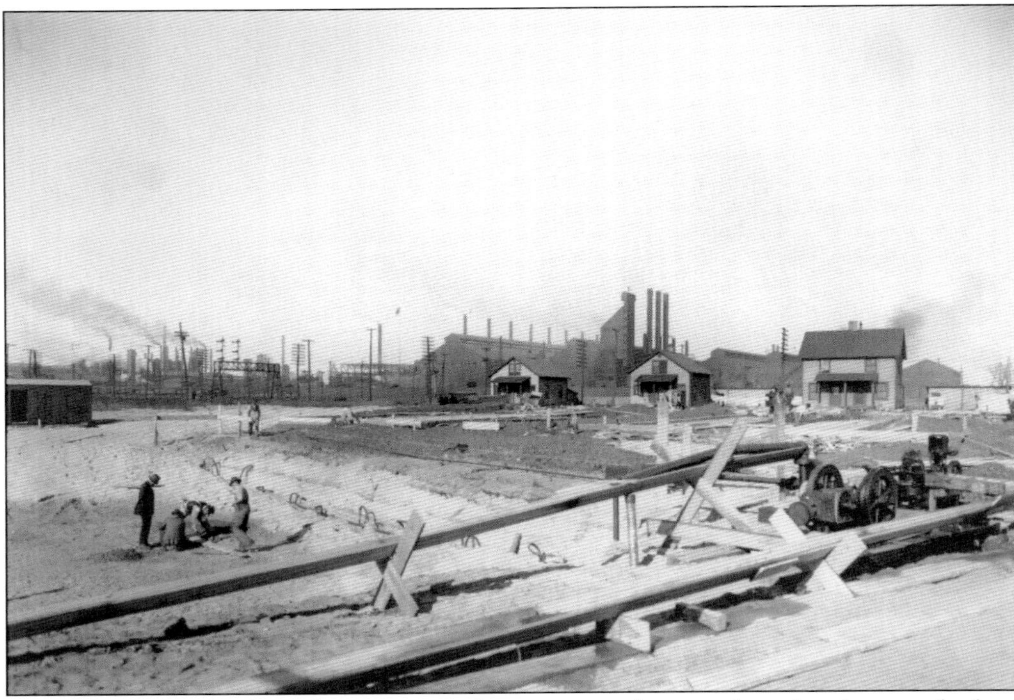

Building of the Inland Steel Community Center was underway when the photograph above was taken on October 21, 1918. Construction included the expansion of the clock house and employment center, resulting in the new office seen below in November 1918. (Both, courtesy of the Calumet Regional Archives, Indiana University.)

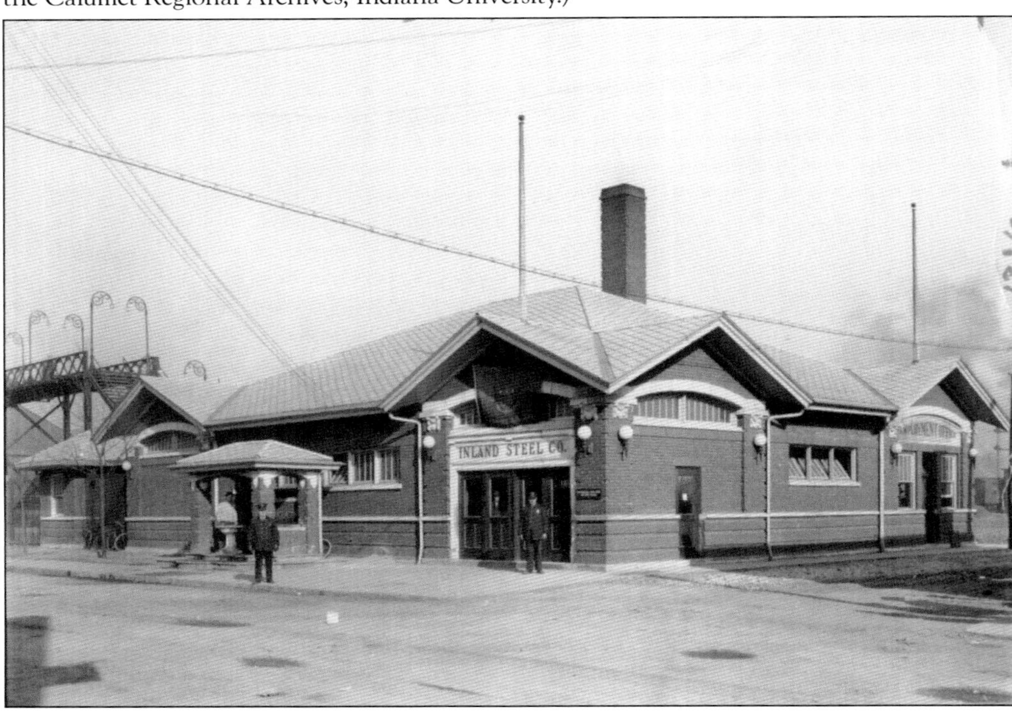

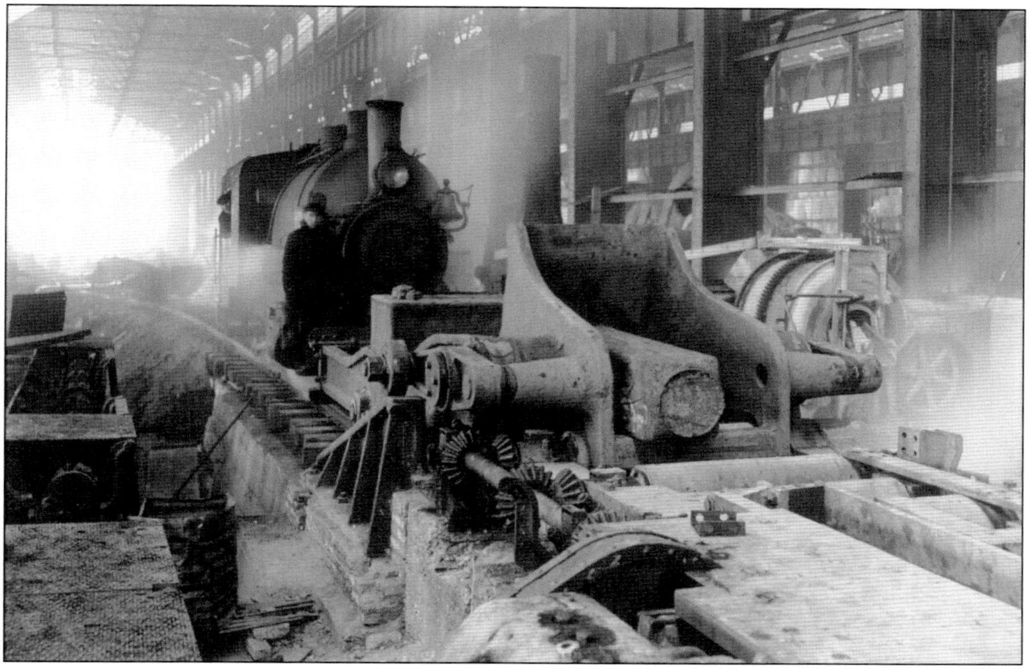

By the time this photograph of an ingot buggy delivering an ingot to the roll tables was taken on December 27, 1916, Indiana Harbor was a boomtown. The population soared to 19,098 residents in 1910. (Courtesy of the Calumet Regional Archives, Indiana University.)

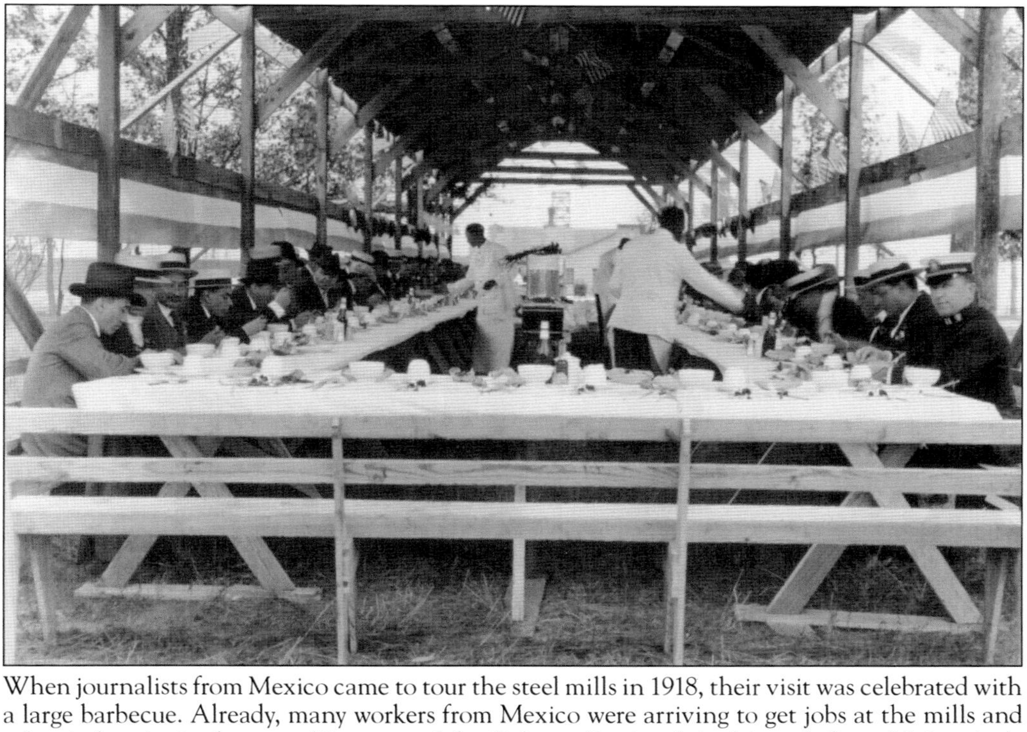

When journalists from Mexico came to tour the steel mills in 1918, their visit was celebrated with a large barbecue. Already, many workers from Mexico were arriving to get jobs at the mills and other industries in the area. (Courtesy of the Calumet Regional Archives, Indiana University.)

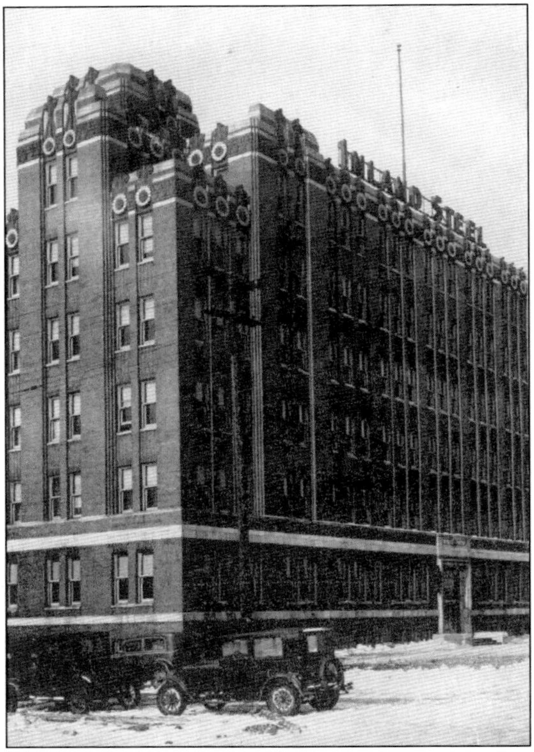

The six-story headquarters of Inland Steel was the city's second high-rise. Built in the Art Deco style, it opened in May 1930, just a few months after the 1929 stock market crash. (Courtesy of the East Chicago Public Library.)

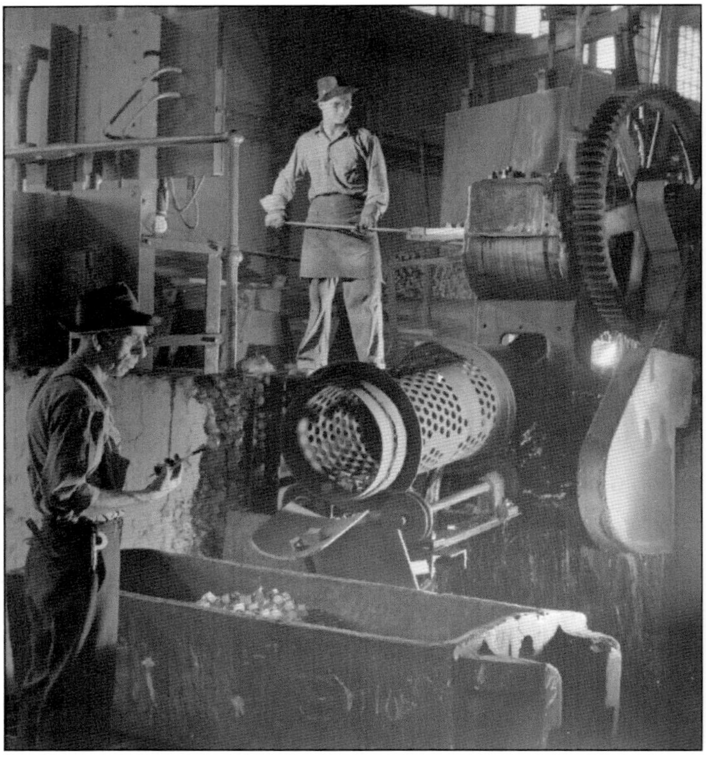

This 1930 photograph shows the bolt and spike department at Inland Steel. (Courtesy of the Calumet Regional Archives, Indiana University.)

This photograph shows many aspects of the Inland Steel Company, a complex world of its own that included blast furnaces, ore boats, and the canal. (Courtesy of the Calumet Regional Archives, Indiana University.)

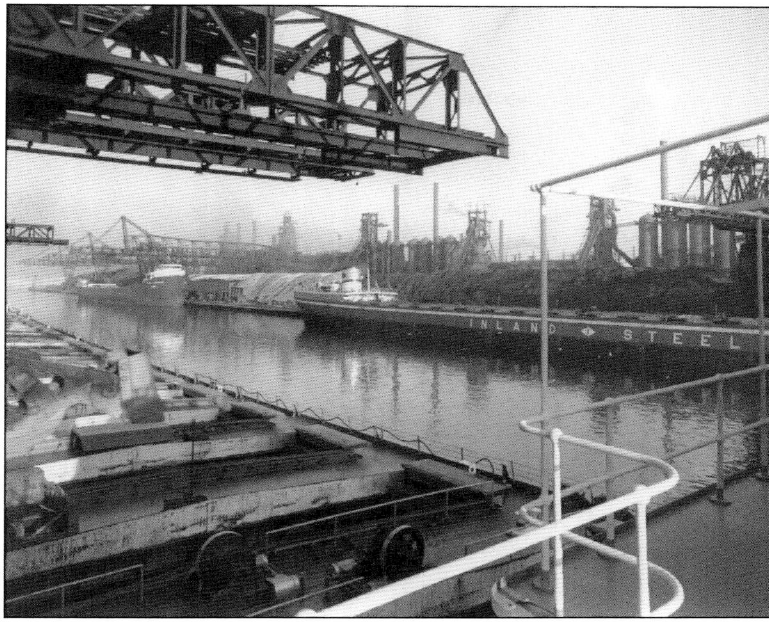

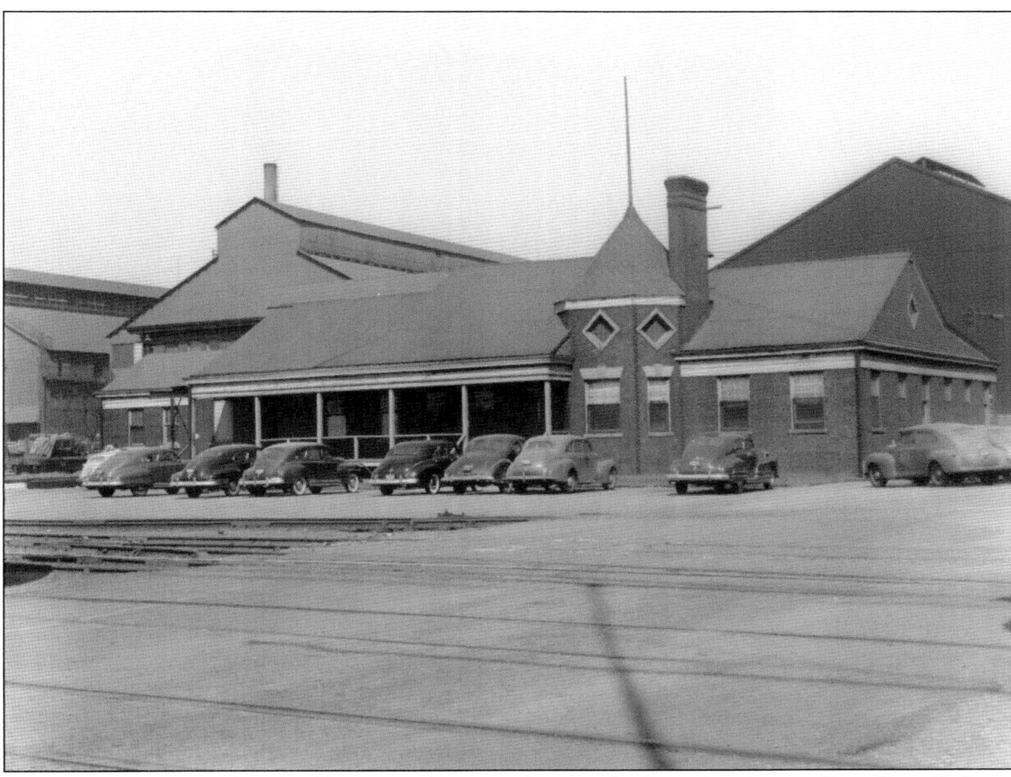

This is the old main office building at Indiana Harbor Works. By 1930, the number of people living in the Indiana Harbor section of East Chicago had increased dramatically again. By this time, the population was 35,967. (Courtesy of the Calumet Regional Archives, Indiana University.)

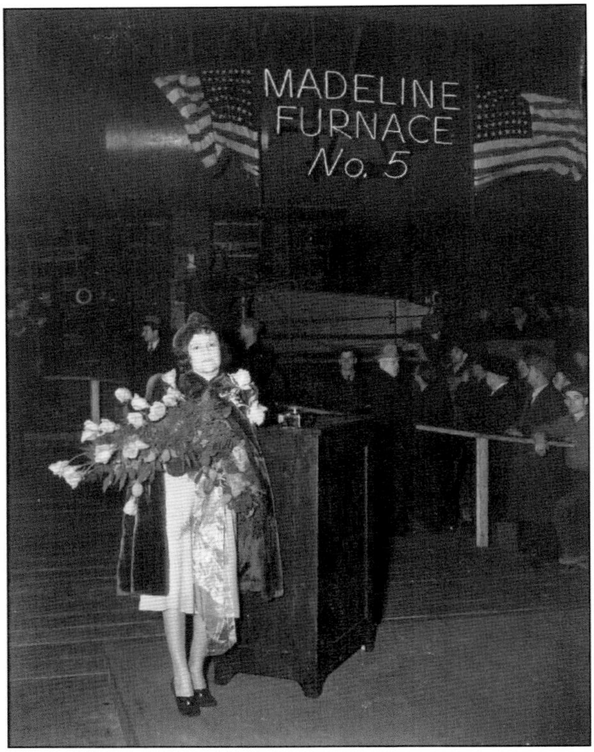

Madeline Block Straus is seen here at the lighting of the Madeline No. 5 blast furnace for Inland Steel of Indiana Harbor Works in 1939. (Courtesy of the Calumet Regional Archives, Indiana University.)

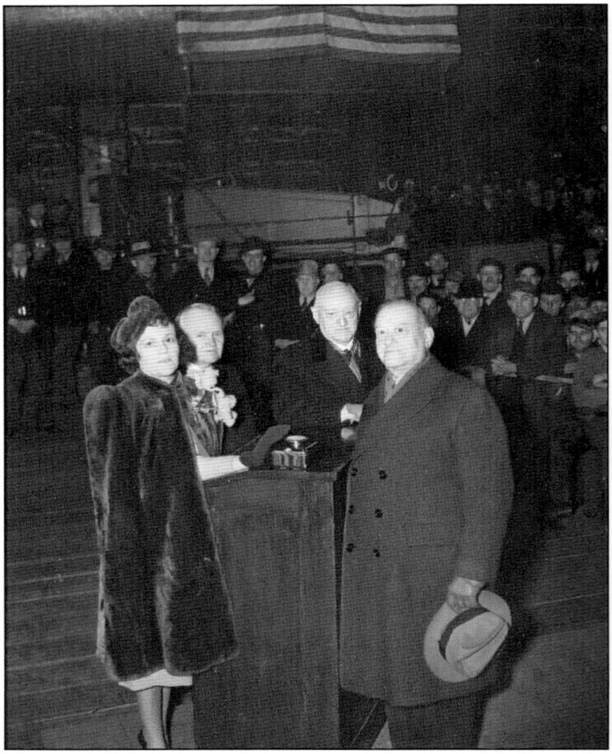

Madeline Block Straus is pictured with family members at the Madeline No. 5 blast furnace lighting in 1939. Her father, Philip Block, was one of the founders of Inland Steel and served as its president from 1919 to 1941. (Courtesy of the Calumet Regional Archives, Indiana University.)

Optical pyrometer testing is pictured during the pouring of ingot molds at Inland Steel in 1943. East Chicago had four major population waves that characterized and influenced the Twin City. First were immigrants from Scotland, Wales, England, and Germany. The European wave came from middle and southeastern Europe until 1914, when World War I brought about a change in immigration laws. (Courtesy of the Calumet Regional Archives, Indiana University.)

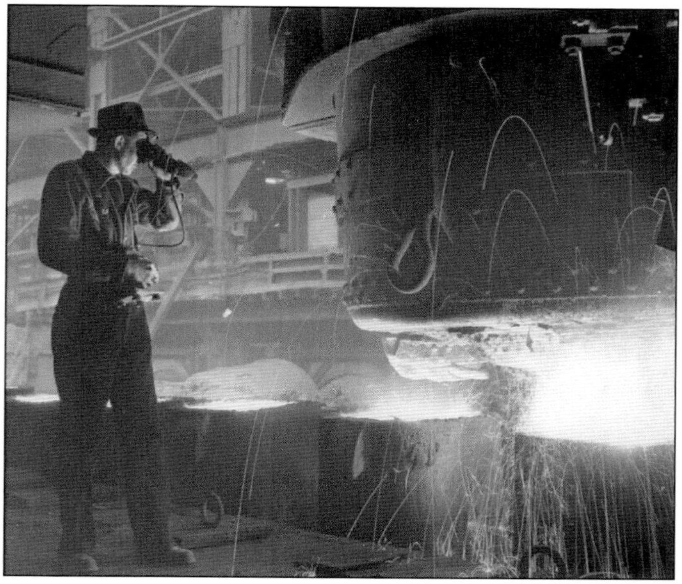

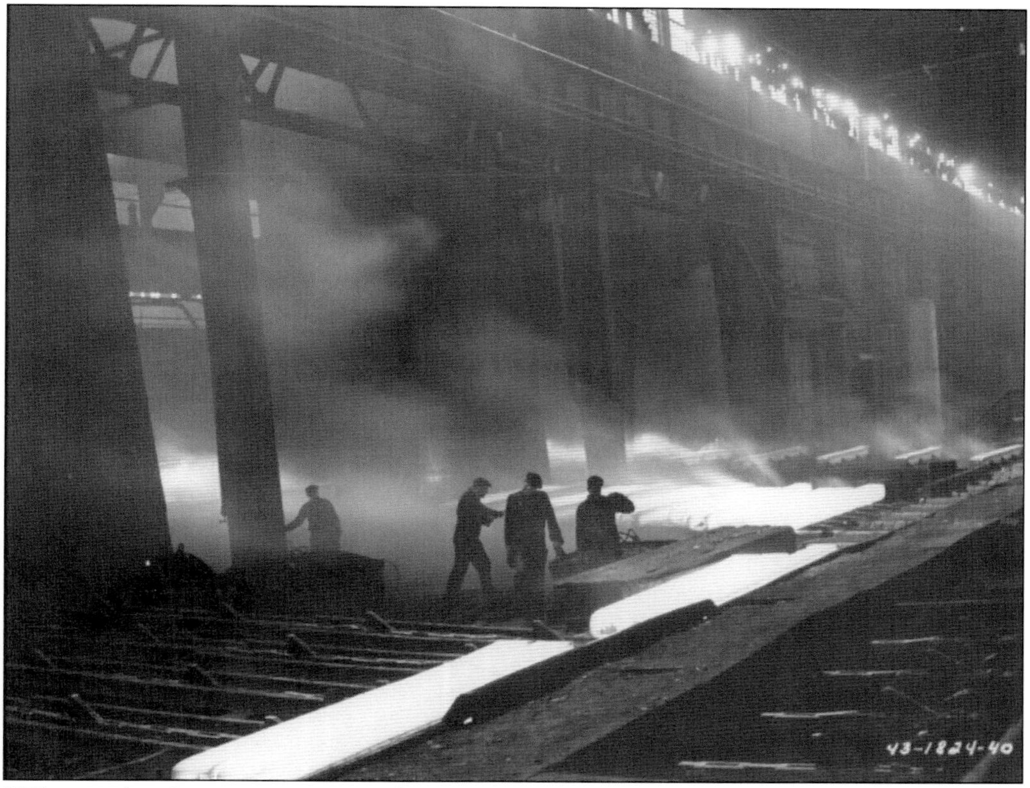

"Where rail and water meet" was a slogan referencing how the shipping facilities and rail lines made for the booming success of the steel industry—and other industries. In this 1943 photograph, intermediate-stage pieces of steel (blooms) are cooled at the storage hotbed before they are scarfed (removal of surface defects). (Courtesy of the Calumet Regional Archives, Indiana University.)

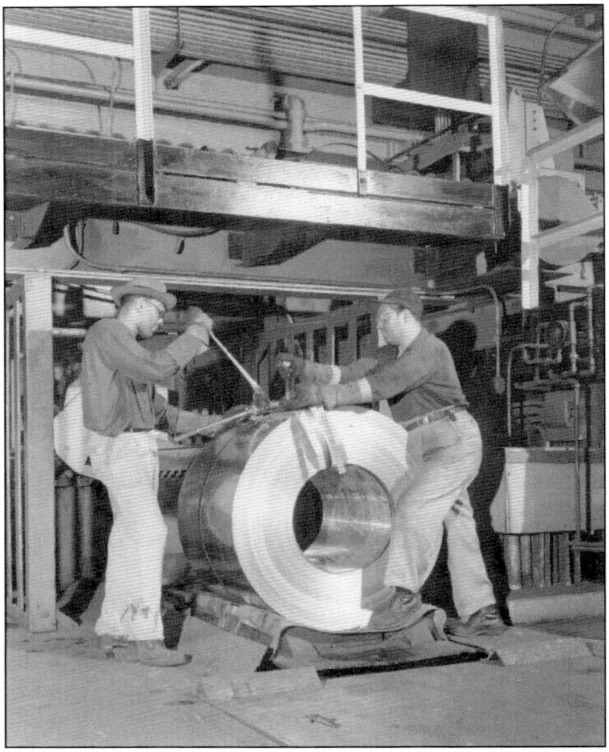

Working in the steel mills was a dangerous, hot, and exhausting job. In this 1954 photograph, crews band a coil. (Courtesy of the Calumet Regional Archives, Indiana University.)

In 1957, Madeline Block Straus officiated at the 50th anniversary of operation at the Madeline No. 1 at Indiana Harbor Works. She sounded a siren, signaling the start of the golden anniversary. A noted community volunteer with many years of service to Chicago institutions, she was a founder and board member of the Prentice Women's Hospital of Northwestern University Medical Center. During World War II, she was a volunteer with the American Red Cross and a Gray Lady at the US Naval Training Center in Great Lakes. (Courtesy of the Calumet Regional Archives, Indiana University.)

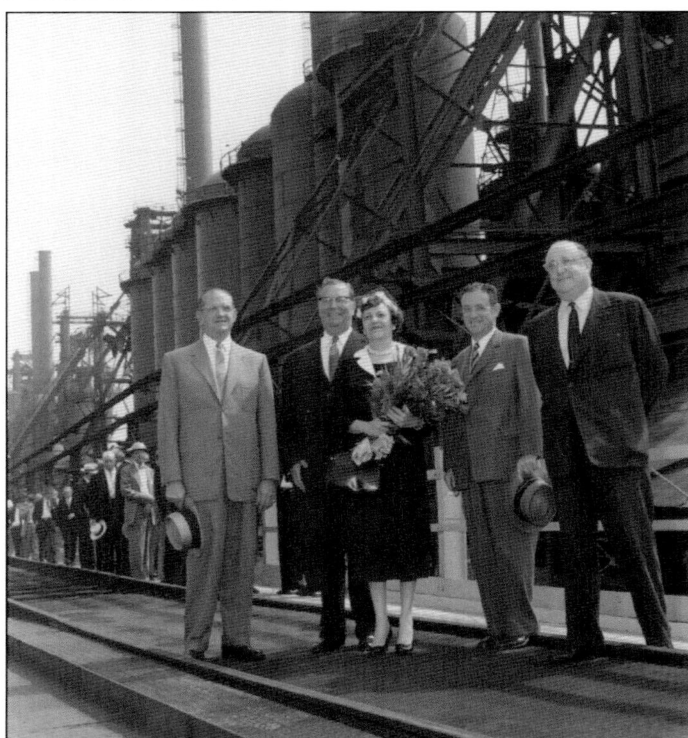

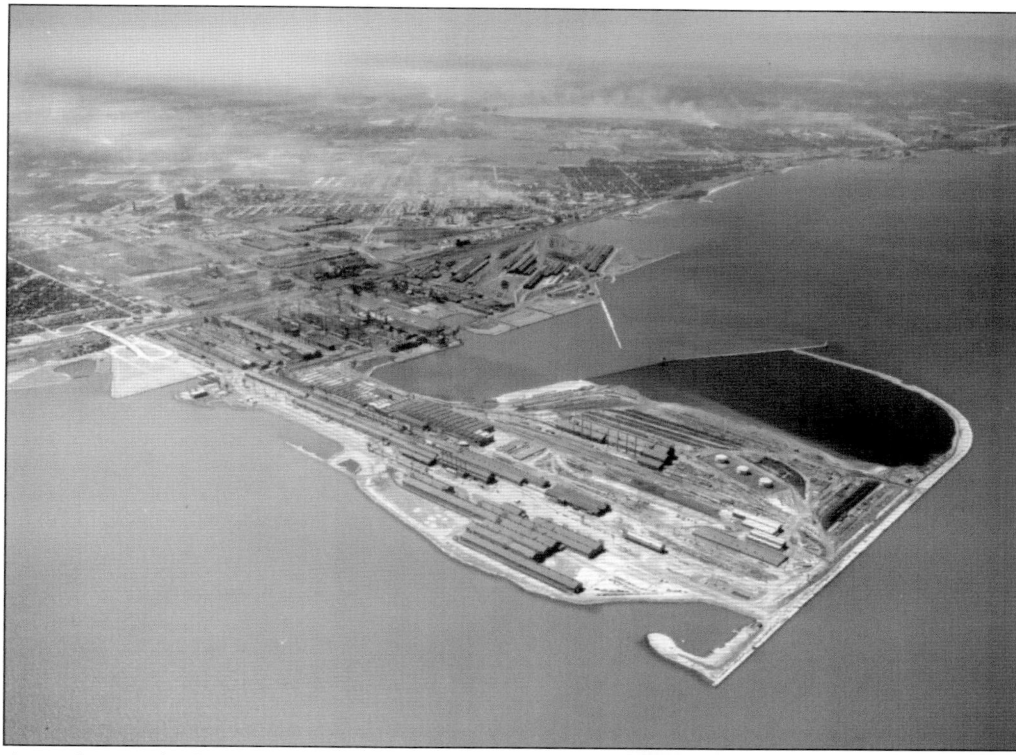

According to the US census, by 1956, East Chicago's population was 57,669 and seemed unstoppable. This 1959 aerial photograph of the Indiana Harbor Works shows the mills functioning at peak performance. (Courtesy of the Calumet Regional Archives, Indiana University.)

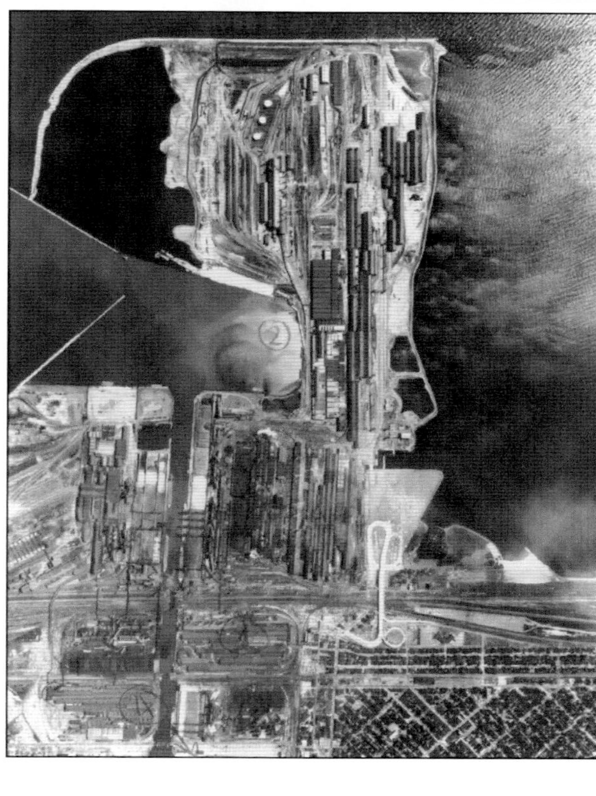

This aerial view from November 1961 shows Plants 1, 2, and 3. (Courtesy of the Calumet Regional Archives, Indiana University.)

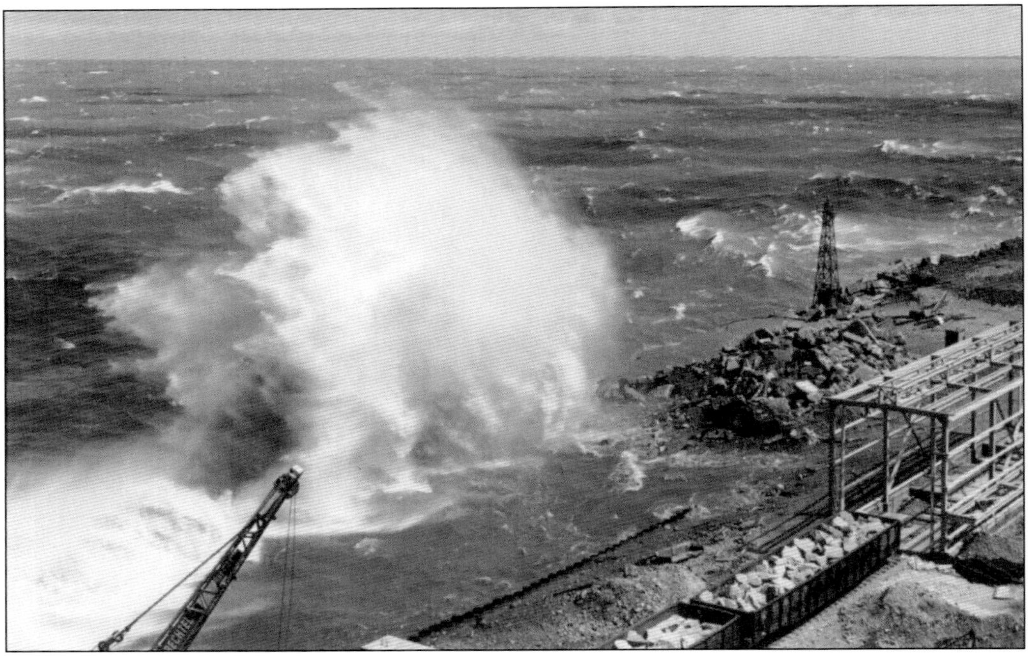

Wild waves from a stormy Lake Michigan pound the Indiana Harbor Works shoreline in 1963. (Courtesy of the Calumet Regional Archives, Indiana University.)

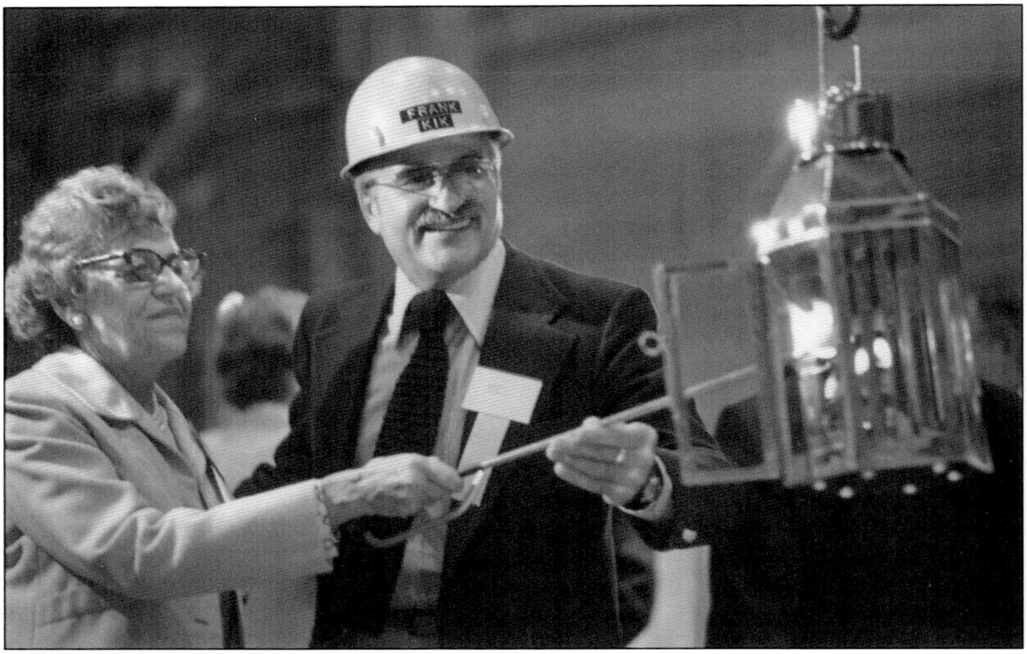

In 1980, Madeline Block Straus Willner lit a lantern to provide the flame for Madeline No. 7. At the time, Inland's newest blast furnace was one of the two largest in the western hemisphere. Madeline Block Straus married Inland vice president Henry Horner Straus, who died in 1965. A year later, she wed Benton J. Willner, a retired Inland sales executive. (Courtesy of the Calumet Regional Archives, Indiana University.)

Three

Getting Around

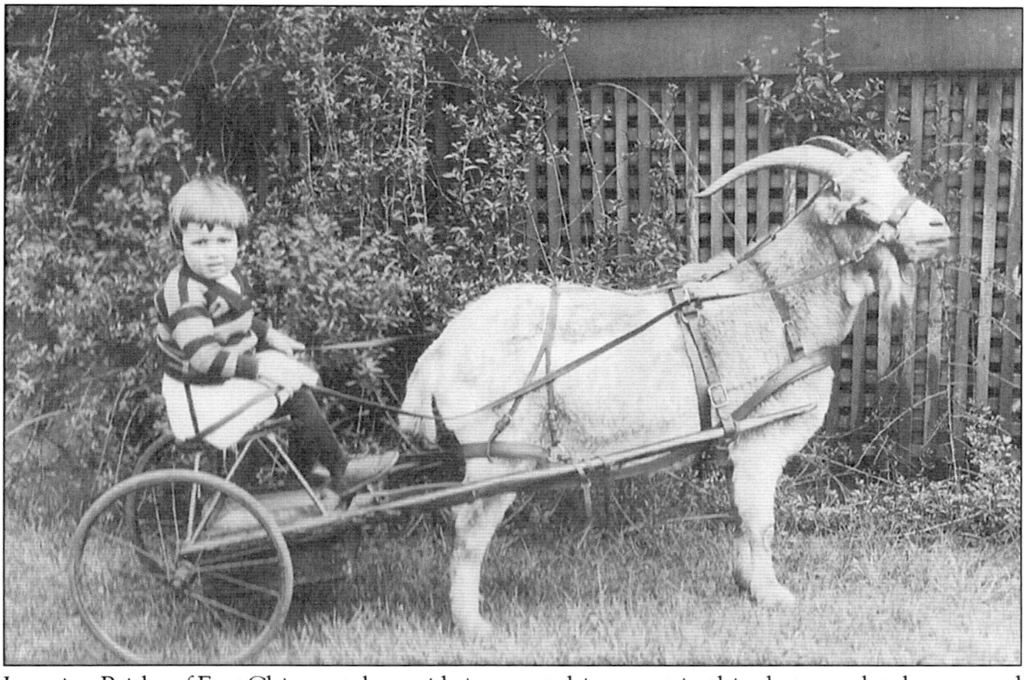

Lorraine Briska of East Chicago takes a ride in a goat-driven cart in this photograph taken around 1910. (Courtesy of the Briska family.)

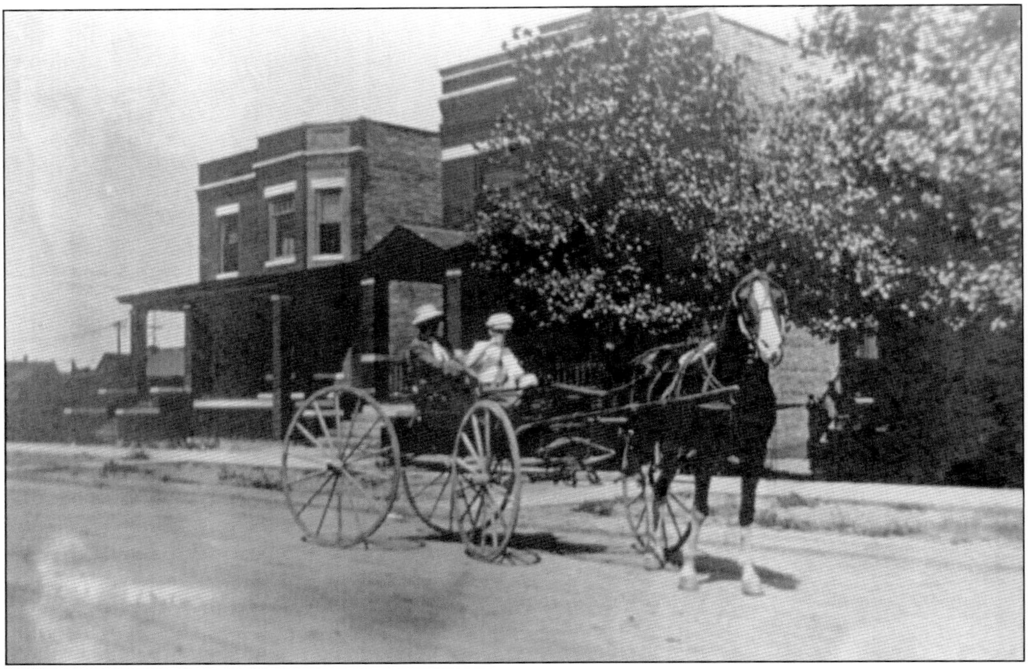

George Huish, the publisher of the *Calumet News*, travels by horse and buggy down Hemlock Avenue. Huish moved to Indiana Harbor in 1902 from Muncie, served in World War I, and became a noted citizen and commander of American Legion Post 266. (Courtesy of the East Chicago Public Library.)

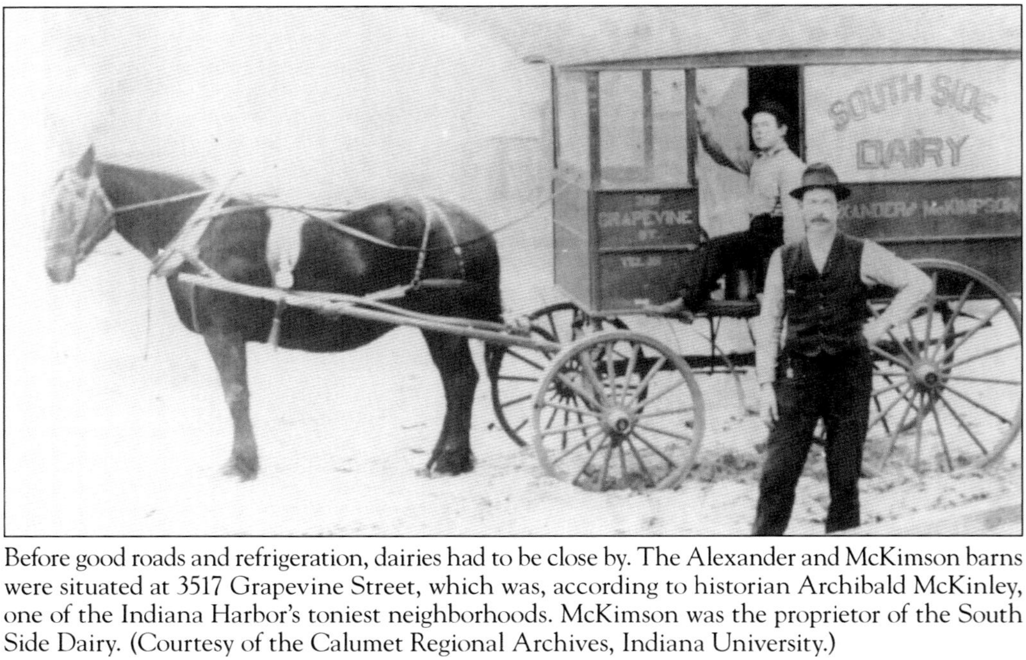

Before good roads and refrigeration, dairies had to be close by. The Alexander and McKimson barns were situated at 3517 Grapevine Street, which was, according to historian Archibald McKinley, one of the Indiana Harbor's toniest neighborhoods. McKimson was the proprietor of the South Side Dairy. (Courtesy of the Calumet Regional Archives, Indiana University.)

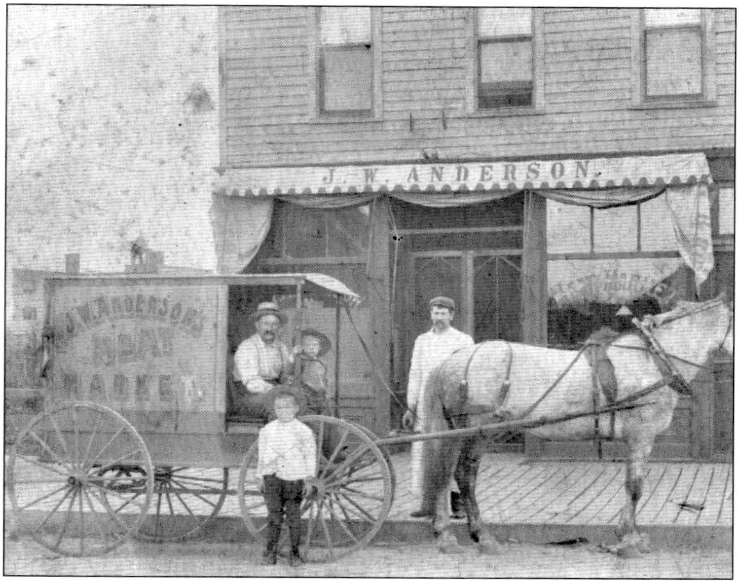

J.W. Anderson Market made home deliveries. Unfortunately, the streets were so impassable that goods often had to be unloaded and put into wheelbarrows to be delivered to homes. (Courtesy of the Calumet Regional Archives, Indiana University.)

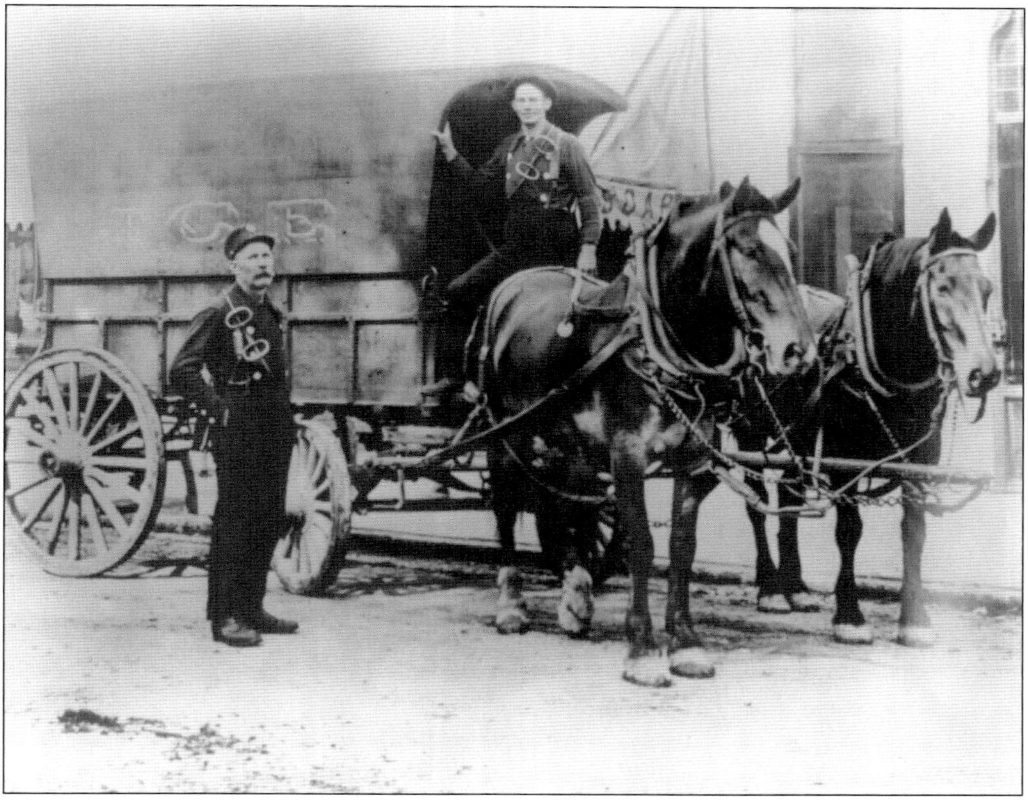

Before refrigeration, ice had to be cut from lakes and rivers and stored in hay to prevent melting during warm weather. It was then delivered to homes and businesses. (Courtesy of the Calumet Regional Archives, Indiana University.)

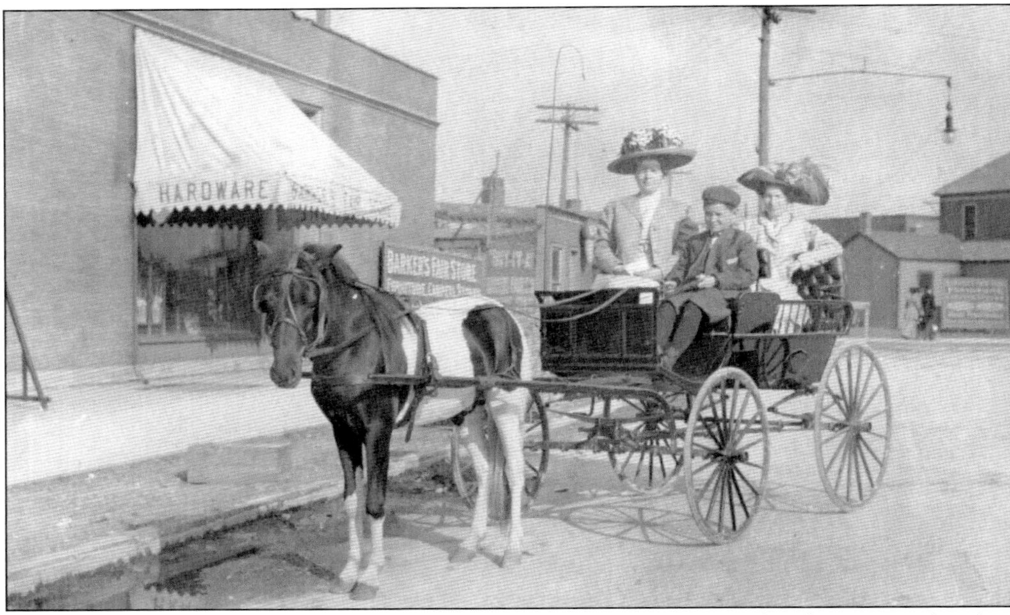

Mrs. Henry Barker is pictured with her son and her daughter Marian Barker (later Janson) in front of the second Barker's Fair Store, which was rebuilt following the cyclone of 1904. Her husband, Henry Barker (née Barkofski), was killed in the cyclone. After his father's death, Henry Barker opened a second store. He also introduced the city's first home delivery service, something so revolutionary that a majority of the community showed up to see it. (Courtesy of the East Chicago Public Library.)

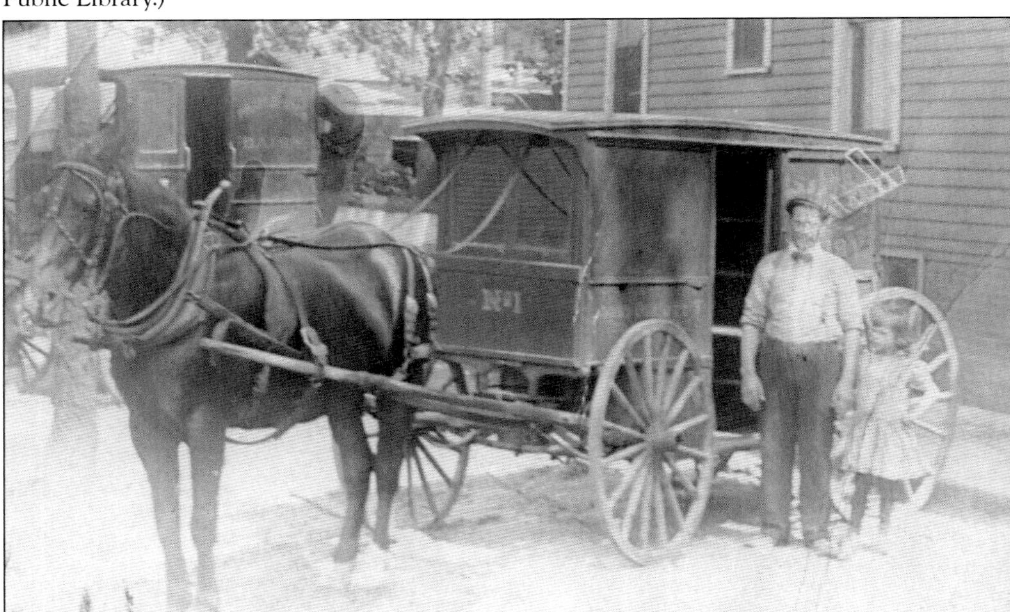

Small dairies were typical during the early part of the 20th century, before refrigeration allowed milk and other dairy products to be stored farther from the source. (Courtesy of the Calumet Regional Archives, Indiana University.)

Though horse and buggies were still standard, automobiles began to reshape cities like East Chicago. (Courtesy of the Calumet Regional Archives, Indiana University.)

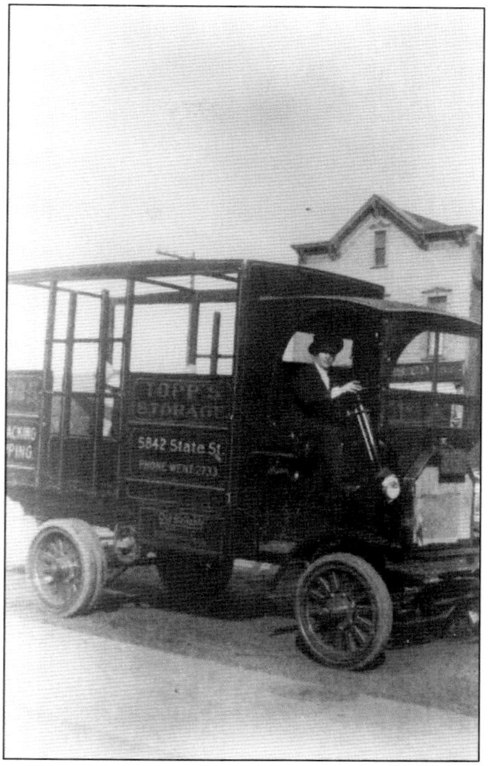

Trolley cars ran down such major thoroughfares as Michigan and Euclid Avenues as well as Main and Guthrie Streets. Here, a trolley passes a parade of horse-pulled floats on Michigan Avenue. (Courtesy of the East Chicago Public Library.)

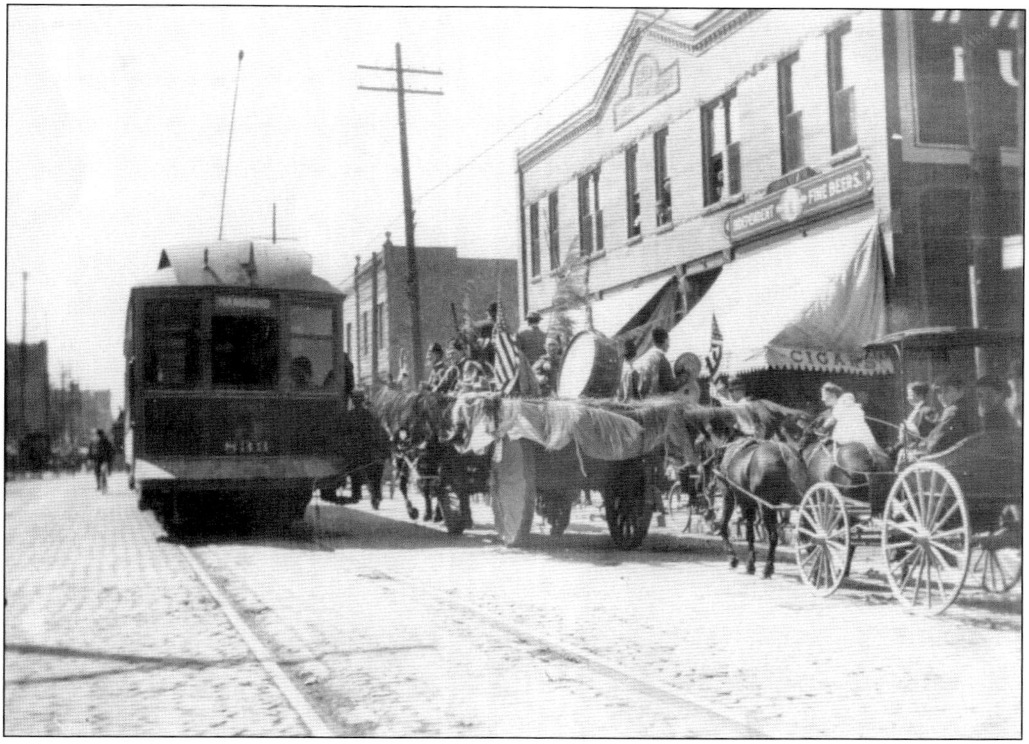

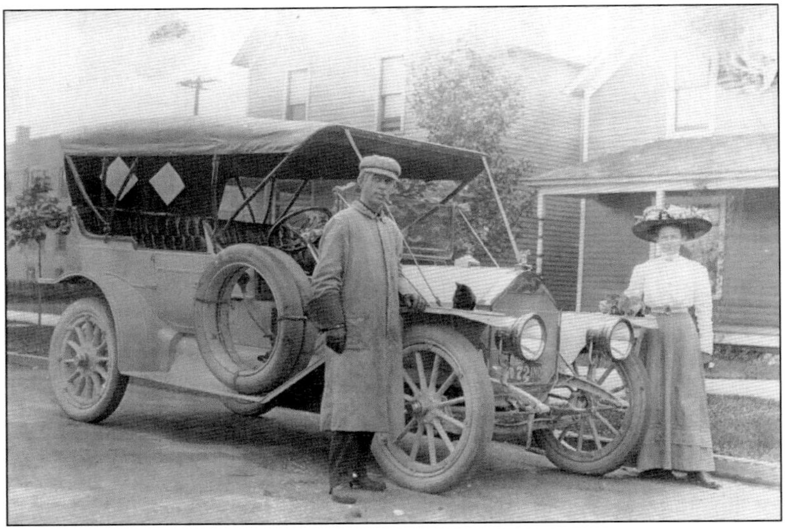

Riding in open air cars was a dusty business before paved roads. In this 1911 photograph, an East Chicago couple are dressed for traveling on city streets. (Courtesy of the Calumet Regional Archives, Indiana University.)

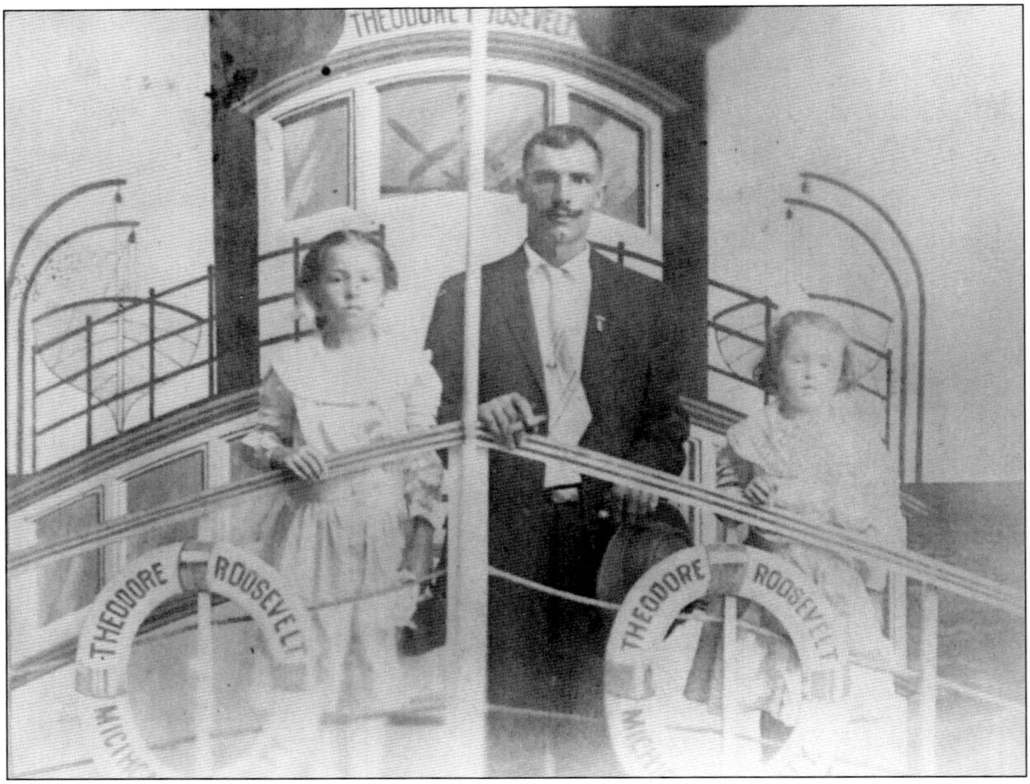

In this 1912 photograph is Steve Kish aboard the *Theodore Roosevelt*, which sailed to Michigan City that year as part of the Inland Steel annual employee picnic. The company began these outings the year before, when it also formed the Inland Steamship Company. According to historian Arch McKinlay, families including children boarded a ship at the blast furnace dock in the morning and returned that evening after a day's excursion. These trips were discontinued in 1915 after the *Eastland* overturned in the Chicago River, killing 812 people during the Western Electric Company's annual picnic. (Courtesy of the Calumet Regional Archives, Indiana University.)

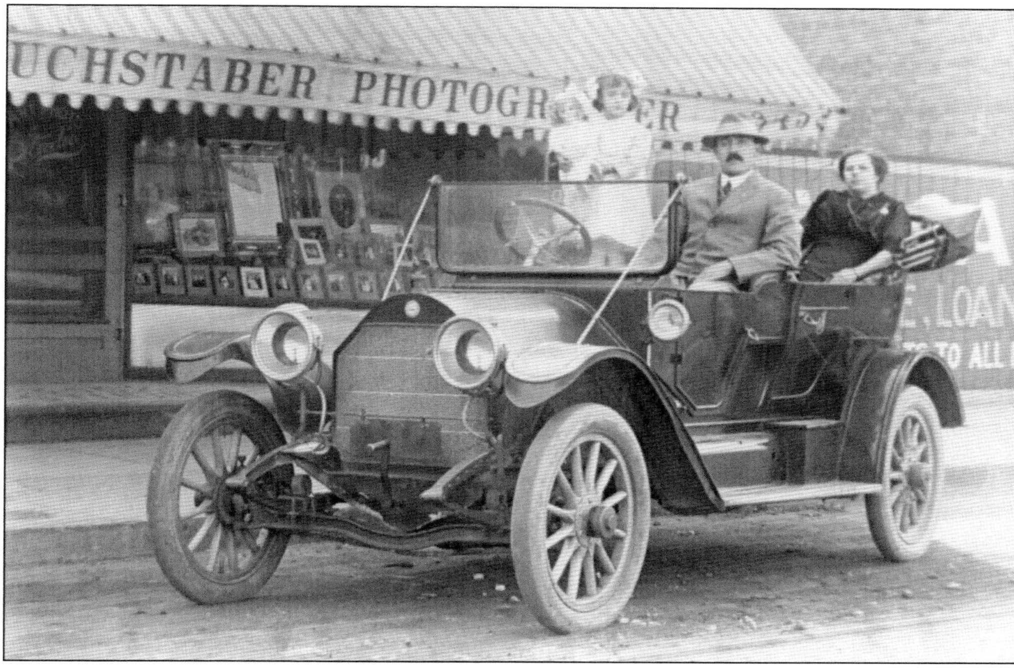

Essack Buchstaber, shown here with his wife, Bertha, was a noted photographer in East Chicago. He often used his car as a prop for photographs. (Courtesy of the East Chicago Public Library.)

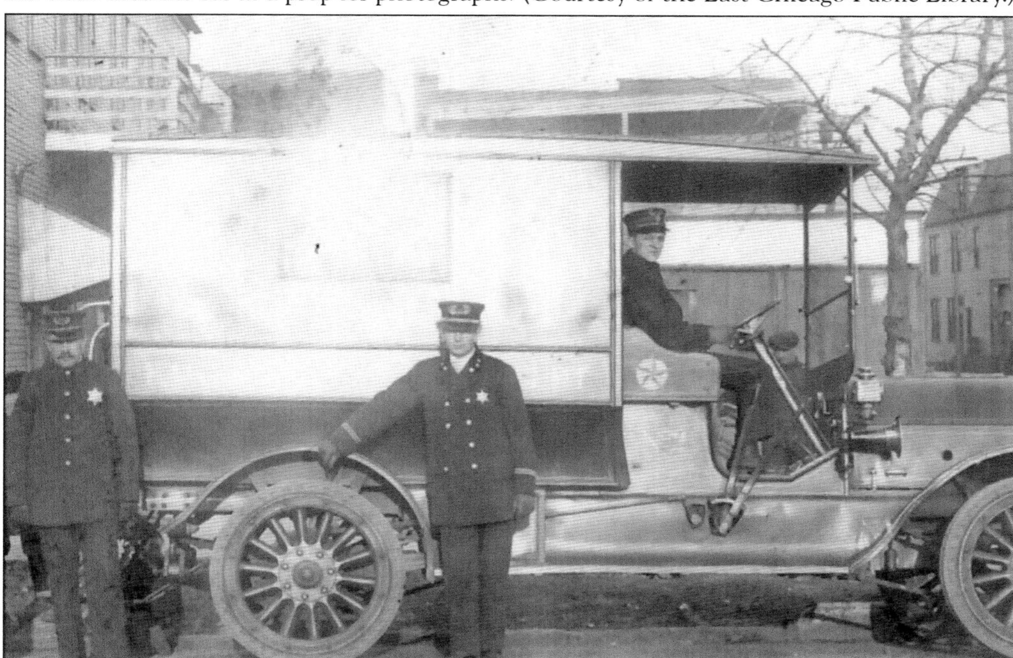

When Capt. Michael Gorman joined the police department in 1898, there had never been a horse-drawn police wagon. Lawbreakers were often put in a wheelbarrow and pushed through the sand to the two-by-four-foot jail. This photograph shows one of the city's first motorized paddy wagons. (Courtesy of the East Chicago Public Library.)

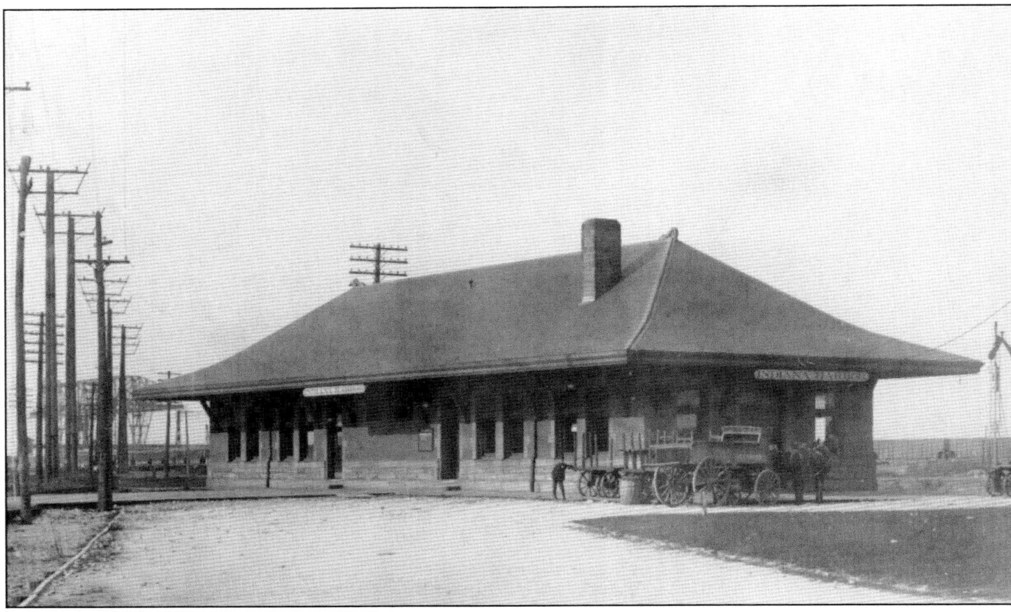

Construction workers arrived in Indiana Harbor from South Chicago in 1901 to begin building both the town and the new Inland Steel mill. For many years, trains were the main transportation between Chicago and Indiana Harbor, and by 1909, 125 trains stopped at the latter every day. One of the important lines was the South Shore & Michigan Southern Railway, whose Indiana Harbor depot is pictured. (Courtesy of the Calumet Regional Archives, Indiana University.)

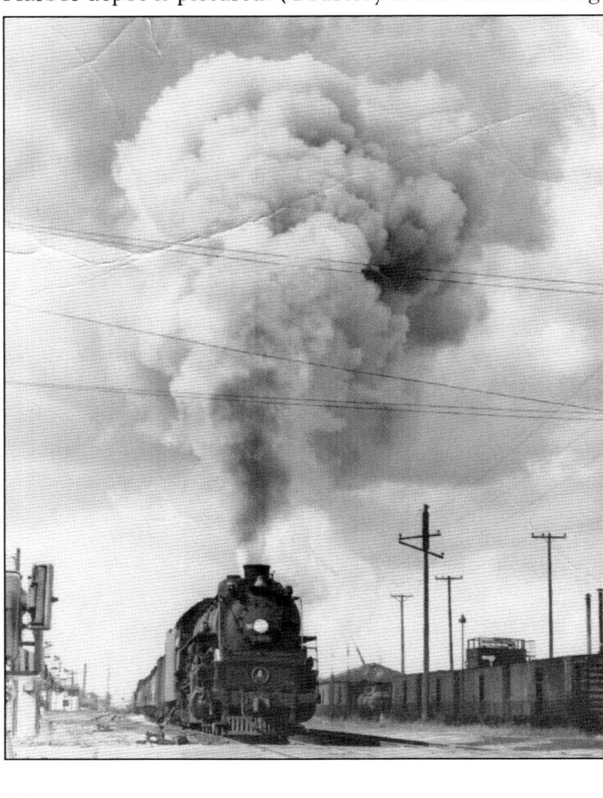

The first train on the Indiana Harbor line ran in December 1905. In the beginning, summoning a train was pretty rudimentary. Those wanting to flag down the New York Central trains climbed trees to see if they were coming around the bend and waved their hands to get them to stop. (Courtesy of the Calumet Regional Archives, Indiana University.)

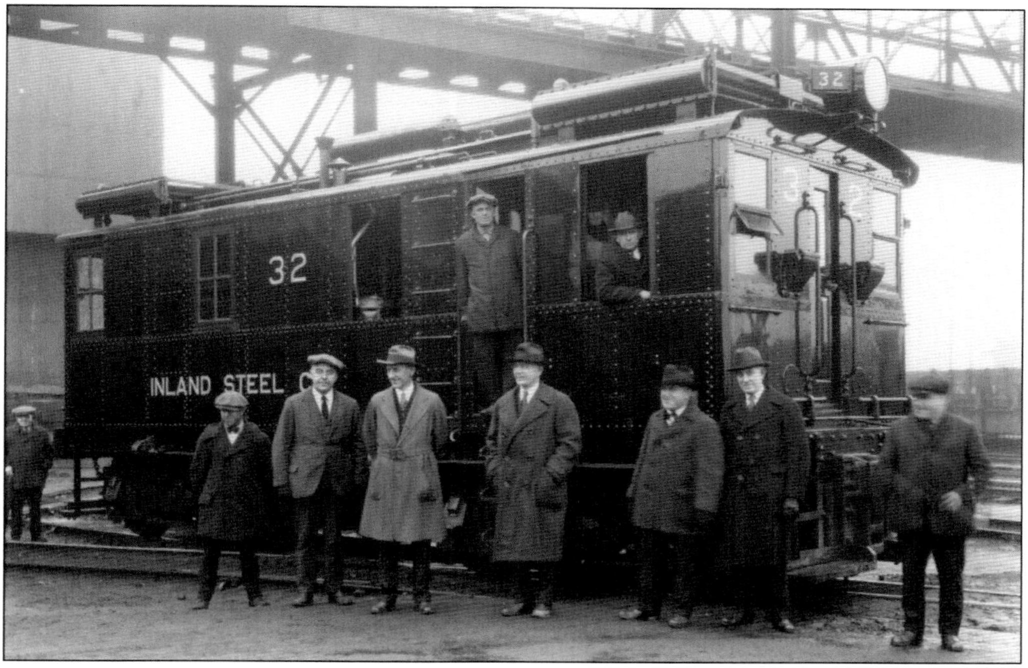

Locomotive No. 32 went into service on Thanksgiving Day at Inland Steel. When East Chicago celebrated its 75th anniversary in 1968, the combined payroll of local industries was more than $500 million annually. (Courtesy of the Calumet Regional Archives, Indiana University.)

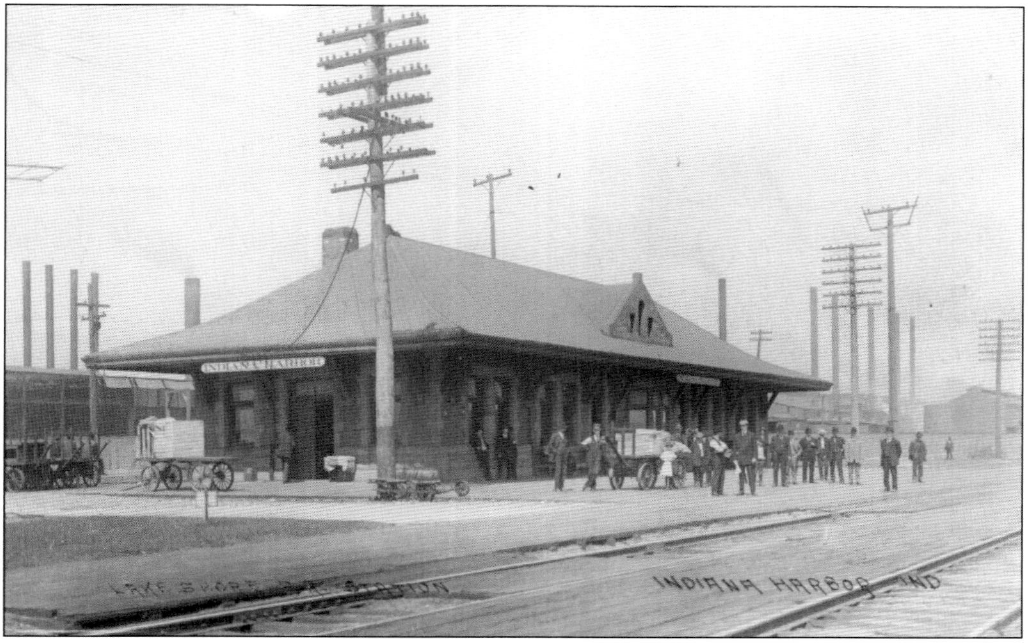

This early postcard shows the Indian Harbor depot. Besides passenger trains, three belt line railroads connected with all 23 trunk lines entering Chicago. East Chicago also had three streetcar systems carrying hundreds of passengers a day. (Courtesy of the Calumet Regional Archives, Indiana University.)

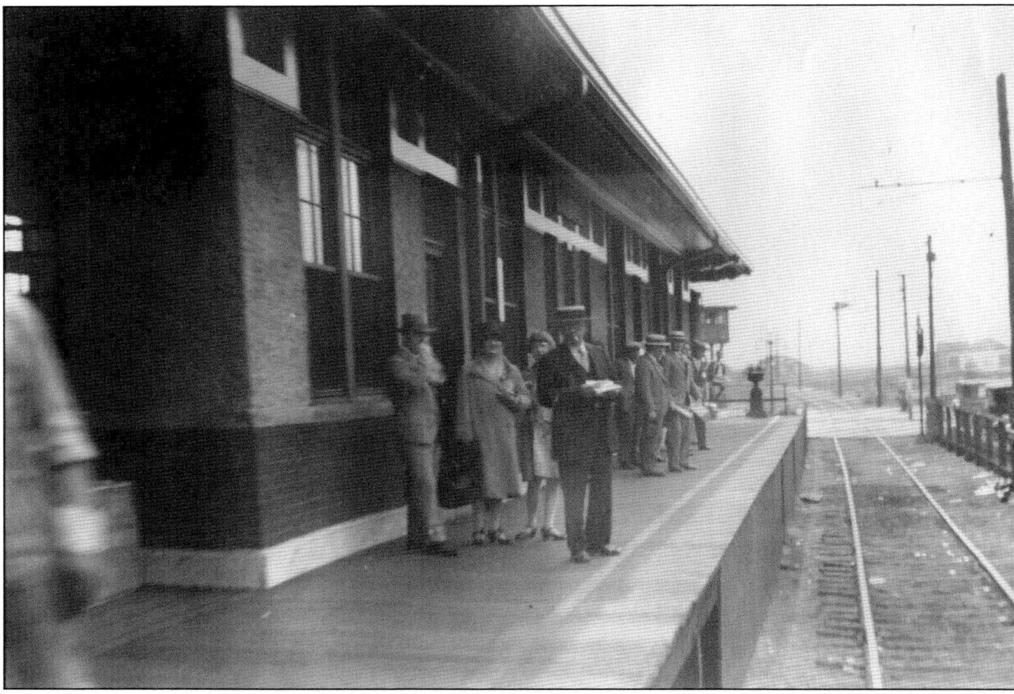

In this 1928 photograph, passengers wait for the train in front of the depot on Chicago Avenue. (Courtesy of the East Chicago Public Library.)

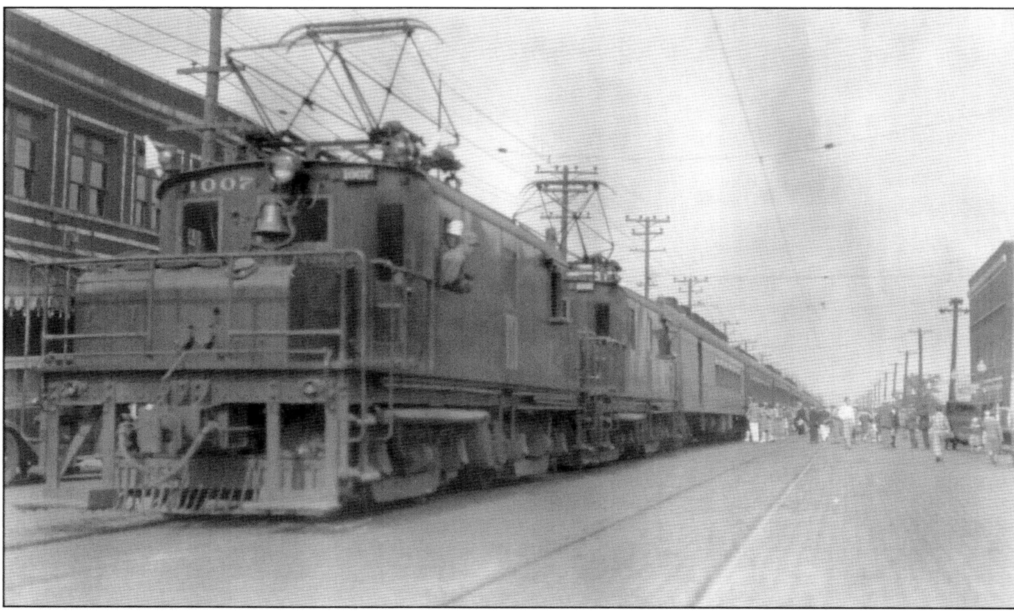

Four years after the start of the 20th century, 45 passenger trains made daily stops at Indiana Harbor, and the South Shore & Michigan Southern Railway was in the process of erecting a $15,000 passenger station on Regent Street, 300 feet north of Watling Street. The South Shore trolley connected Indiana Harbor with East Chicago. (Courtesy of the Calumet Regional Archives, Indiana University.)

Four

Our Community

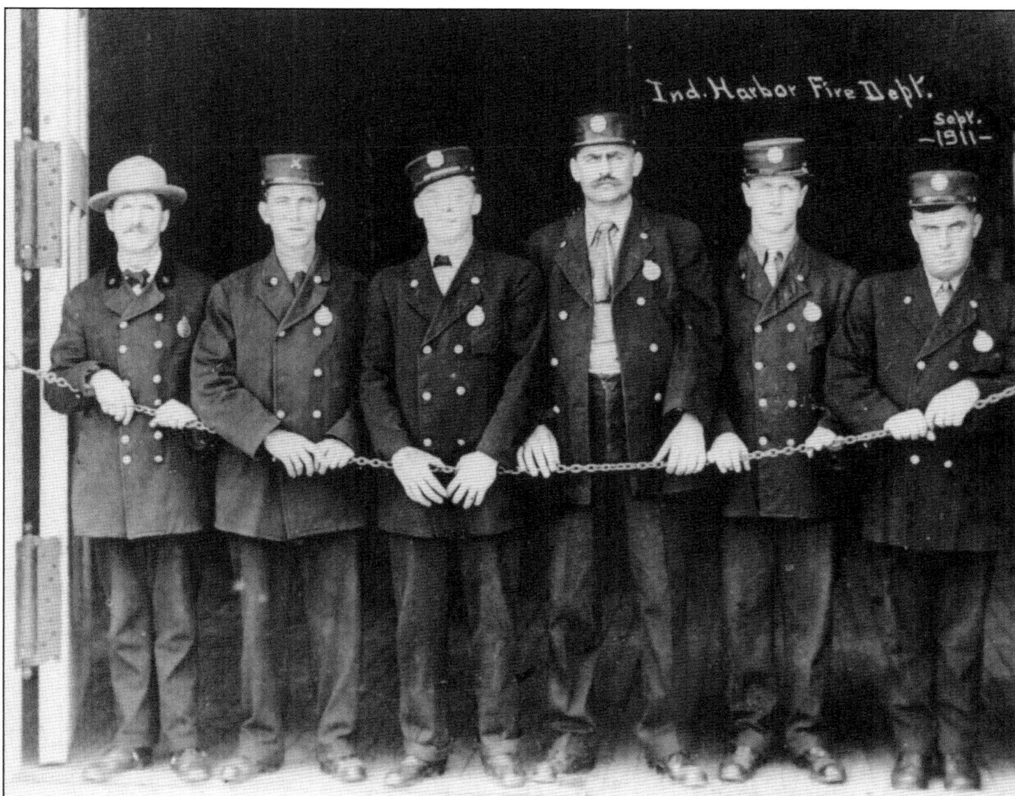

In 1911, members of the East Chicago Fire Department posed for this photograph in Indiana Harbor. (Courtesy of the Calumet Regional Archives, Indiana University.)

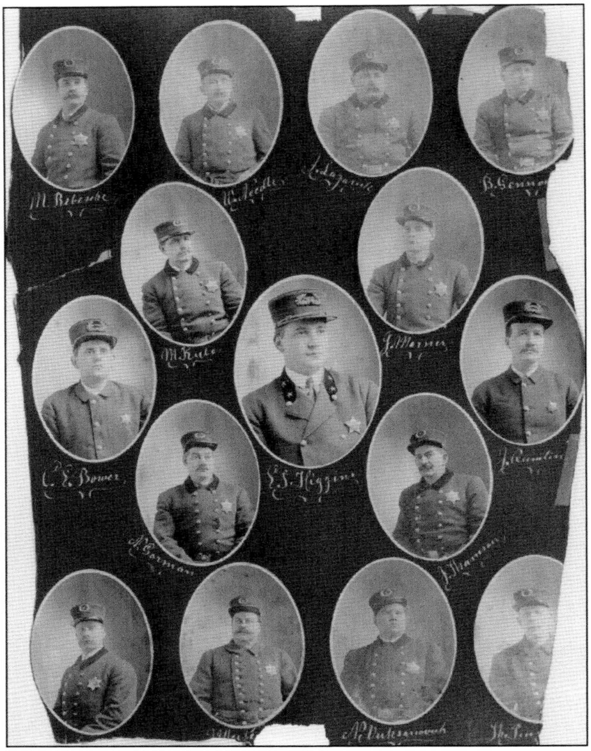

In 1904, the police station was located at Block and Watling Streets, and on Saturday night, a borrowed wagon and team of horses were used to collect the weekend drunks. (Courtesy of the Calumet Regional Archives, Indiana University.)

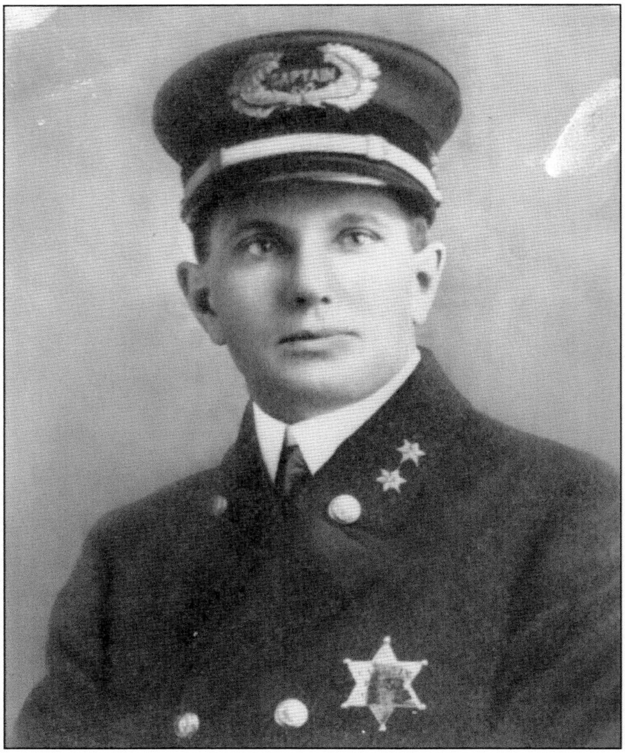

Crist Struss served twice as chief of the East Chicago police in the 1920s and became so disenchanted and upset over policing in the notoriously corrupt Twin City that he spent time in a sanitarium in Battle Creek, Michigan. Struss died in his home at 3821 Ivy Street on May 14, 1926. An excerpt of his obituary read, "His conduct in office was marked by a strict devotion to duty and even his political enemies praised him for the work which he accomplished." (Courtesy of the East Chicago Public Library.)

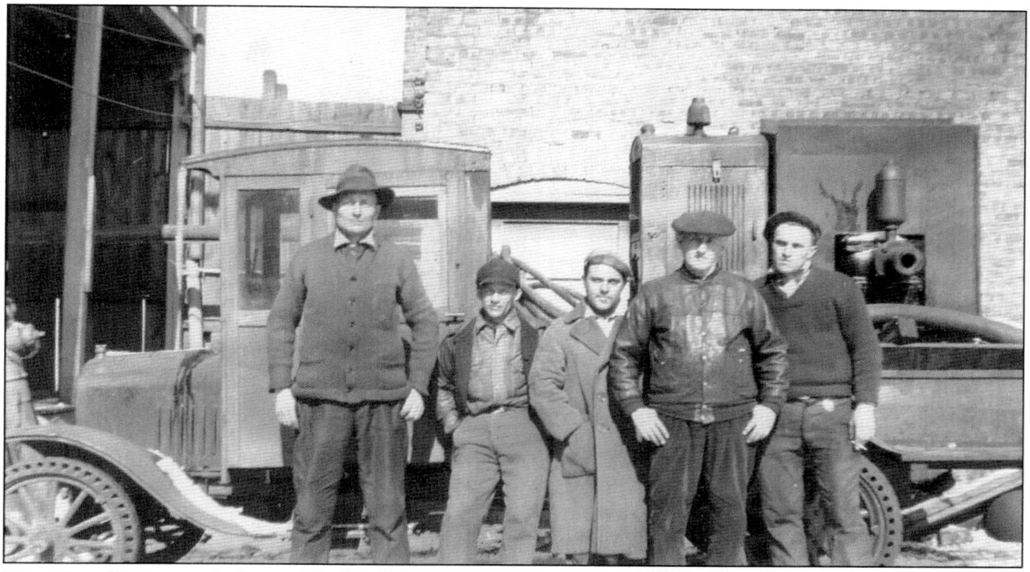

The East Chicago–Indiana Harbor Water Company was in operation from 1907 to 1924, when the city bought it. Pictured here are water plant workers in 1914. (Courtesy of Archibald McKinlay.)

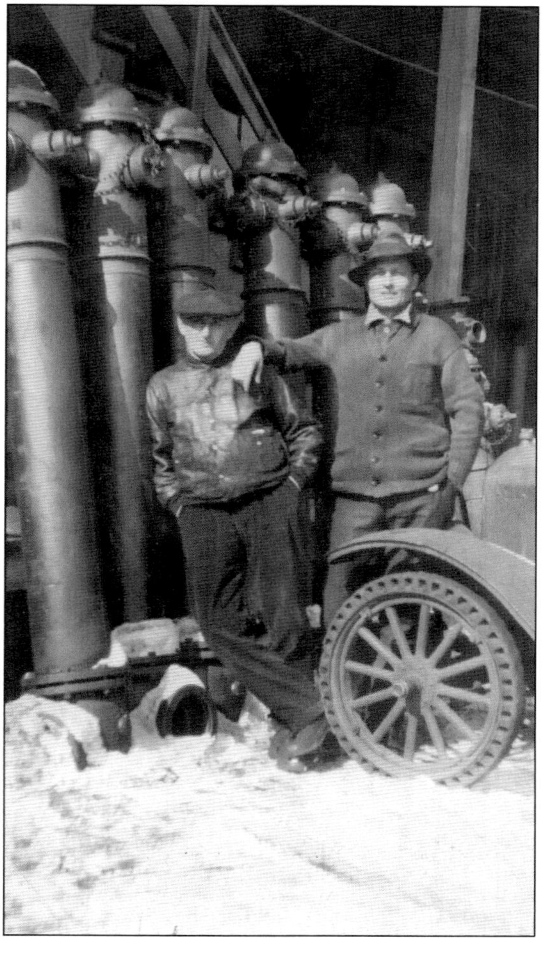

Before paved roads (and even some main streets in Indiana Harbor were not paved in the 1910s), roads were dusty in dry weather and muddy and sometimes impassable during wet weather. Oiling down dusty roads helped keep drivers and their passengers from becoming covered in a film of dirt. (Courtesy of Archibald McKinlay.)

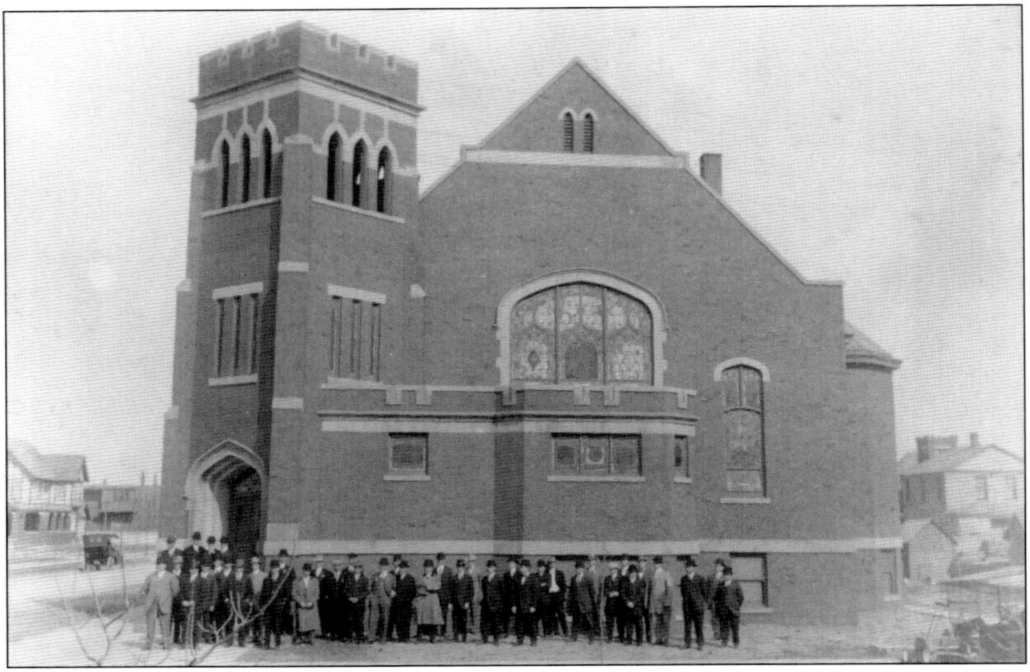

According to historian Arch McKinlay, the Methodist church, pictured in 1916, began when Reverend Leazenby hiked through swamps and over dunelands after hearing about a tent city filled with people who had arrived to work in Indiana Harbor. A cry from one of the tents made him stop, and he found a woman holding a dead baby and sobbing, "Why, oh why God, did you lead us to this forsaken land?" Seeing the reverend, she begged him for a Christian burial for her child. People from differing religious backgrounds joined in the service, and by 1904, eight churches were organized and holding services. (Courtesy of the Calumet Regional Archives, Indiana University.)

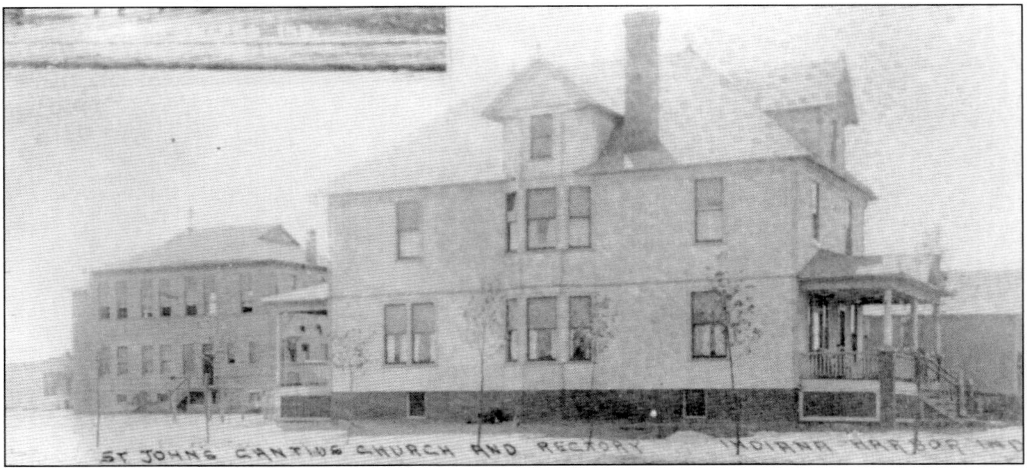

St. John Cantius Church and Rectory was founded in 1905 by 26 Polish immigrant families. The church was named for a Polish priest and theology professor, St. John Cantius, who was declared a patron of Poland and Lithuania by Pope Clement XII in 1737. The Franciscan Sisters of Chicago (then known as the Franciscan Sisters of Blessed Cunegundes) opened a school in the parish the same year. (Courtesy of the Calumet Regional Archives, Indiana University.)

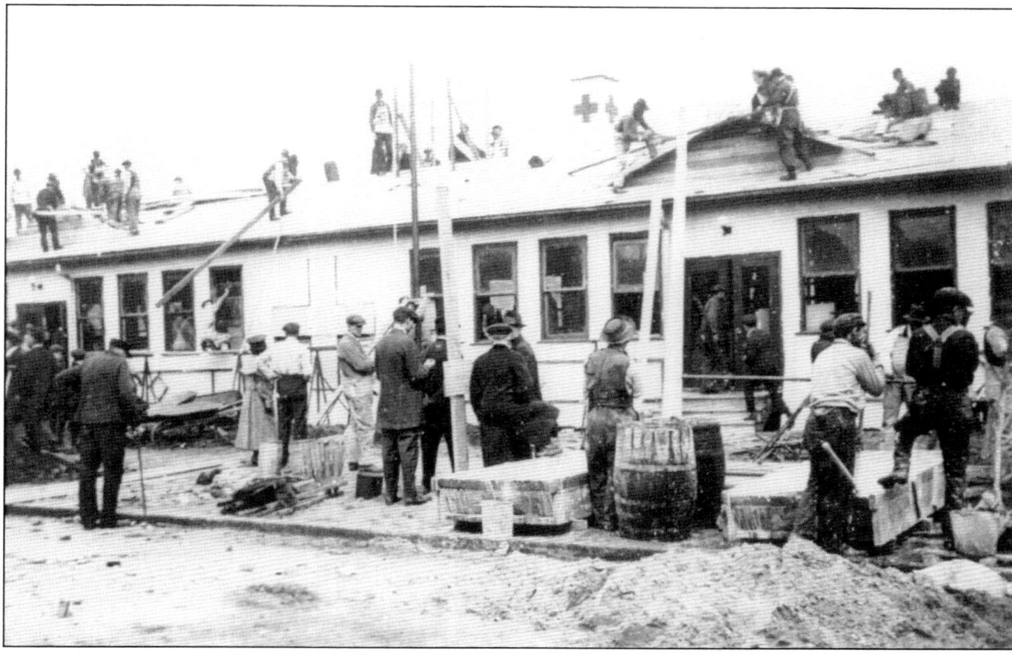

Built in a single day in 1917, the Red Cross on Fir Street near Michigan Avenue in Indiana Harbor was used by women who collected and made medical supplies for the troops during World War I. (Courtesy of the Calumet Regional Archives, Indiana University.)

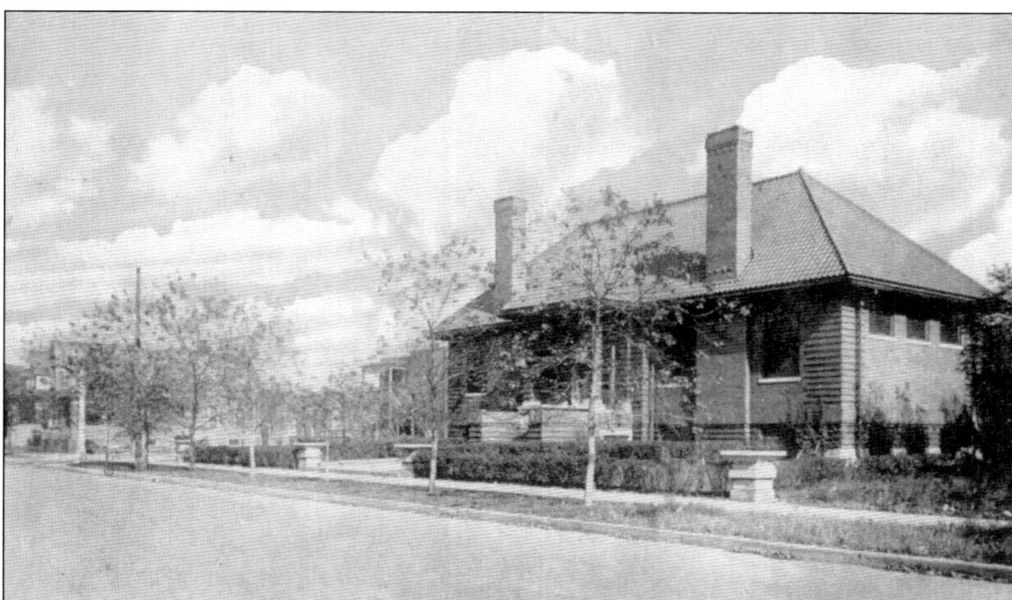

The East Chicago Library, situated at the corner of 136th Street and Grapevine Avenue (now Grand Boulevard), was one of 164 Carnegie libraries in 155 communities in Indiana. Indiana has more libraries created through an endowment by steel magnate Andrew Carnegie than any other state. Listed in the National Register of Historic Places, the library was constructed in the Arts and Crafts style in 1913. (Courtesy of the Calumet Regional Archives, Indiana University.)

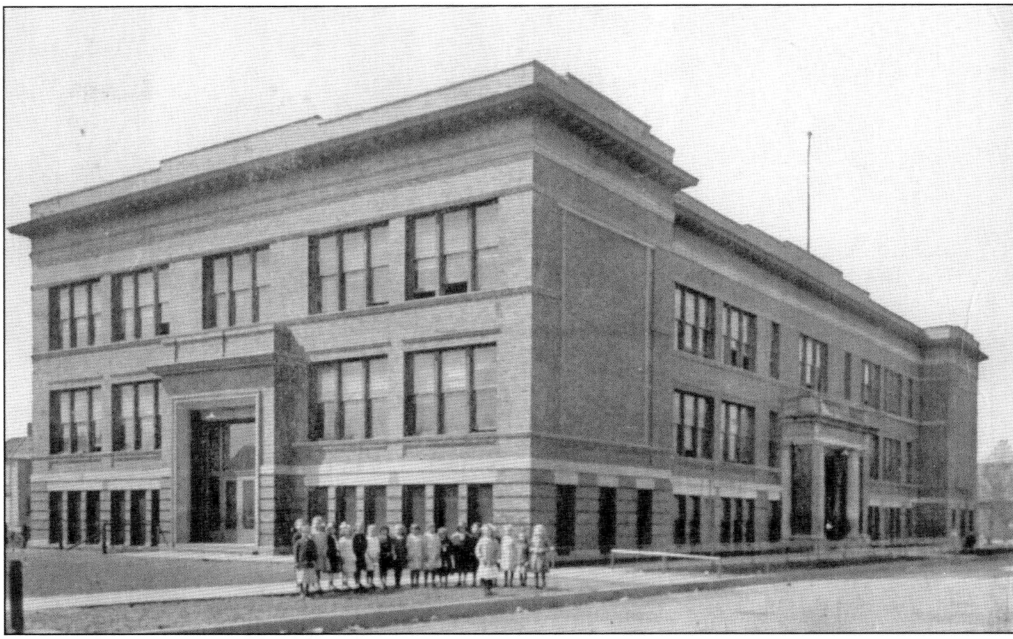

James Whitcomb Riley Elementary School was one of many schools in Indiana named after the state's poet, who is probably now best known for his poem "Little Orphan Annie." (Courtesy of the Calumet Regional Archives, Indiana University.)

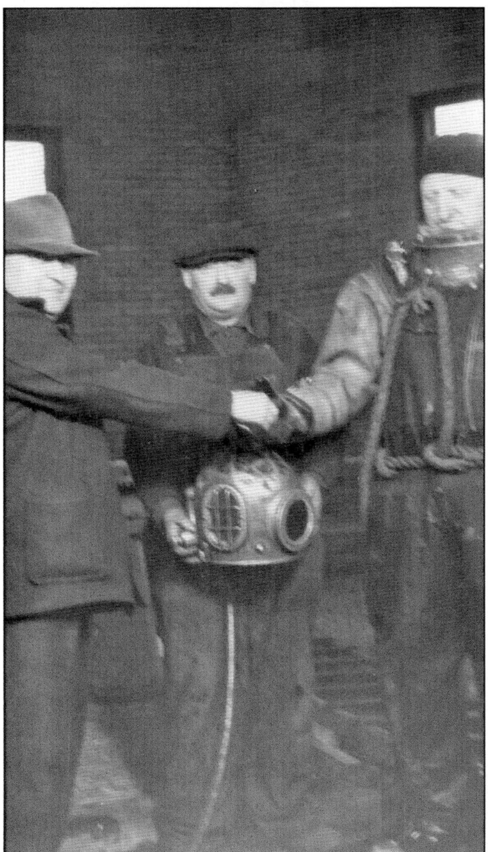

Construction and upkeep of the ship canal required commercial divers trained in hazardous underwater building. (Courtesy of the Calumet Regional Archives, Indiana University.)

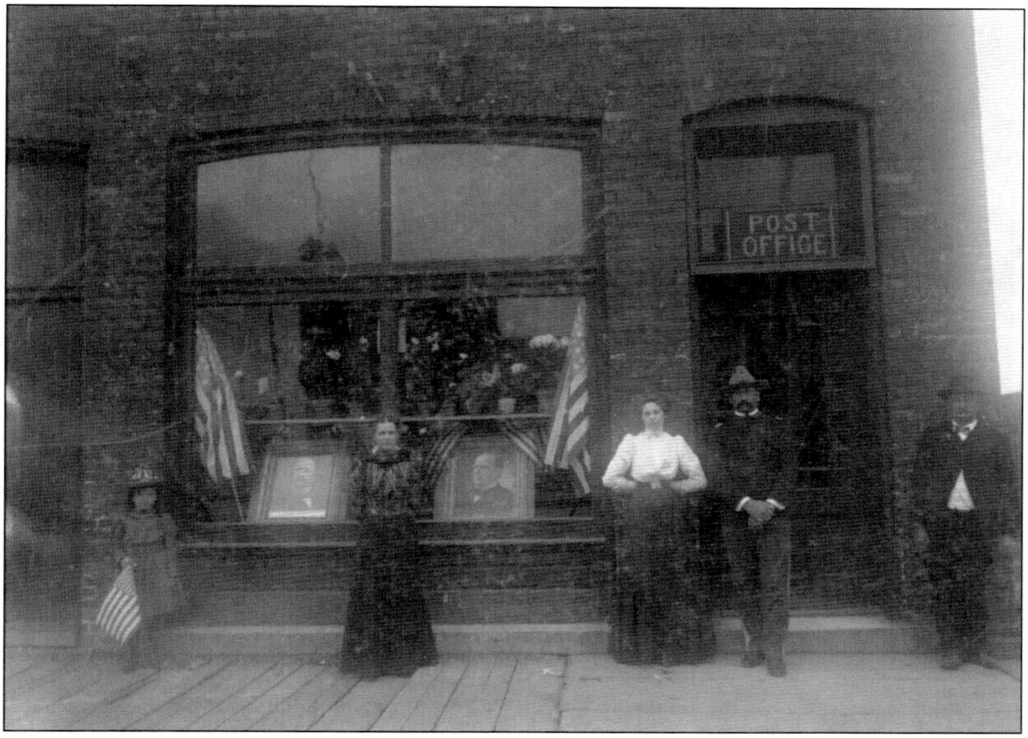

The East Chicago Post Office is pictured in 1899. (Courtesy of the Calumet Regional Archives, Indiana University.)

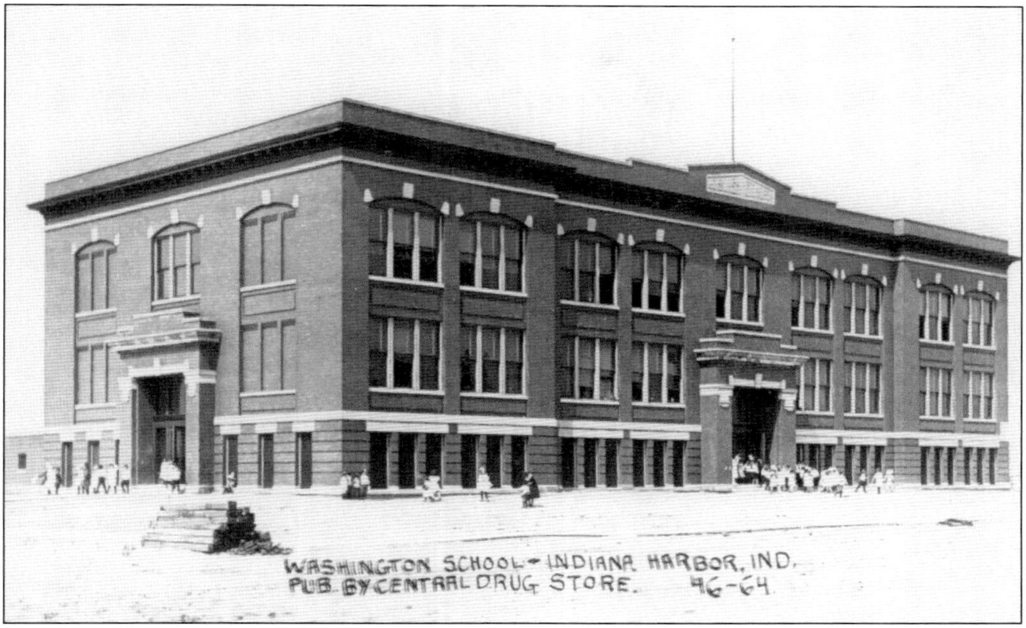

Built in 1919, East Chicago Washington High School was located in Indiana Harbor. Residents in East Chicago attended Roosevelt High School. Both schools have been torn down and replaced by Central High School. (Courtesy of the Calumet Regional Archives, Indiana University.)

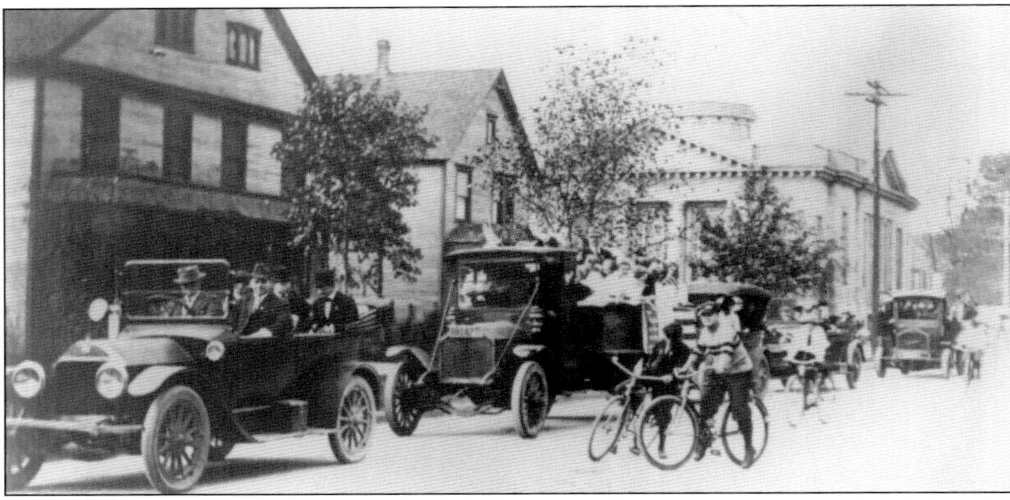

The Neoclassical-style First Congregational Church on 140th Street was designed in 1913 by East Chicago architect Carl D. Norris, who also designed Roosevelt High School, the Masonic Lodge buildings, and the 1931 wing added to the Grand Boulevard Library. The church, built of Indiana limestone, is known for its beautiful stained-glass windows. The dedication parade for the church is pictured here. (Courtesy of the Calumet Regional Archives, Indiana University.)

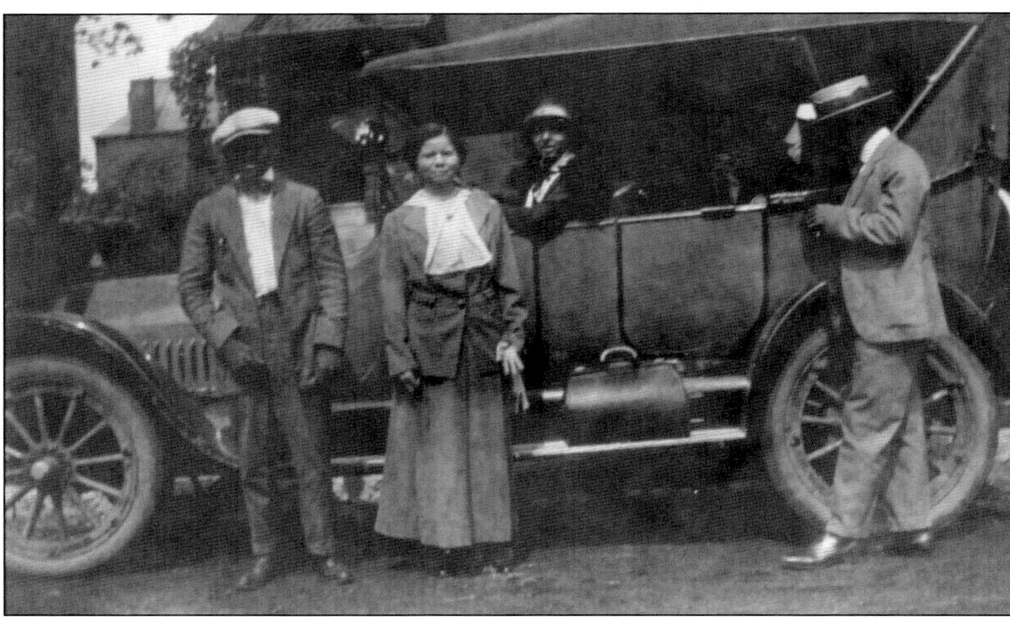

Robert Brown, pictured in 1928, was one of the first African Americans to serve on the East Chicago police force. (Courtesy of the East Chicago Public Library.)

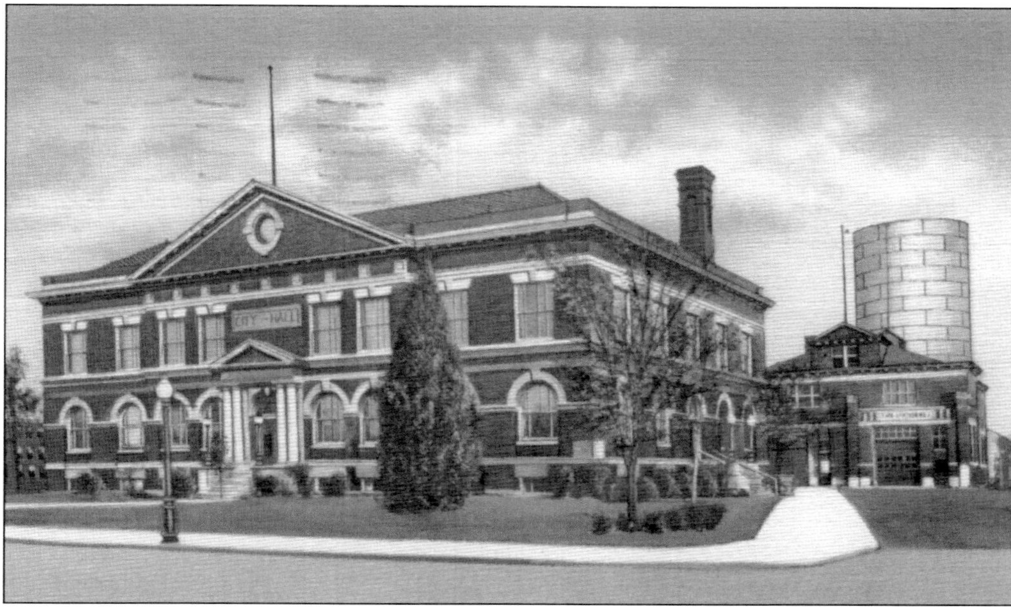

East Chicago City Hall, built in 1907 on Indianapolis Avenue, has been renovated through the years but its center staircase made of cast iron with marble treads remains. When it first opened, the city's jail was located on the bottom floor. (Courtesy of the Calumet Regional Archives, Indiana University.)

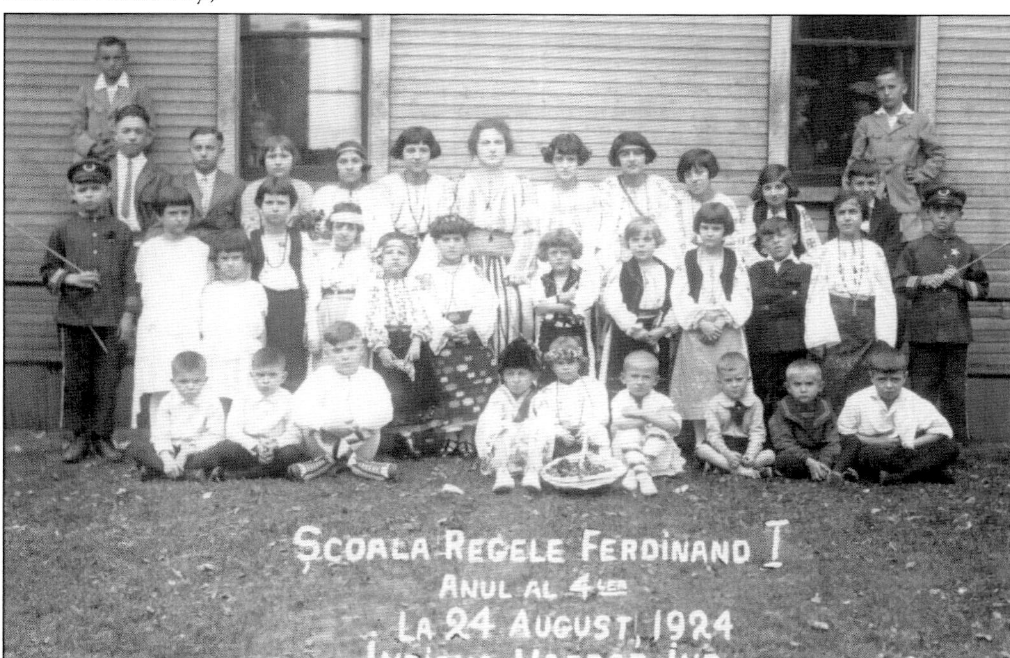

Mary Ben Young, who was born in 1922 in Indiana Harbor and lived there most of her life, remembers that as soon as school was out for the summer, Romanian children would attend the Romanian school and learn the history and language of their country. However, most already spoke it since that was the primary language at home. (Courtesy of the Simon family.)

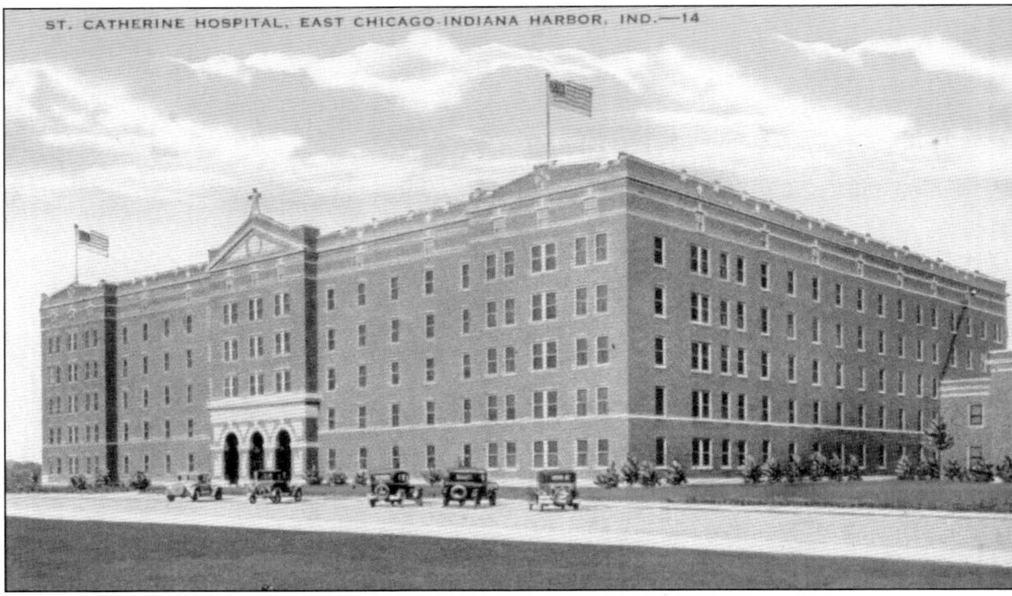

On April 32, 1927, banker and philanthropist Col. Walter J. Riley was the first to break ground at the site of St. Catherine Hospital. When the hospital was completed, it had such modern facilities as a main kitchen and state-of-the-art operating room. St. Catherine Hospital has expanded over the years and is still considered one of the best hospitals in the region. (Courtesy of the Simon family.)

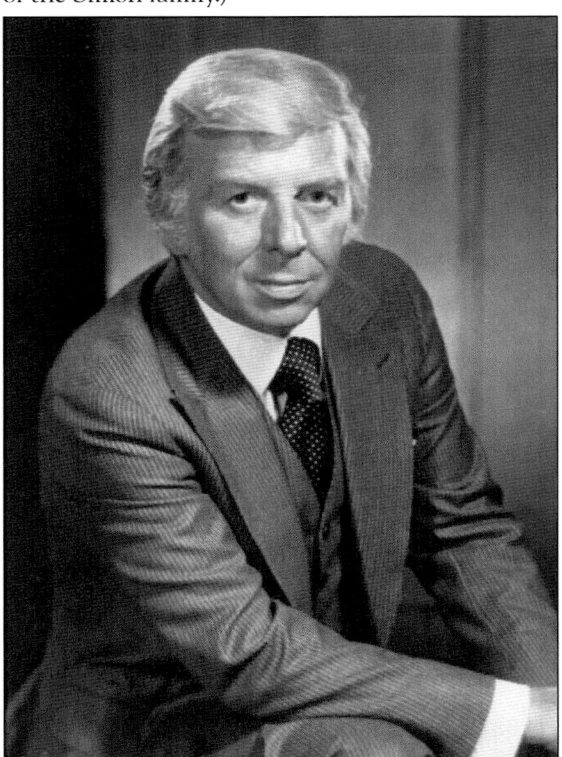

Robert A. Pastrick, mayor of East Chicago, was long a powerful political force in the Democratic Party and a Calumet region political icon since beginning his career in the early 1950s. His tenure as mayor for more than three decades is one of the longest in the country. (Courtesy of the Calumet Regional Archives, Indiana University.)

Five

The Melting Pot

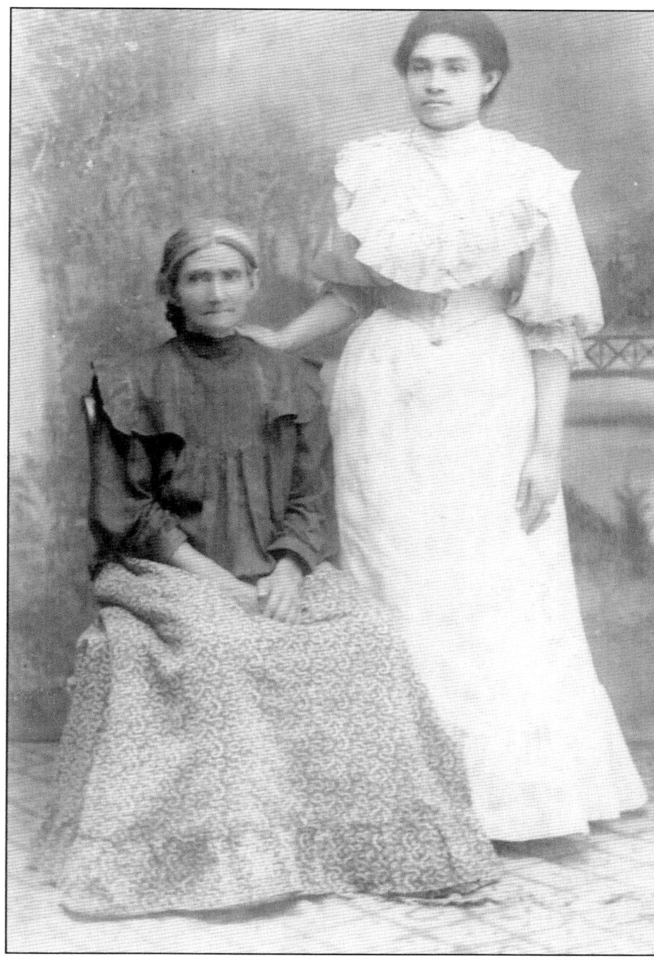

Maria's Journey, a book published by the Indiana Historical Society about the family of Maria Arredondo and written by her son Ray Arredondo and his wife, Trisha, traces their journey from the Mexican Revolution to the mid-1950s. Maria raised her 10 children in East Chicago under harsh conditions but saw them succeed. Her youngest son, Lorenzo Arredondo of East Chicago, served on the bench for 34 years. He was the longest-serving Hispanic state trial judge in the nation when he stepped down in 2011. (Courtesy of Ramon and Trisha Arredondo.)

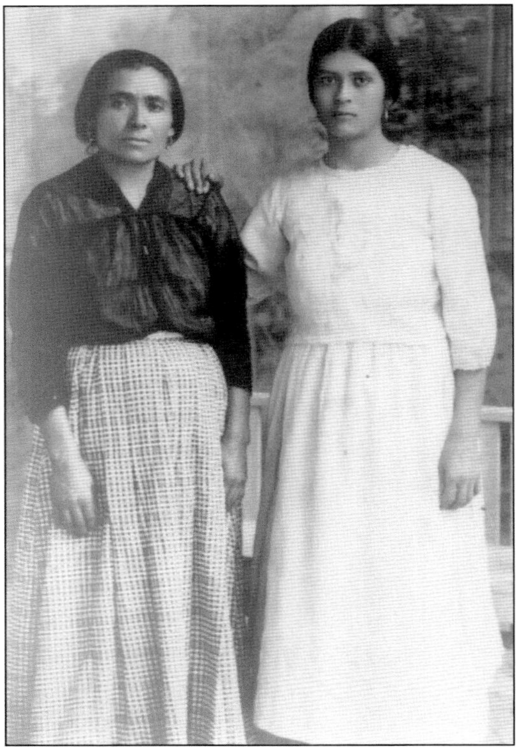

"Watching Maria evolve from a shy young child accepting an arranged marriage at age 14 to a strong and persevering woman trudging through the perilous path of the immigrant wife and mother was nothing short of spectacular," says Trish Arredondo about her mother-in-law, Maria. (Courtesy of Ramon and Trisha Arredondo.)

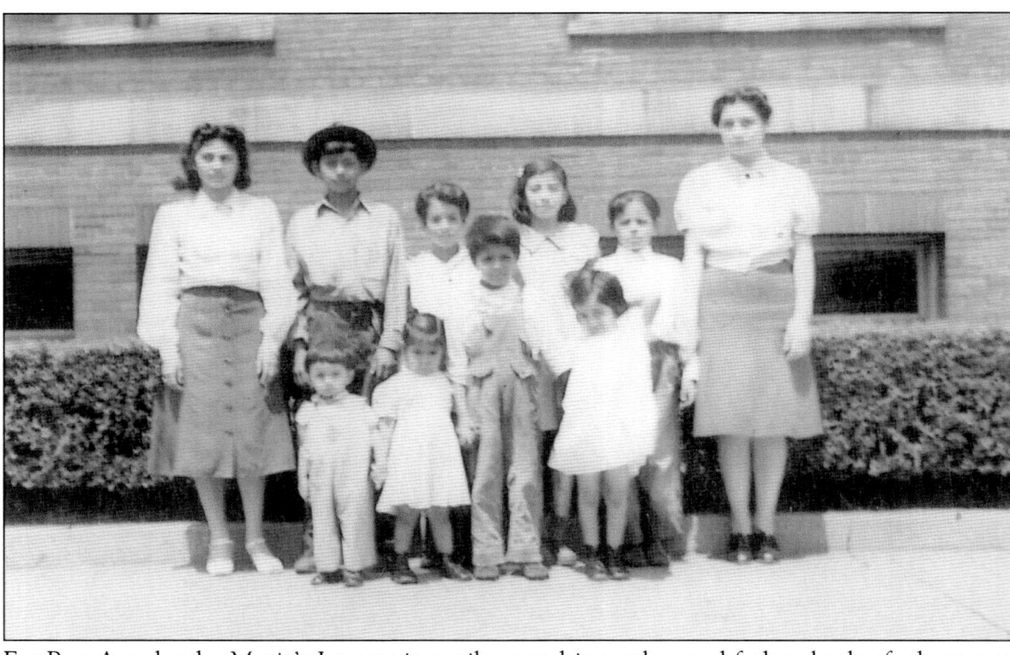

For Ray Arredondo, *Maria's Journey* is a tribute to his mother and father, both of whom were strong-willed and determined people who looked at the world through different eyes—she as a mother wishing a better life for her children and he as a global thinker who felt it his mission to change the world of the worker. (Courtesy of Ramon and Trisha Arredondo.)

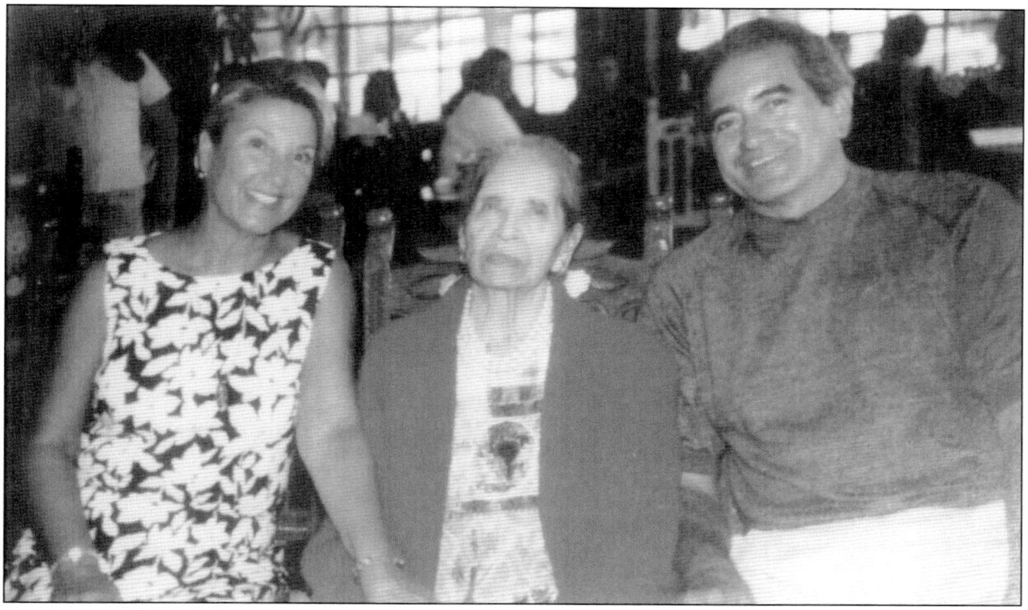

On her 95th birthday, Maria Arredondo is flanked by Trisha Hull Arredondo and Ramon Arredondo in this photograph taken in September 2002. This picture appears on the cover of their book about the Arredondo family. (Courtesy of Ramon and Trisha Arredondo.)

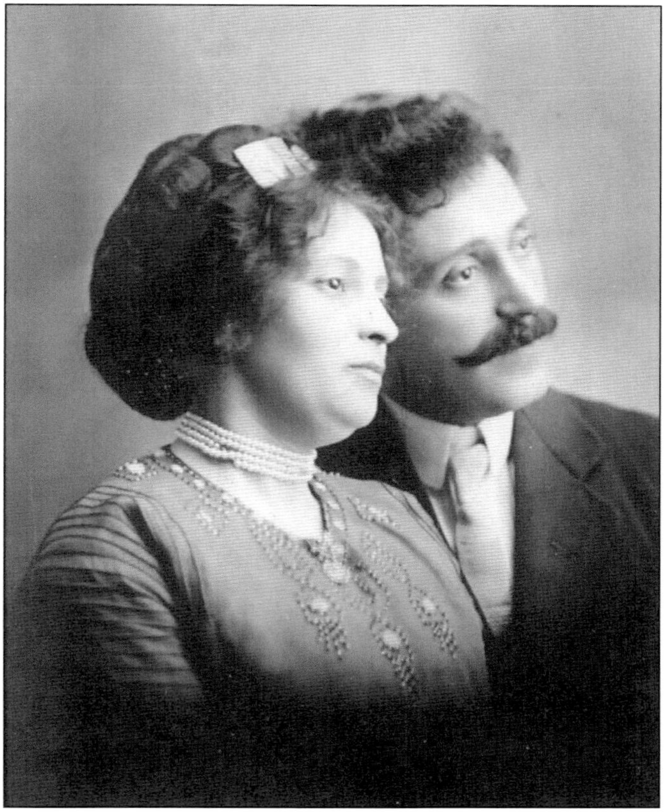

Essack Buchstaber, shown here with his wife, Bertha, was born in Russia in 1880. He came to the United States in 1903 and became a successful photographer until his untimely death in an automobile accident in 1920. (Courtesy of Pamela Buchstaber.)

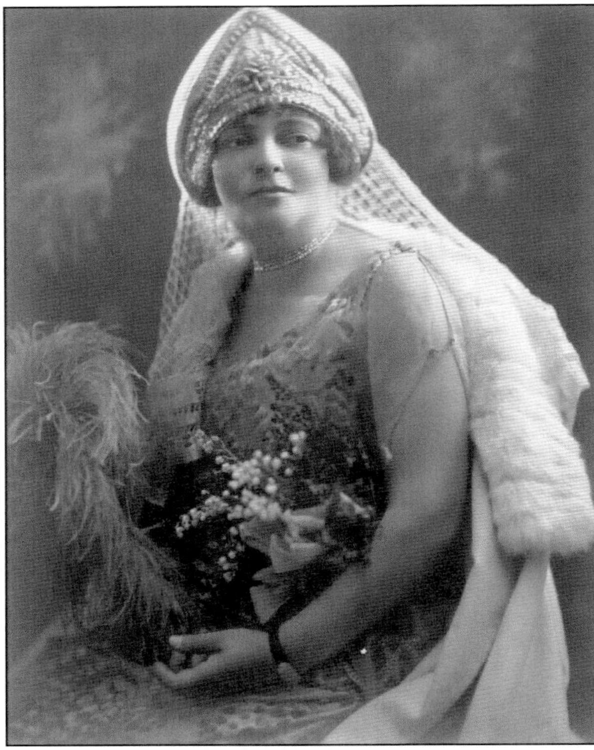

Born in Russia, Bertha Sterling (née Fleischer) came to the United States at age 20, married, and settled in East Chicago. She and her first husband, Essack, had three sons and one daughter: Sam, David, Fred, and Elizabeth. (Courtesy of Pamela Buchstaber.)

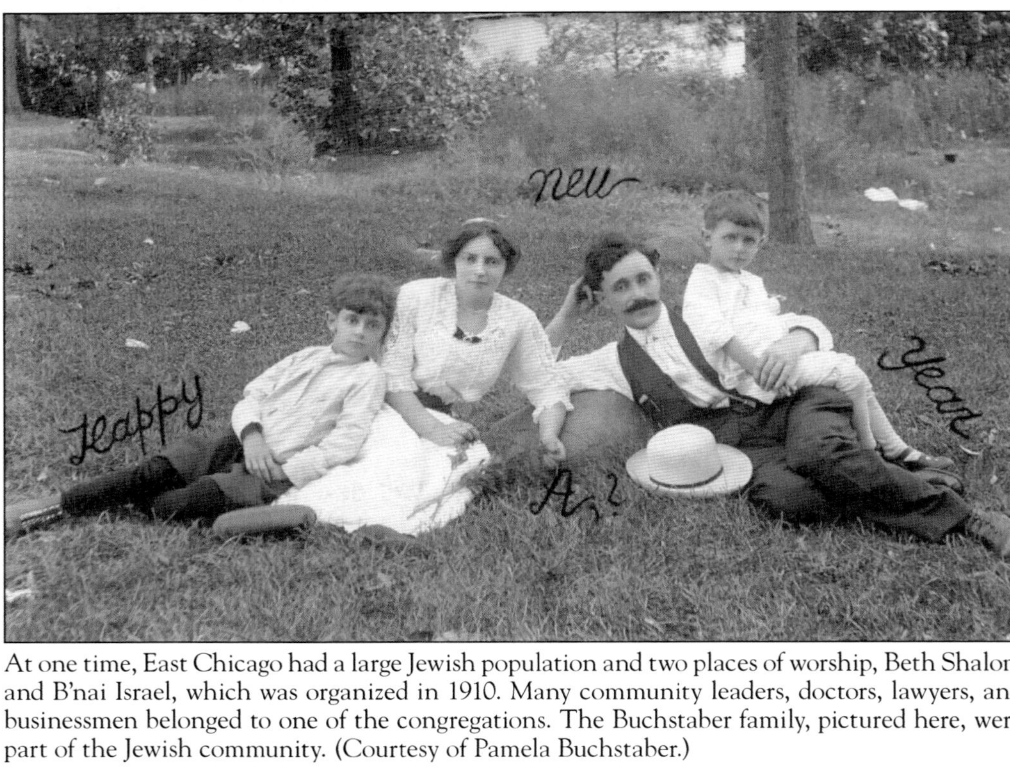

At one time, East Chicago had a large Jewish population and two places of worship, Beth Shalom and B'nai Israel, which was organized in 1910. Many community leaders, doctors, lawyers, and businessmen belonged to one of the congregations. The Buchstaber family, pictured here, were part of the Jewish community. (Courtesy of Pamela Buchstaber.)

The young boy in the center is Harry Dellahan, who was born in Greece and immigrated to East Chicago. He married and had two children, Daniese and Thomas. (Courtesy of Daniese Sprague.)

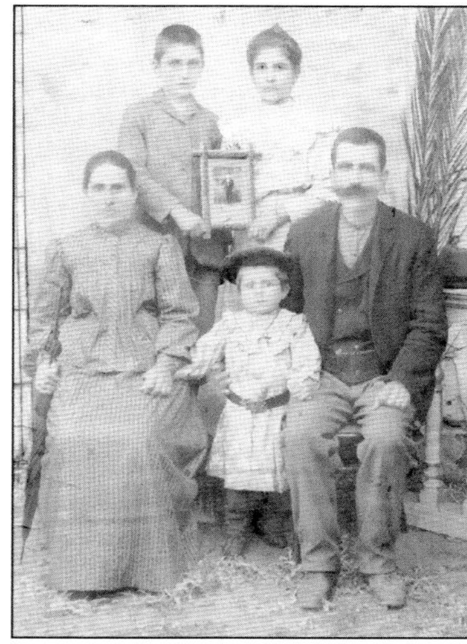

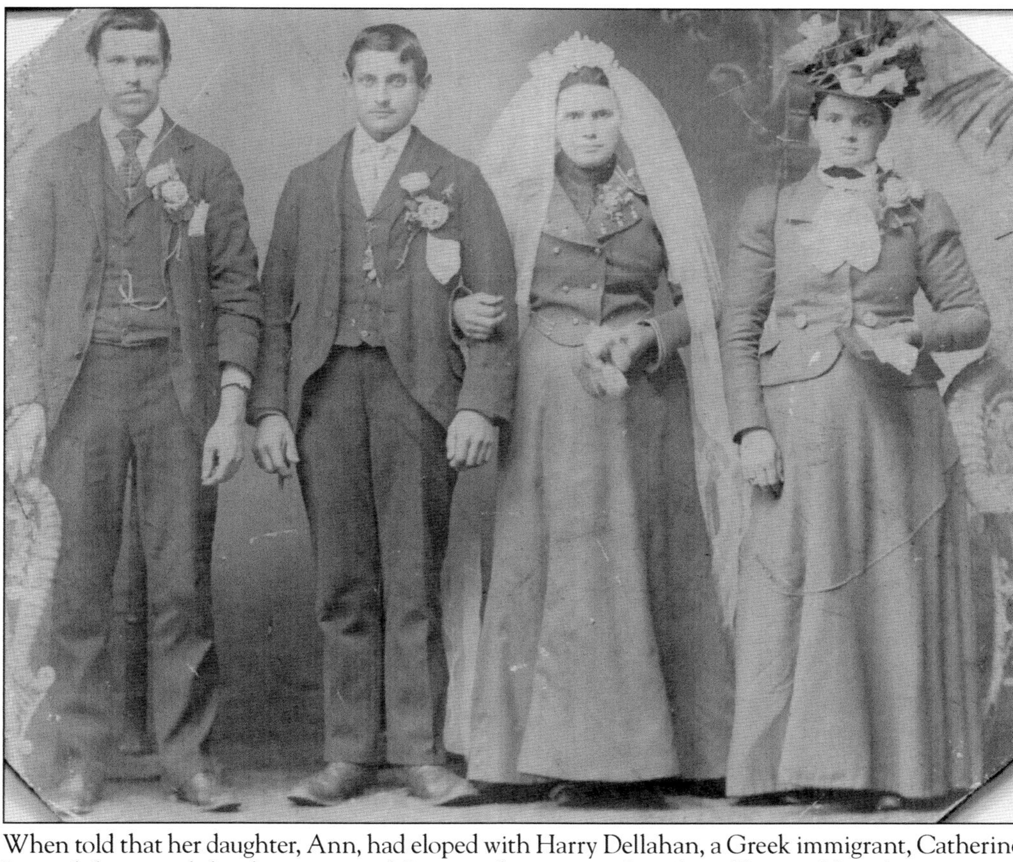

When told that her daughter, Ann, had eloped with Harry Dellahan, a Greek immigrant, Catherine Lapaich lamented that he was not of Croatian heritage and predicted he would get her pregnant and then abandon her to return to Greece. Instead, when Catherine died suddenly at age 58 in 1937, Thomas took care of his wife's family, which included Catherine's widowed husband, godmother, and three siblings, as well as his own two young children. Obviously, Catherine's fears were ill-founded. (Courtesy of Daniese Sprague.)

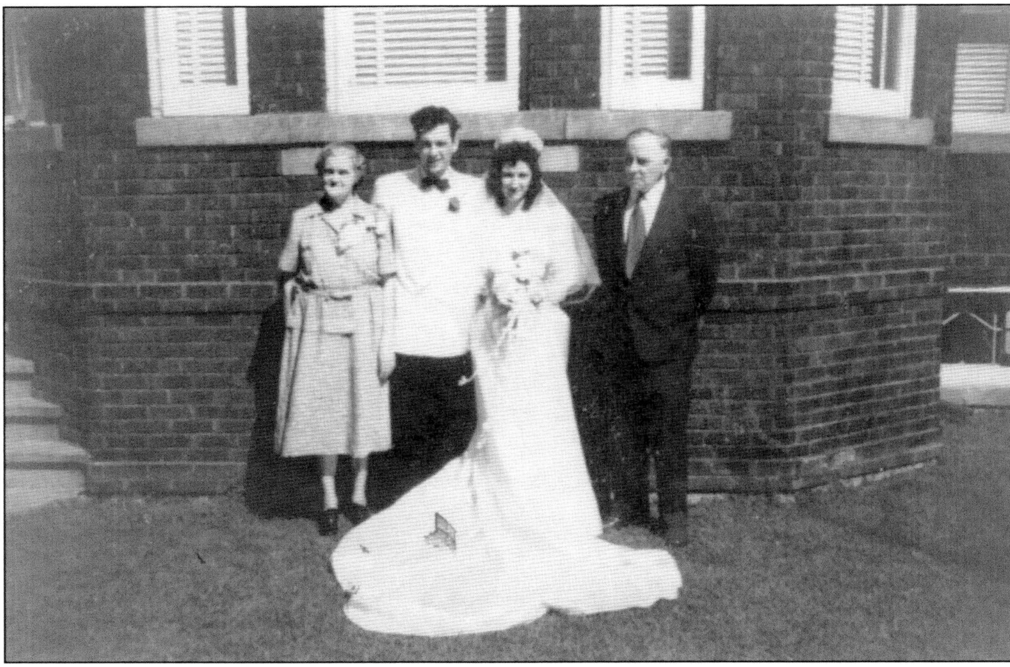

Immigrants who came to America first wanted to keep with the old ways and have their children choose spouses of the same nationality. But while many first generation Americans did follow those traditions, others married for different reasons than just country of origin, creating a true melting pot. In 1948, Robert Briska, whose father was German and mother English (though she was born in the United States), married Daniese Dellahan, a child of Croatian and Greek parentage. (Courtesy of Daniese Sprague.)

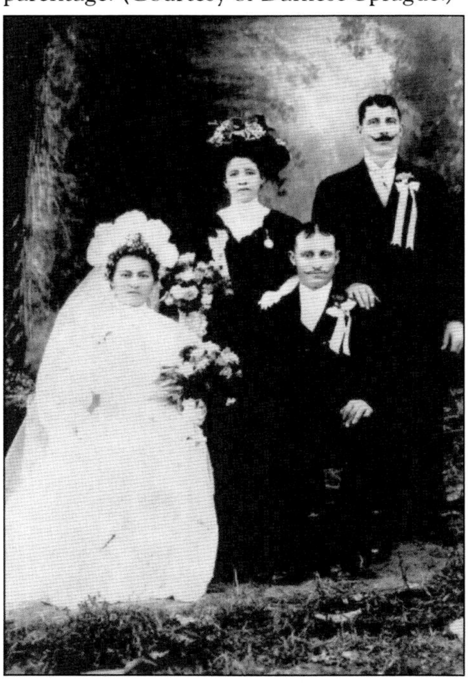

It was not uncommon for men to immigrate from other countries to work in the industries and then, once enough money was saved, send home for a bride. Jon Simon was one such man, marrying Antonia Vulcu, who also was from Romania and crossed the ocean by ship in 1908. The couple married shortly after and had their first son in March 1909. Four other children followed. (Courtesy of the Simon family.)

Dionisie and Maria Simon were first-generation Americans whose parents journeyed across the Atlantic Ocean separately from Romania, married, and started a business. Though they originally had Romanian names, Dionisie became Dan Simon, who was superintendent of East Chicago Public Schools, and Maria was later known as Mary. (Courtesy of the Simon family.)

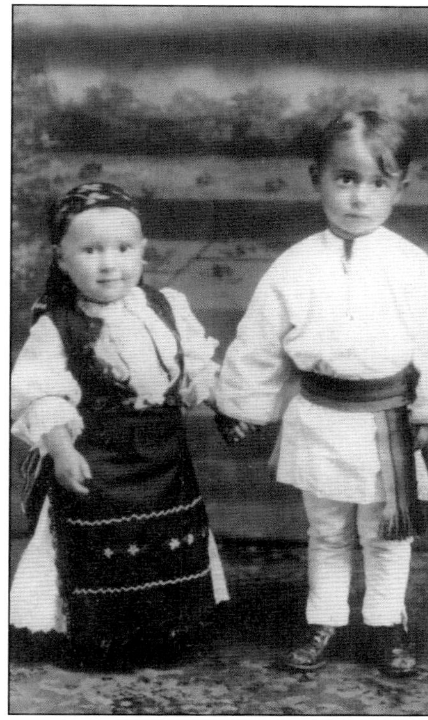

This photograph from around 1920 features a Romanian dance group. Immigrants arriving in East Chicago tended to live in enclaves near each other. For Romanians, that meant living on Block and Pennsylvania Avenues during the early 1900s. They also kept many customs of their homelands. (Courtesy of the Simon family.)

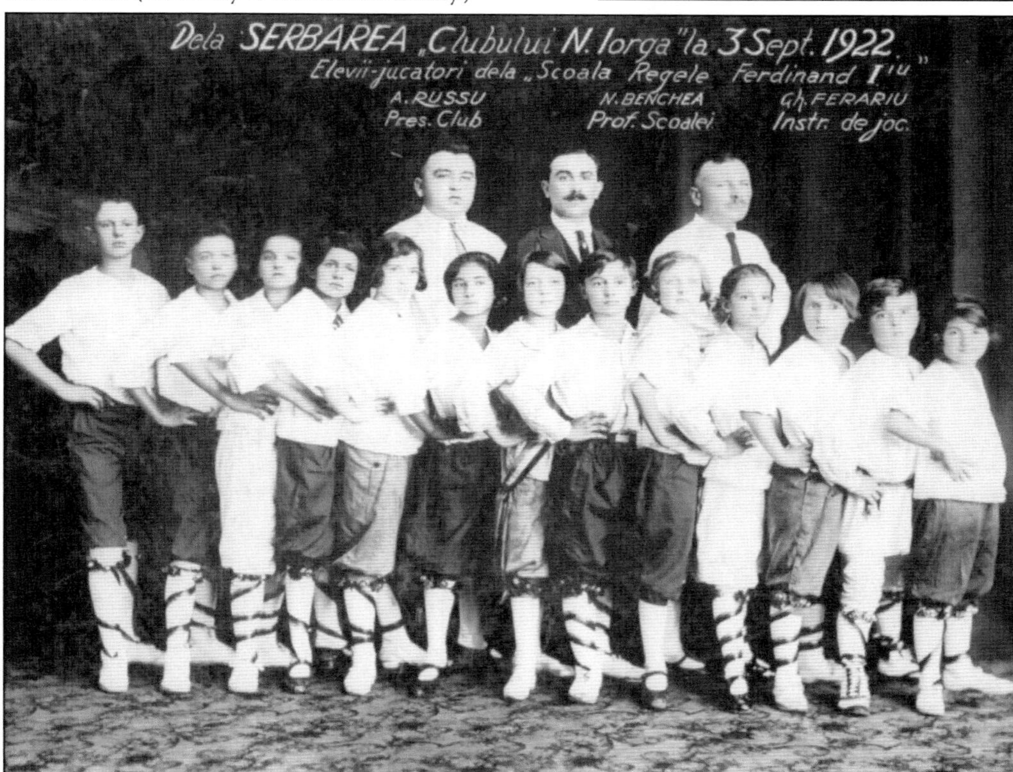

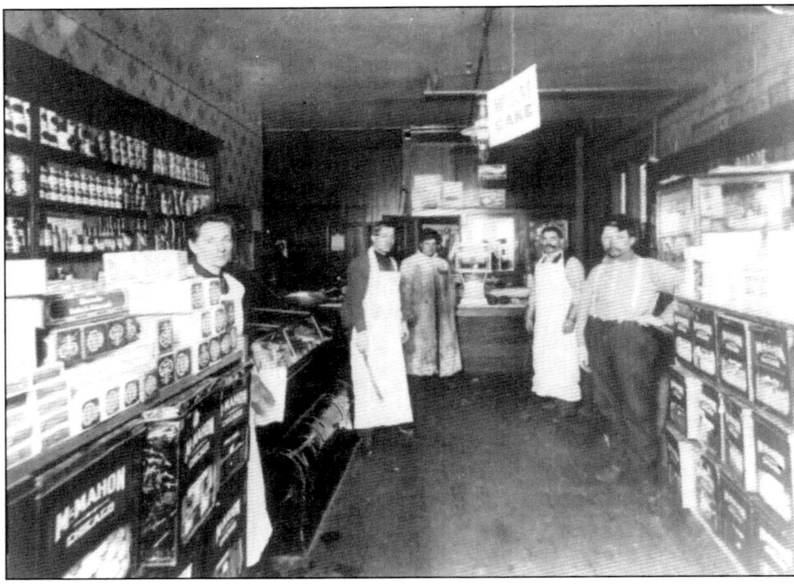

The Meyer's grocery store, seen here in 1910, reflects the hard-working ethic of immigrant families who moved to the Twin City. Note the bloodied coat of the butcher in the back and the cake sign hanging from the ceiling. (Courtesy of the Hammond Public Library.)

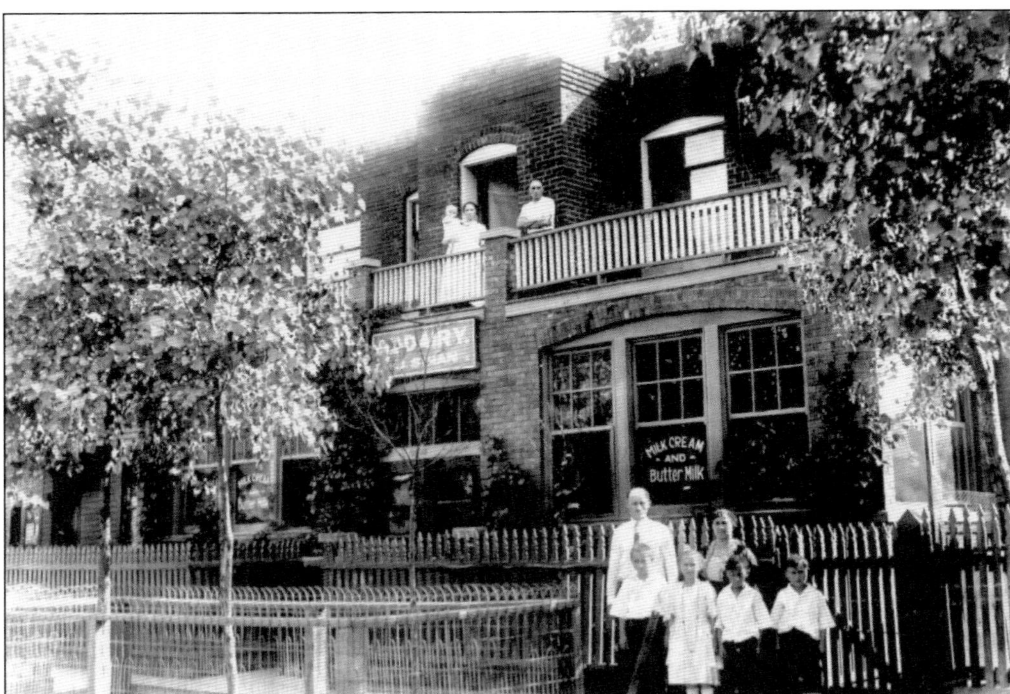

Mary Ben Young is pictured as a young child standing with her parents on the second floor balcony of the Indiana Harbor Dairy. The dairy was owned by Jon and Antonia Simon, who are seen seated in front of the doorway with their children Dionisie, Vasile, Maria, and Ioan. Though Mary was younger than the four Simon children, she interacted with them at church and social gatherings, and also attended Romanian school as they did. (Courtesy of the Simon family.)

Becoming naturalized was of great importance to immigrants. It was the first step to citizenship. Antonia Simon's certificate of naturalization is shown here. (Courtesy of the Simon family.)

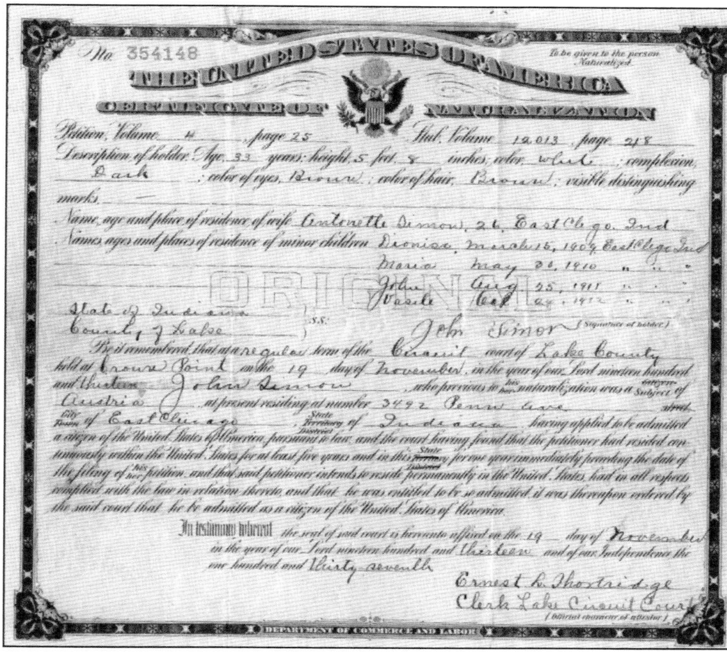

No. 354148 — To be given to the person Naturalized

THE UNITED STATES OF AMERICA

CERTIFICATE OF NATURALIZATION

Petition, Volume 4 page 25 Stub Volume 12013 page 248

Description of holder: Age, 33 years; height, 5 feet, 8 inches; color, white; complexion, Dark; color of eyes, Brown; color of hair, Brown; visible distinguishing marks, —

Name, age and place of residence of wife Antonette Simon, 26, East Chgo. Ind

Names, ages and places of residence of minor children Dionisa, March 15, 1909 East Chgo Ind
Maria May 30, 1910 " "
John Aug 25, 1911 " "
Vasile Oct 29, 1912 " "

ORIGINAL

State of Indiana, County of Lake } ss: John Simon (Signature of holder)

Be it remembered, that at a regular term of the Circuit court of Lake County held at Crown Point on the 19 day of November, in the year of our Lord nineteen hundred and thirteen John Simon, who previous to his naturalization was a subject of Austria, at present residing at number 3492 Penn Ave street, City of East Chicago, State of Indiana, having applied to be admitted a citizen of the United States of America pursuant to law, and the court having found that the petitioner had resided continuously within the United States for at least five years and in this State for one year immediately preceding the date of the filing of his petition, and that said petitioner intends to reside permanently in the United States, had in all respects complied with the law in relation thereto, and that he was entitled to be so admitted, it was thereupon ordered by the said court that he be admitted as a citizen of the United States of America.

In testimony whereof the seal of said court is hereunto affixed on the 19 day of November in the year of our Lord nineteen hundred and thirteen and of our Independence the one hundred and thirty seventh

Ernest L. Shortridge
Clerk Lake Circuit Court (Official character of attester)

DEPARTMENT OF COMMERCE AND LABOR

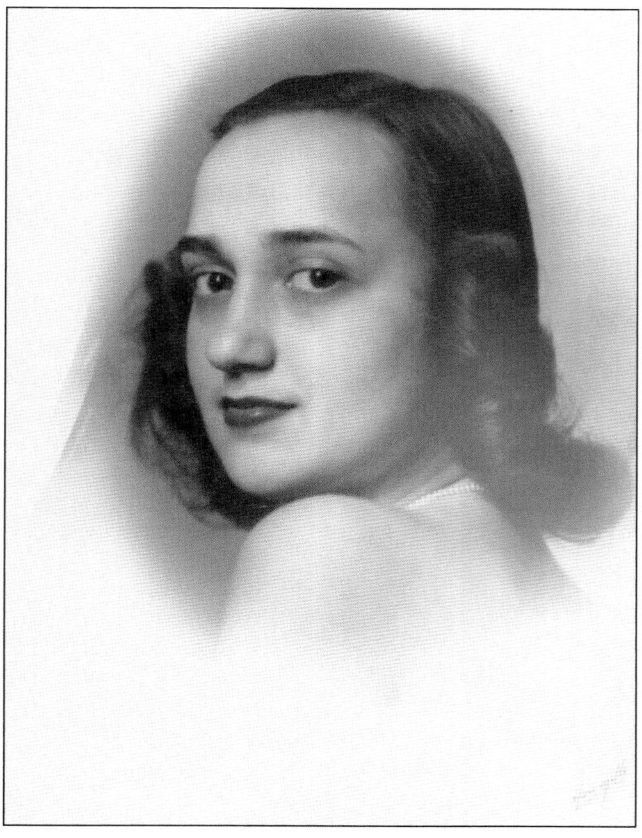

Violet Simon was the youngest child of Jon and Antonia Simon. Unlike her older brothers and sister, who were born shortly after their parents arrived in Indiana Harbor, she had a more traditional American upbringing, earning a degree in education. She married another first-generation Romanian named Thomas Strimbu. The couple had two children, and Violet taught school and then later worked at social services before retiring. Now 92, she is the last remaining sibling. (Courtesy of the Simon family.)

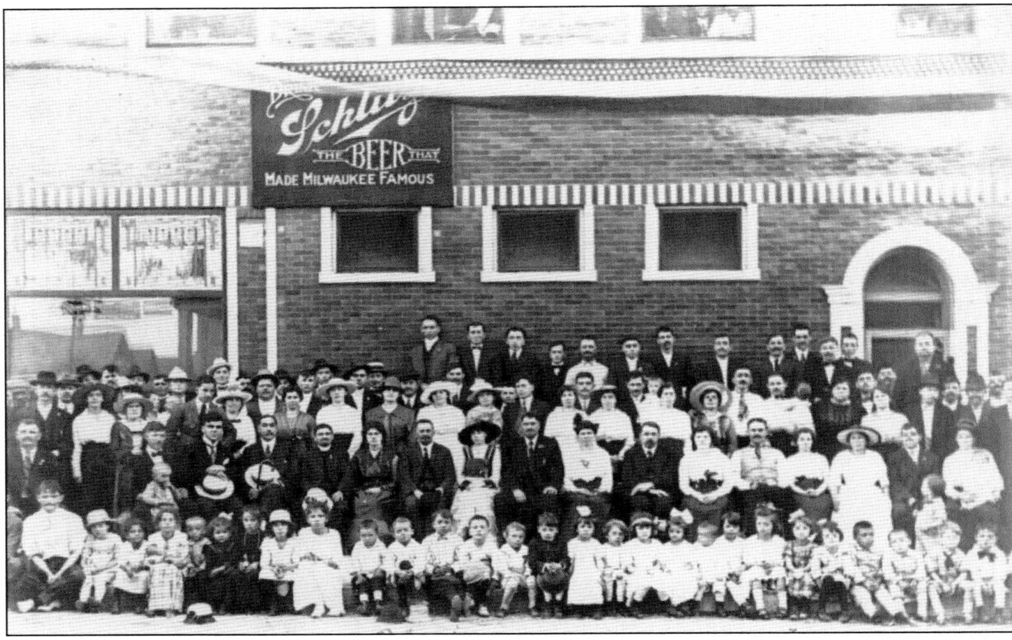

Overwhelmed by their new country, those who migrated to East Chicago continued to speak their native language and follow the customs and cultures of their homelands. Almost every group had a meeting place for dances, dinners, and socialization. Romanians who moved to Indiana Harbor built their own gathering place, the Transylvanian Hall. (Courtesy of the East Chicago Public Library.)

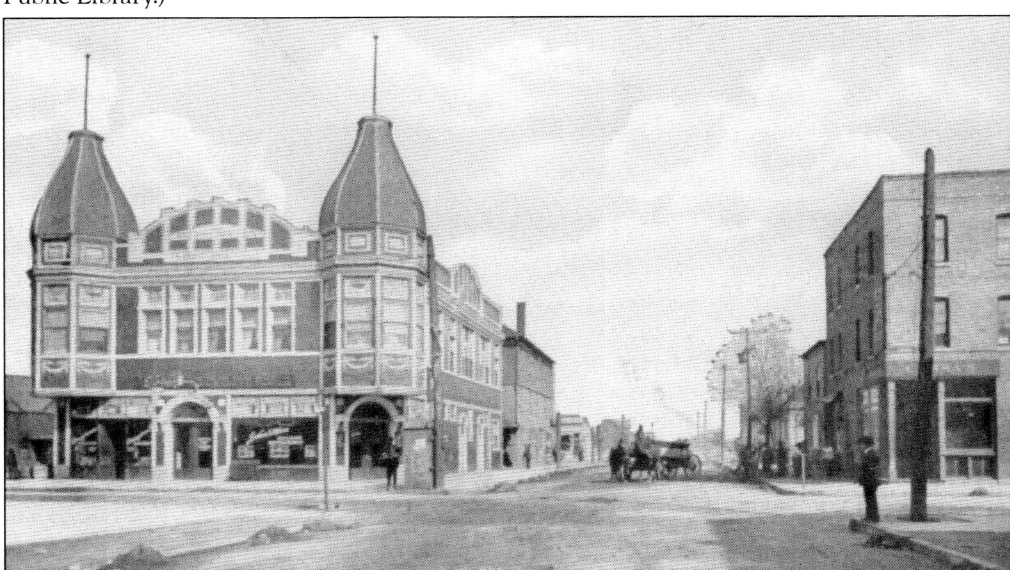

In the perfect melting pot tradition, after the influx of immigrants from Mexico, the Transylvanian Hall, which was next to popular Mexican restaurant Taco Joe's, opened a service window between the two buildings so that Mexican food could easily be served. (Courtesy of the Calumet Regional Archives, Indiana University.)

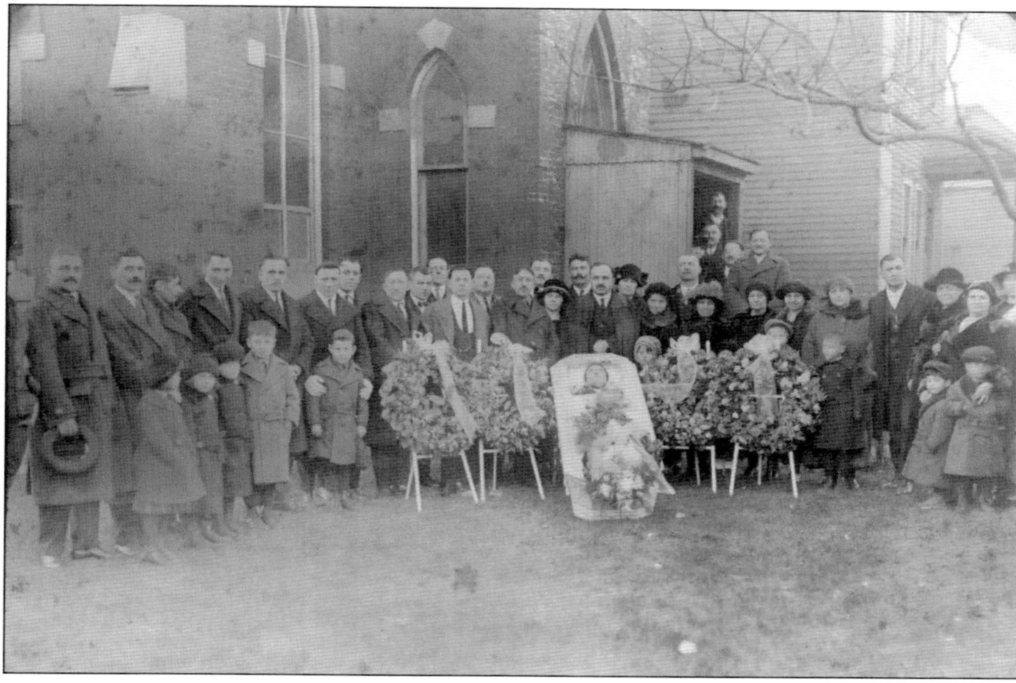

Following the customs of their homeland, many ethnic cultures laid the deceased out in their homes, where people came to pay their respects. Then, prior to burial, the casket was taken through the streets, followed by mourners and musicians playing a dirge. Upon arrival at the church, a photograph was taken. (Both, courtesy of the East Chicago Public Library.)

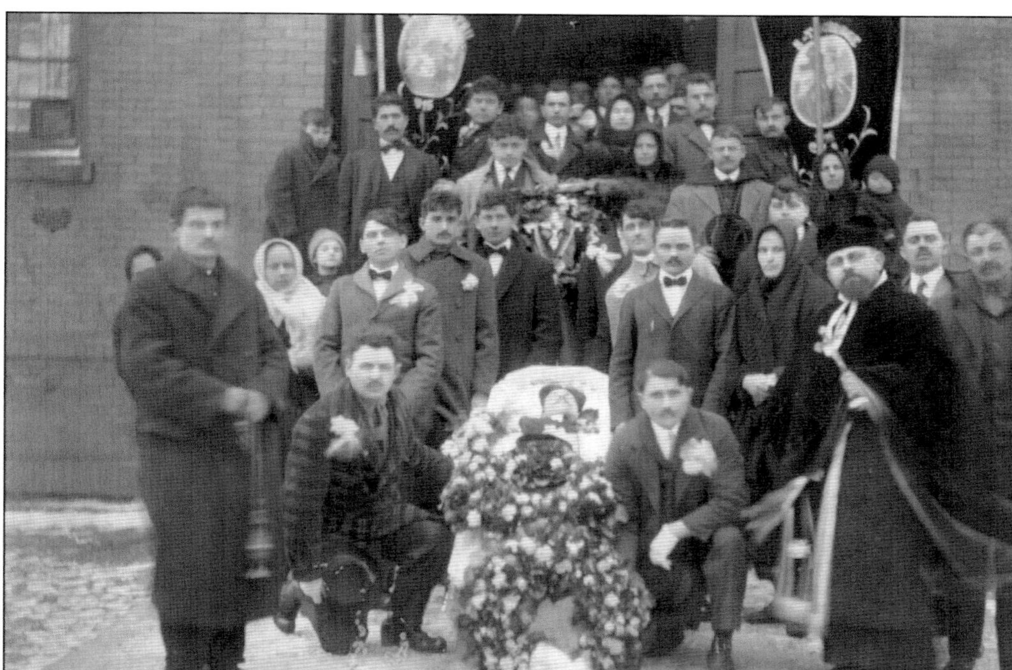

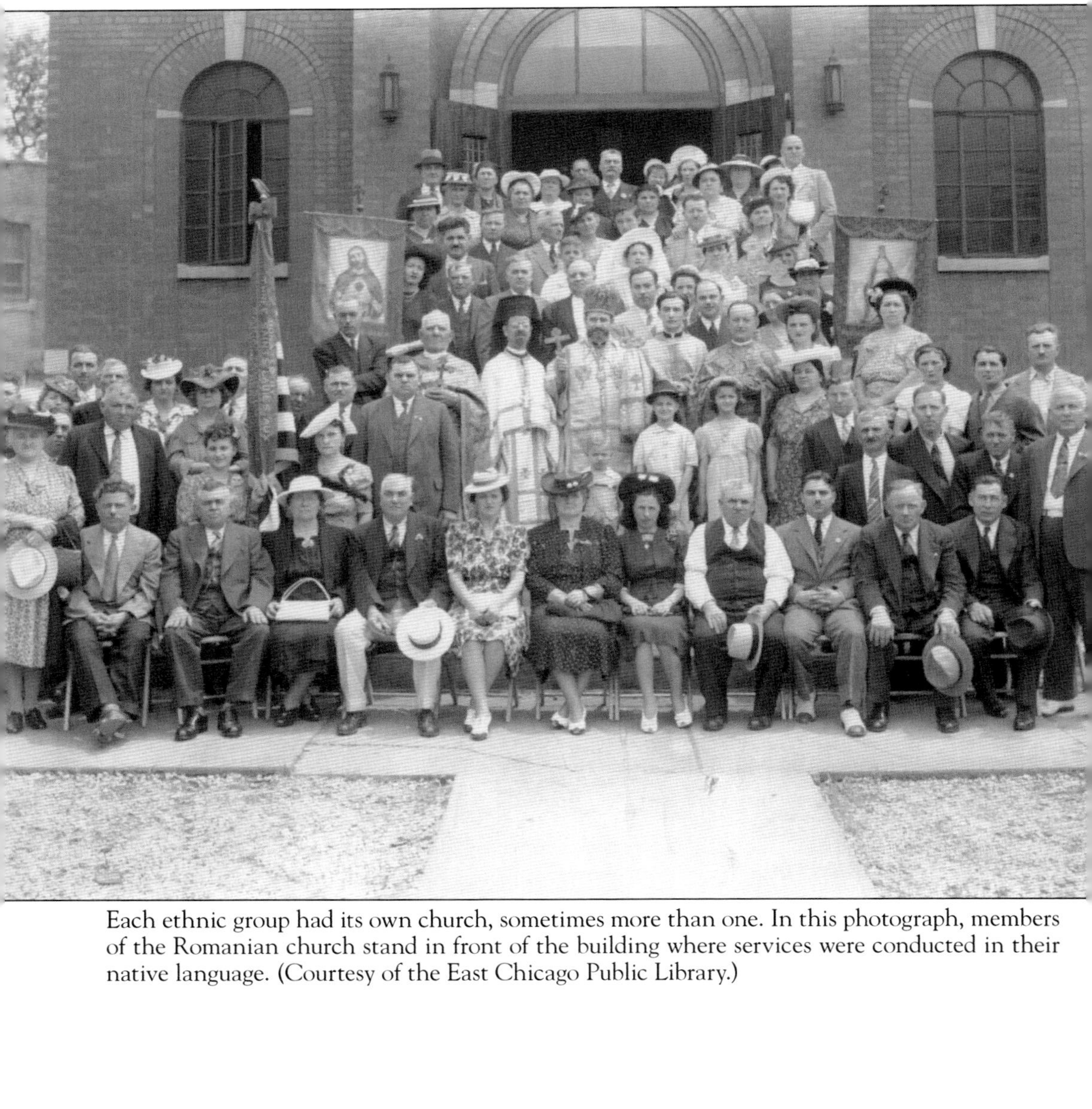

Each ethnic group had its own church, sometimes more than one. In this photograph, members of the Romanian church stand in front of the building where services were conducted in their native language. (Courtesy of the East Chicago Public Library.)

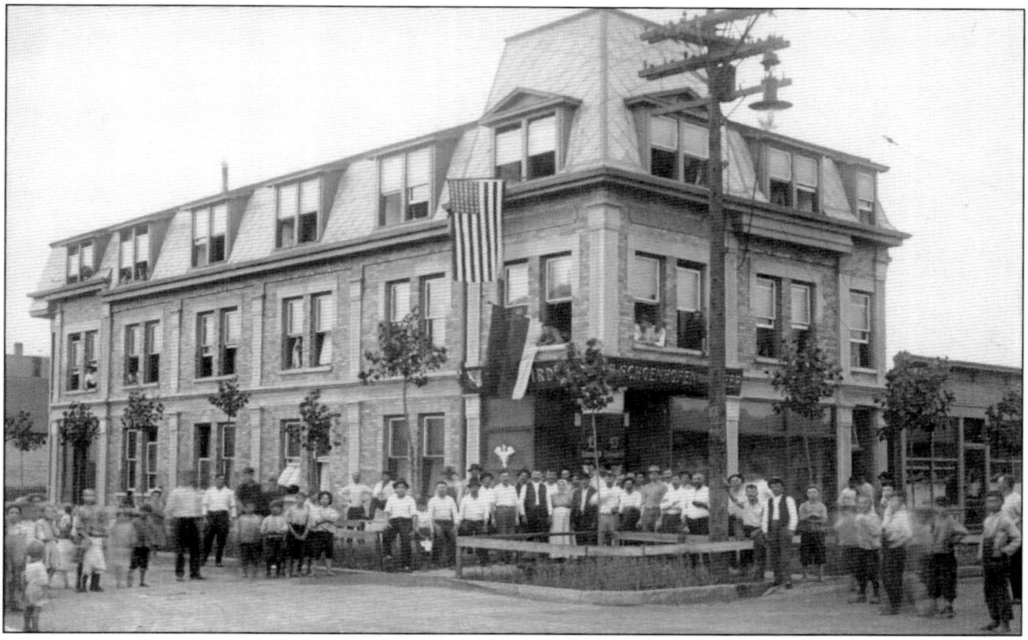

Immigrants from Yugoslavia built this monumental Servian (Serbian) Hall as a place for socializing, dining, and—for the men—imbibing. (Courtesy of Andrew Prieboy.)

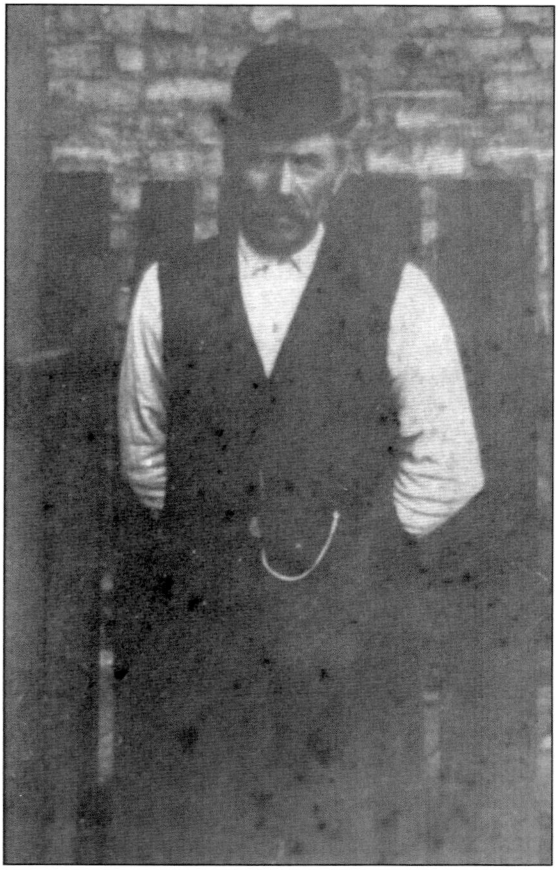

Initially, many workers arriving in East Chicago came from Ireland and Germany. One such family was the Pritzkes, who immigrated to the United States from Germany in the 1880s. Carl Pritzke, pictured here, was a ship's captain and his son William was born in New Zealand. His two other children were Harry and Annie. (Courtesy of the Briska family.)

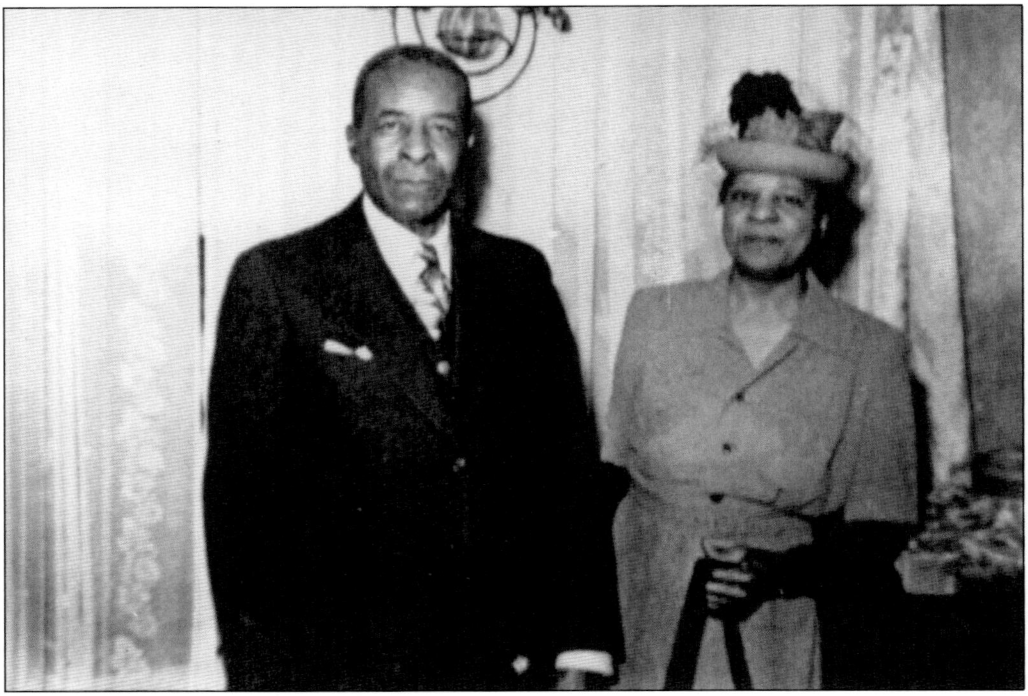

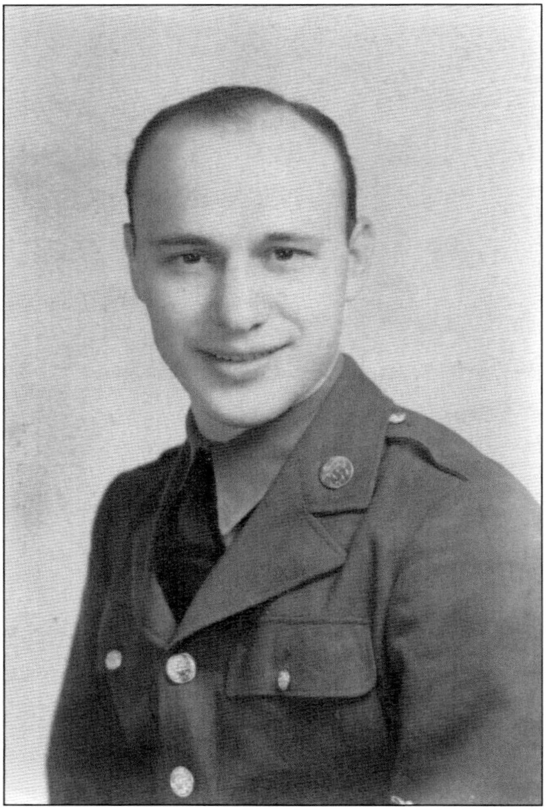

Ben Crawford, pictured with his wife in the 1920s, was the first African American policeman in East Chicago. (Courtesy of the East Chicago Public Library.)

Education was very important to early immigrant families, as they saw it as a passport out of the hard life of factory work. Vasile Simon, born in 1912 to immigrant parents from Romania, would go on to obtain his PhD in English, serve in World War II, and become a college professor. Along the way, he Americanized his first name to Charles. (Courtesy of the Simon family.)

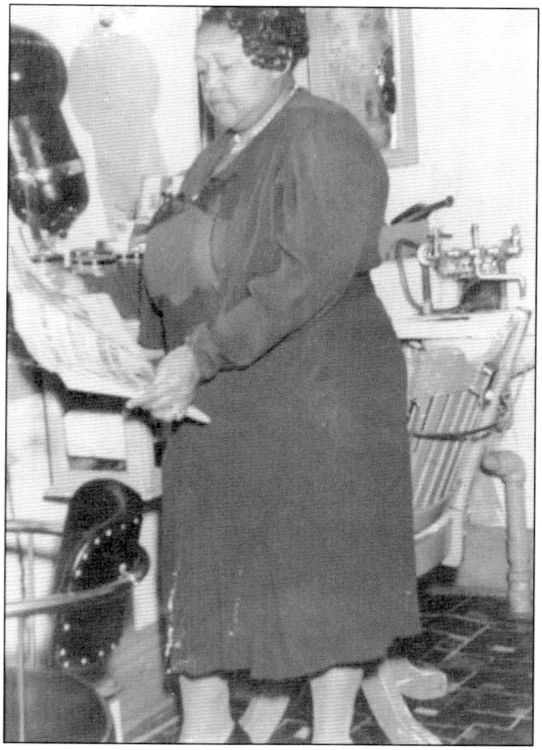

Beulah Draper was the first African American beautician in East Chicago. (Both, courtesy of the East Chicago Public Library.)

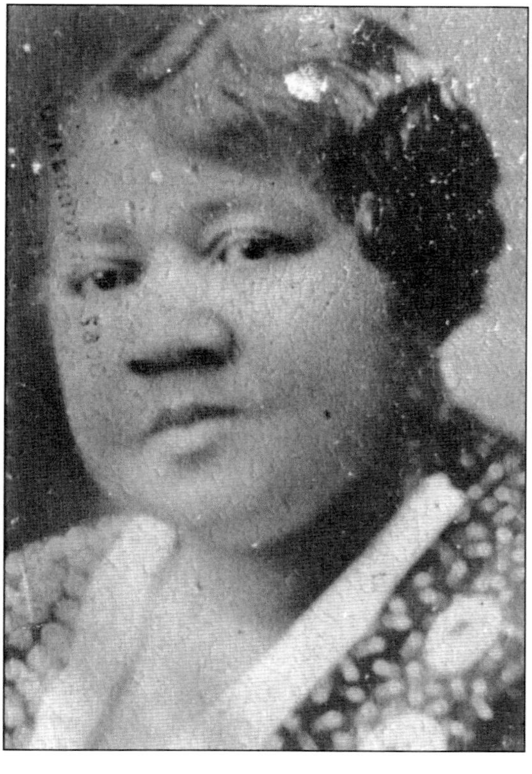

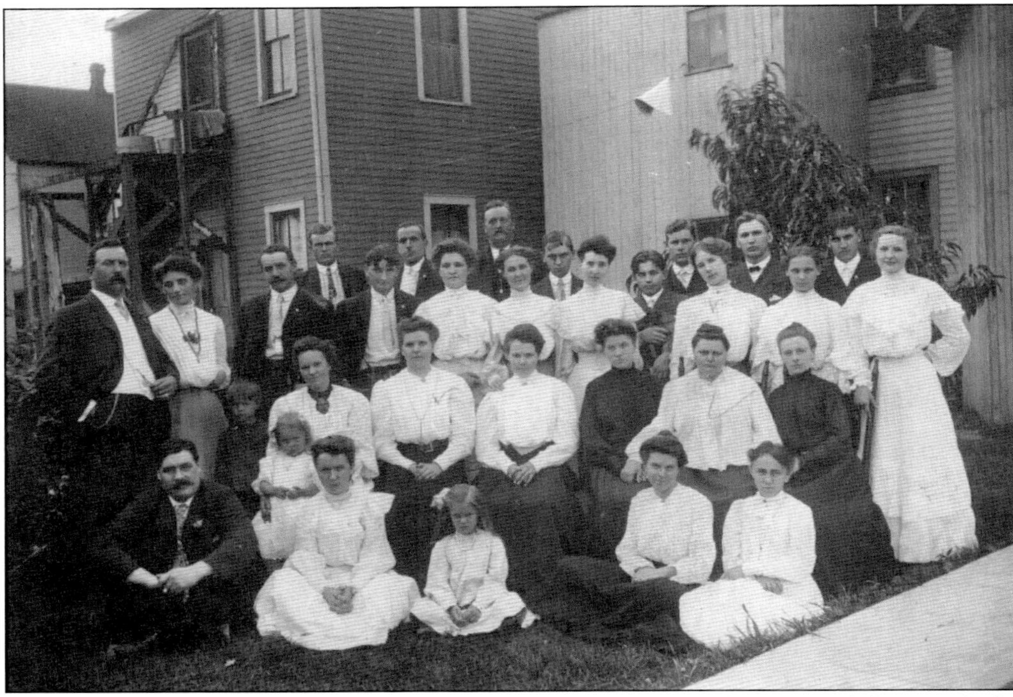

At one time, East Chicago had a large influx of immigrants from Sweden, many of whom worked at Standard Forge. Pictured is the company picnic. (Courtesy of the East Chicago Public Library.)

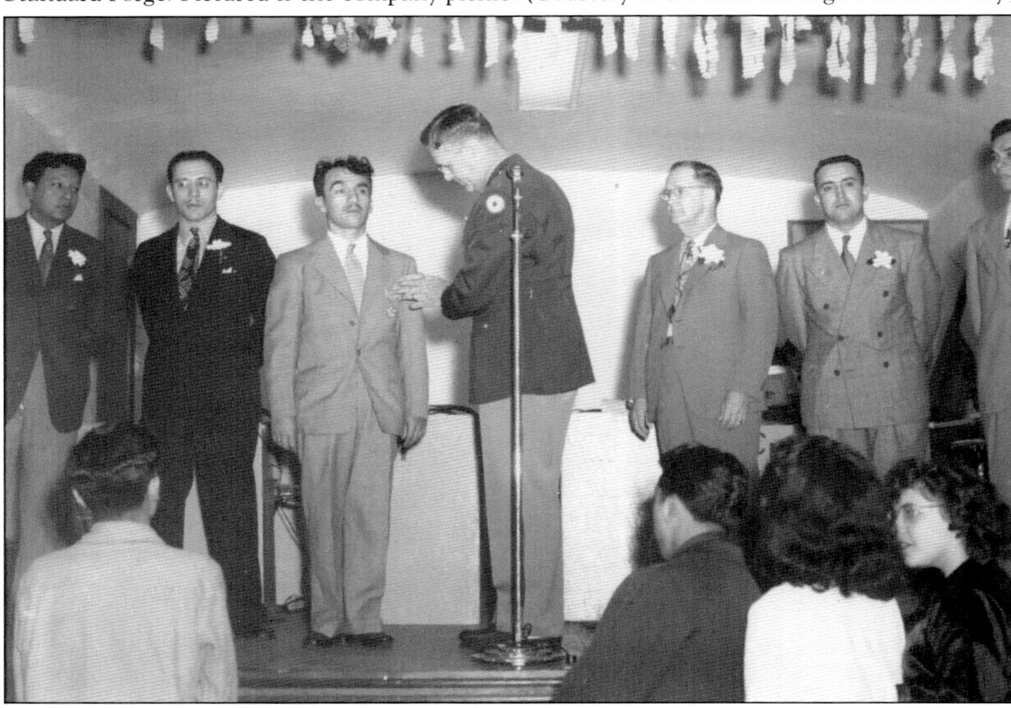

This photograph was taken during the Inauguration Dance at the Latin American Veterans Club in 1946. (Courtesy of the Calumet Regional Archives, Indiana University.)

Six

Marktown

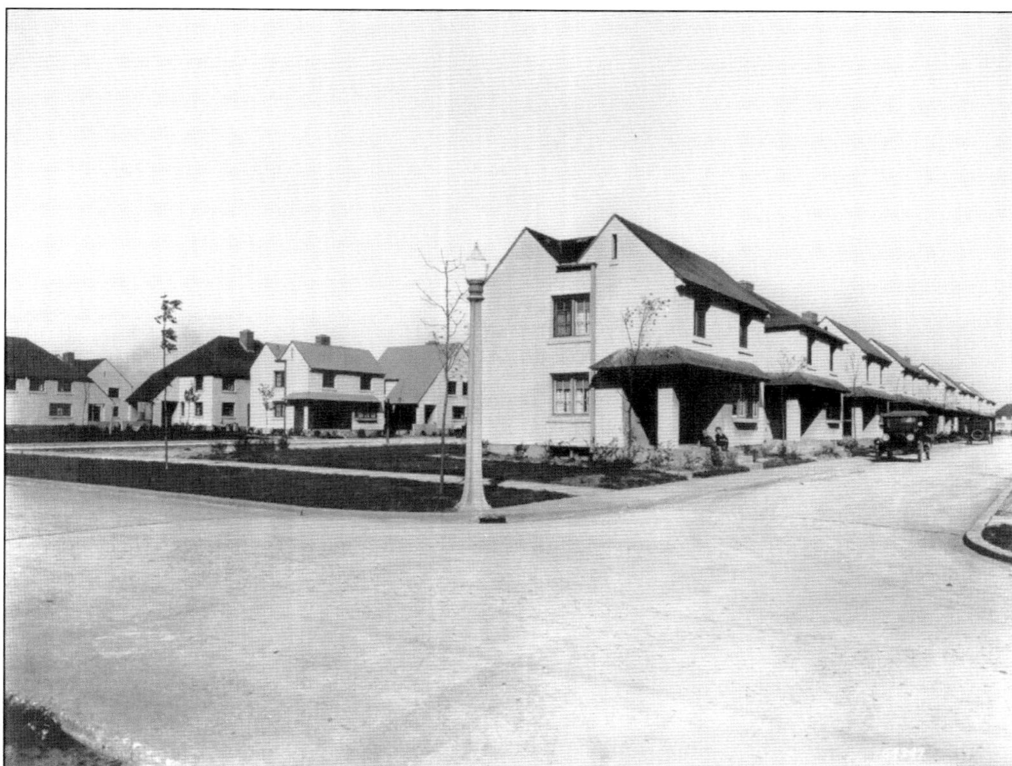

The overall design of the Marktown site included more than 30 sections of housing and businesses for workers, such as these cottages located on Park Street. A prime example of industrial housing, Marktown was listed in the National Register of Historic Places by East Chicago mayor Robert Pastrick in 1975. (Courtesy of the Marktown Preservation Society.)

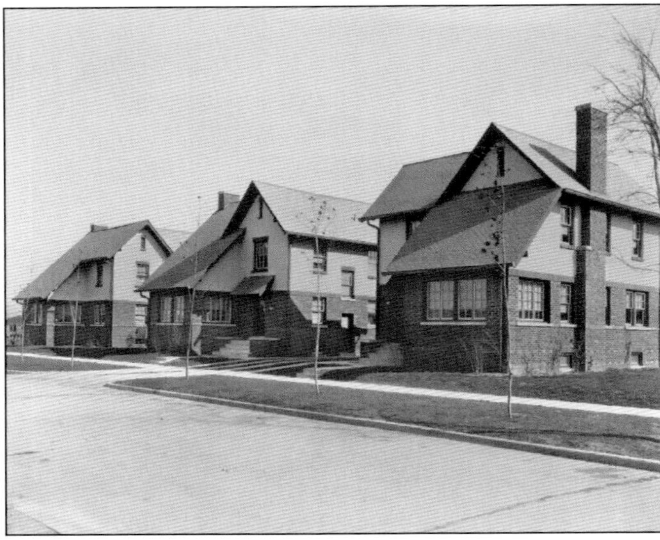

The eight-room home where the supervisor of Mark Manufacturing lived is pictured here. The plan for Marktown was developed with English Garden City concepts in mind, requiring that the homes be well-built and of sturdy, fireproof construction. While all of the homes would not be identical, the design of each home and secondary building was compatible with the other properties in the neighborhood. (Courtesy of the Marktown Preservation Society.)

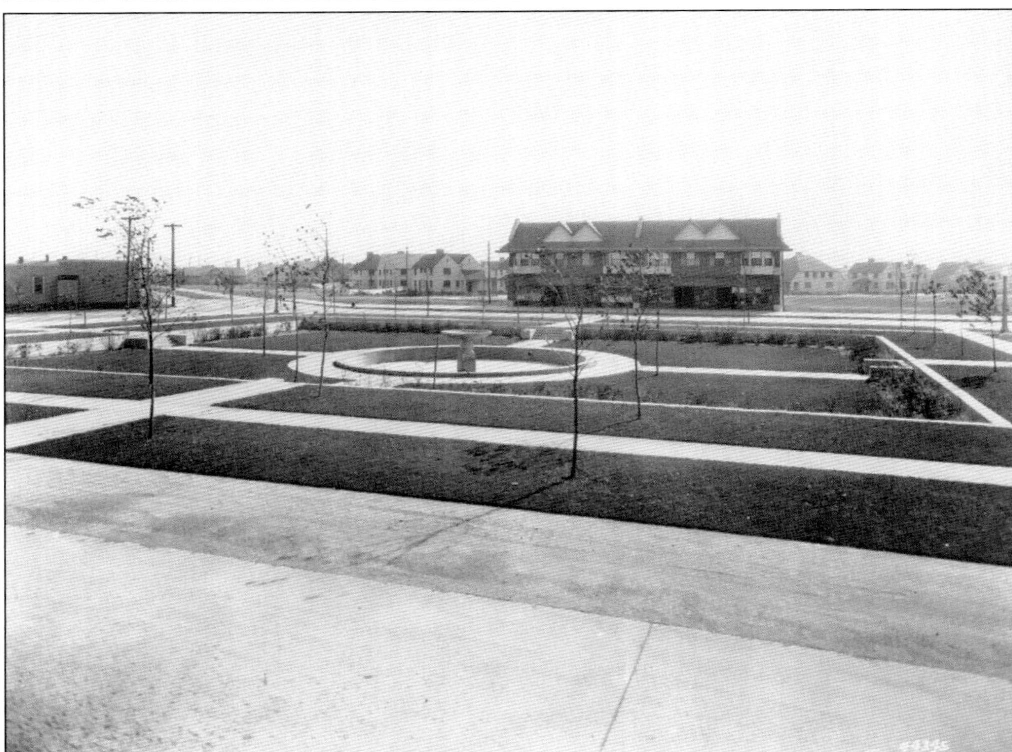

The original designs for Marktown included a market square, set to include more than 20 shops and apartments, a bank, a movie theater, and a post office. Tudor Revival–style homes were complemented by the classic English Garden City concept by renowned Chicago architect Howard Van Doren Shaw. There were no alleys, and houses were to be separated from each other so that the rear windows of one would look out onto the garden area of the house on the next street. With open porches and the backyard of one house looking out onto the front yard of the adjacent home, it created a built-in security system. (Courtesy of the Marktown Preservation Society.)

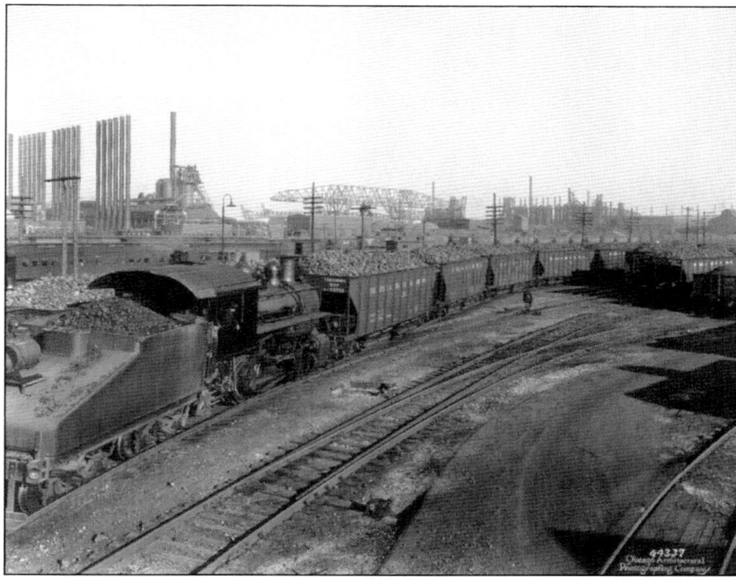

The coke train belonging to Mark Manufacturing is pictured looking east from the coke plant. Beyond the train directly to the left are Pullman railcars, and farther to the right are the company headquarters designed by noted architect Howard Van Doren Shaw, who also designed Marktown. (Courtesy of the Marktown Preservation Society.)

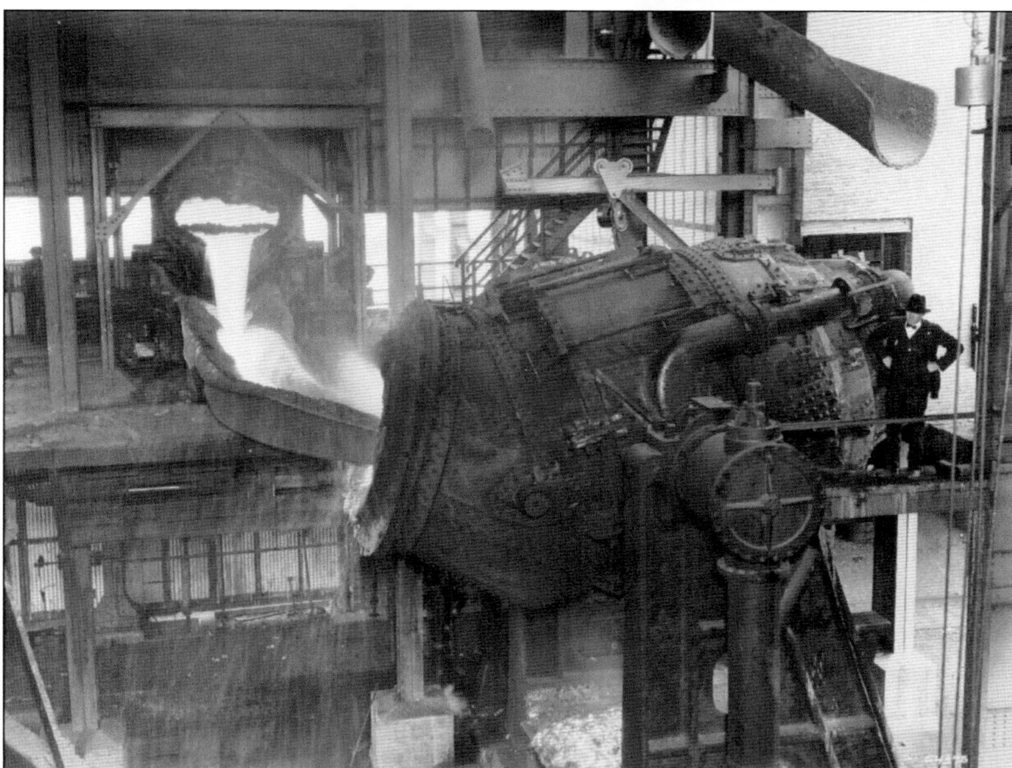

Due to financial problems incurred by the Mark Manufacturing Company during World War I, only four of the 30 sections of housing were ever completed. This high-quality photograph of Mark Manufacturing and others like it were taken in 1920, to be used for a marketing catalogue. In 1923, the company was sold to Youngstown Steel & Tube Company. (Courtesy of the Marktown Preservation Society.)

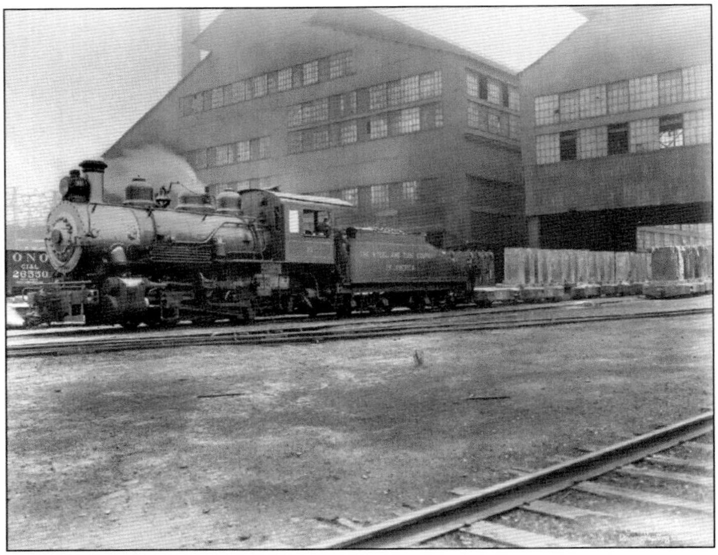

In 1920, Mark Manufacturing merged with Iroquois Iron & Steel and became the Steel & Tube Company. Over the years, it would change hands even more, but Marktown remains. Lake County author Ken Schoon writes in *Calumet Beginnings*: "Marktown is still a quiet residential island surrounded by heavy industry." (Courtesy of the Marktown Preservation Society.)

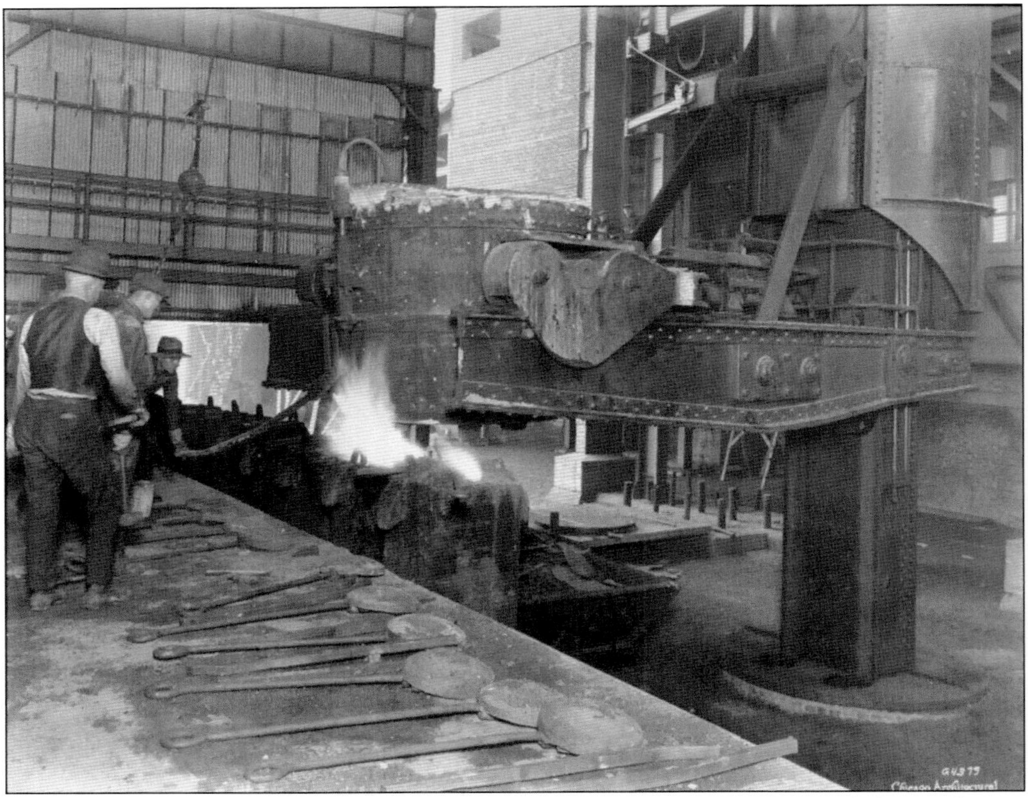

The Stripper Building is seen in this 1920 photograph. Phil Myer organized the Marktown Preservation Society, which curates photographs of the area's past, such as these. He is the executive director and a resident architectural, social, and industrial historian who has lived in the area all his life and whose family first moved to Marktown in 1917. (Courtesy of the Marktown Preservation Society.)

Seven

Our Town

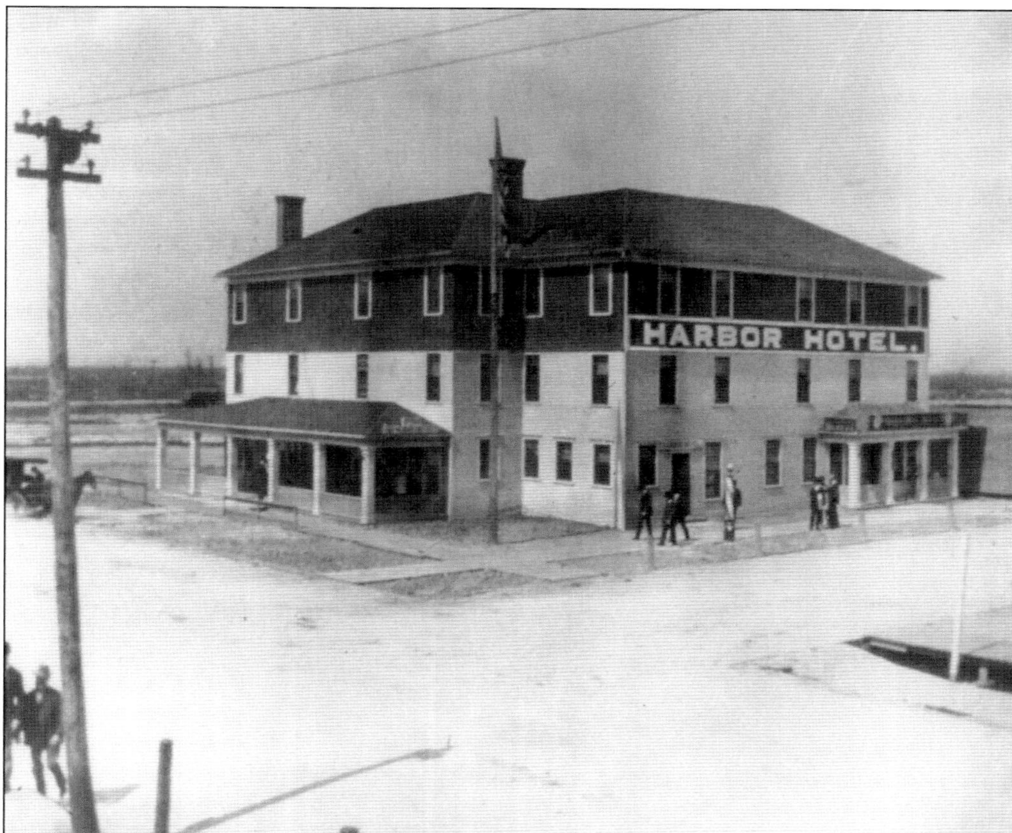

Great Lakes ship captain Charles A. Friedrich opened the Harbor Hotel, shown here in 1901. It was considered one of the finest in Indiana Harbor. According to his biography, Captain Friedrich was the first man who slept in his own bed in the town. (Courtesy of the East Chicago Public Library.)

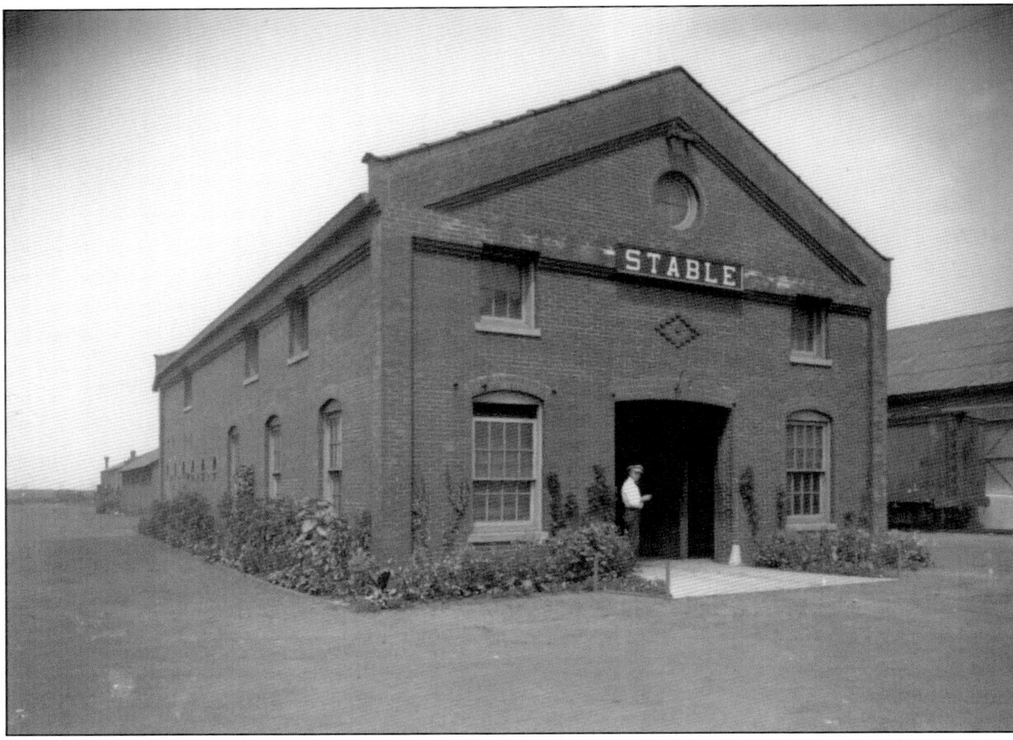

At a time when the horse was king, stables were a major business. (Courtesy of the Calumet Regional Archives, Indiana University.)

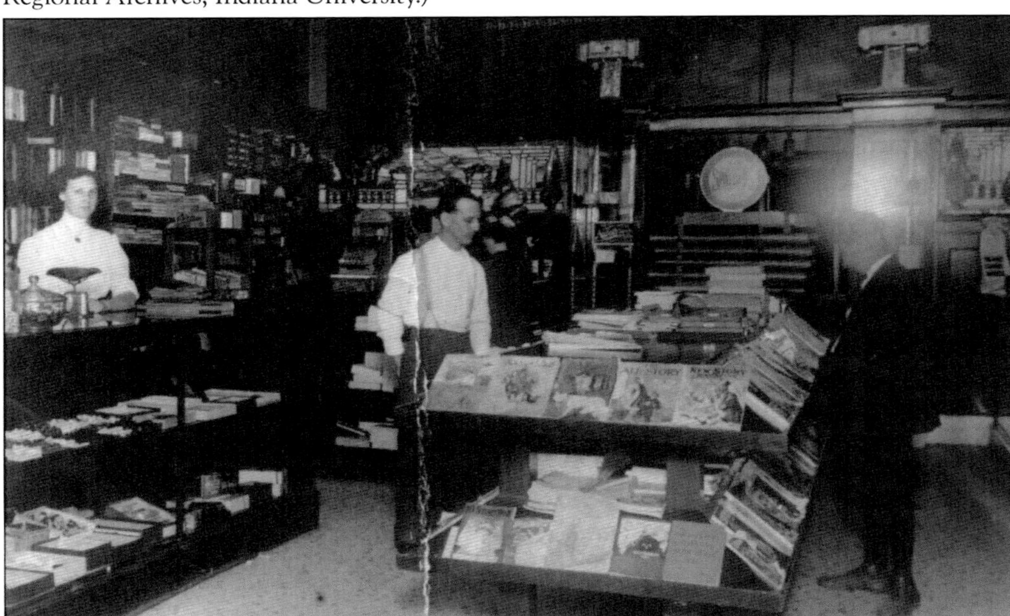
From left to right are Shirley Wick, Harry Thompson, and Charles Nassau inside their business, Nassau & Thompson, founded in 1898. This long-lasting company was a major shop in downtown East Chicago for many decades. (Courtesy of the East Chicago Public Library.)

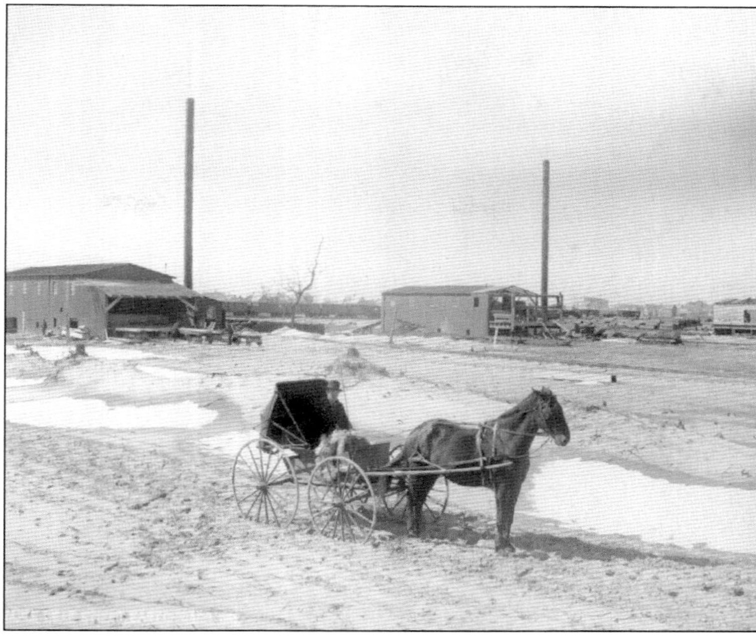

The Irwin & Hascall lumberyards was the only sawmill in the United States to devote itself exclusively to black walnut. Walnut logs arrived by train from Central Indiana, were turned into lumber, and shipped throughout the world. Its location was also known as Saw Mill Park. (Courtesy of the East Chicago Public Library.)

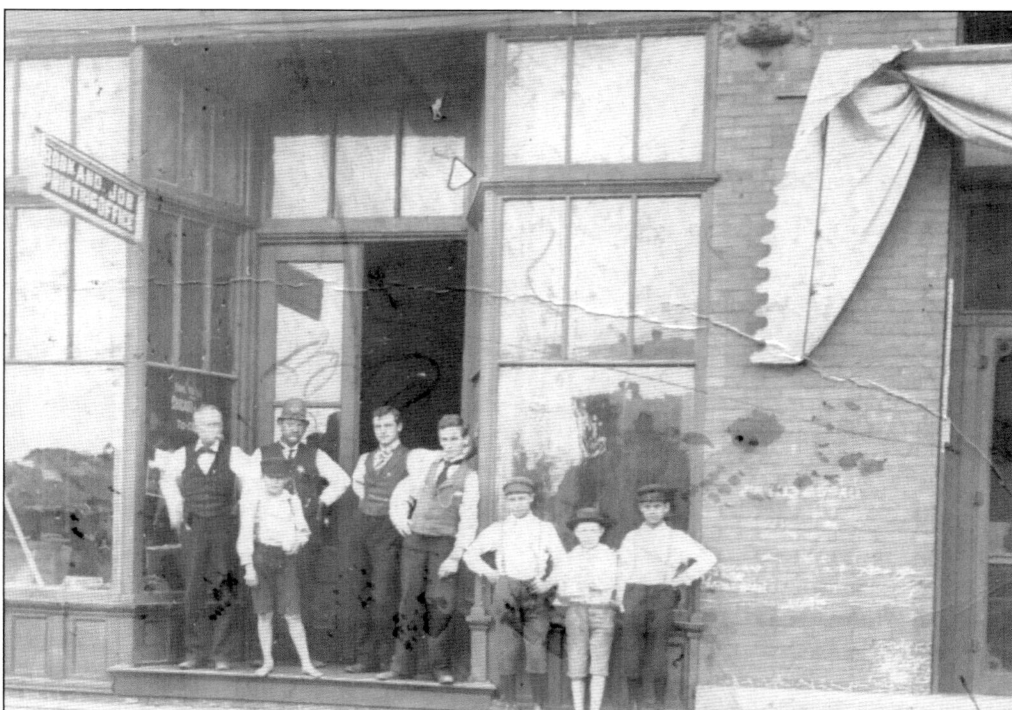

In 1891, Edward Gilbert was the publisher of the *East Chicago Globe*, the first newspaper printed in East Chicago. He also published the *Whiting News* and the *Indiana Harbor News*, besides being Indiana Harbor's first postmaster in 1902 and East Chicago's first city clerk in 1903. Standing next to him in the doorway is town marshal Neil Patterson. (Courtesy of the Calumet Regional Archives, Indiana University.)

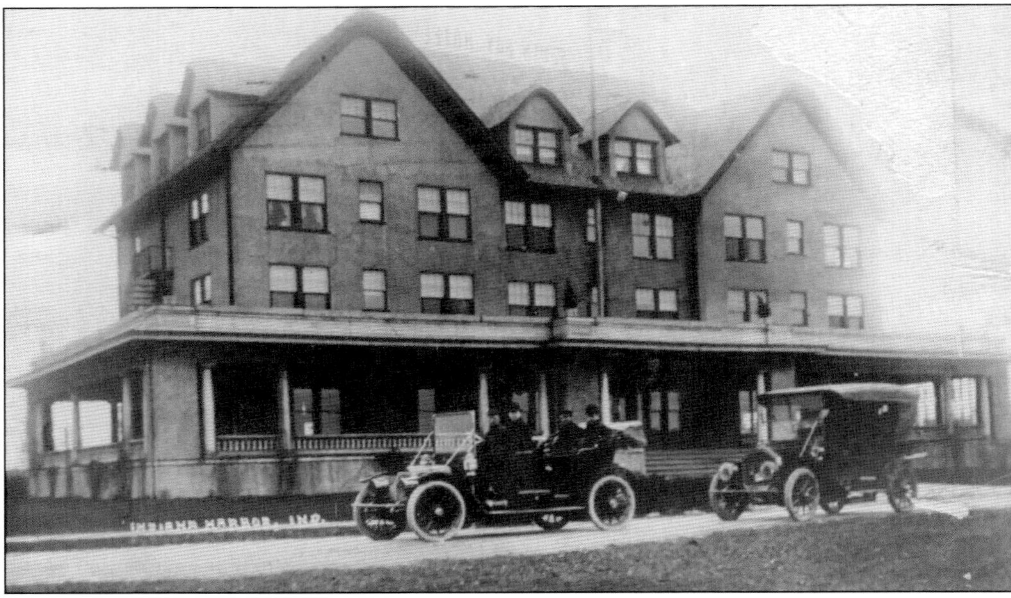

The South Bay Hotel was called the "Atlantic City of the West" and boasted bathing, boating, and fishing as well as excellent cuisine. Their porcelain tubs in every suite were advertised in the *Chicago Daily Tribune*. In the early 1900s, steamships made twice daily stops at the pier near the hotel. (Courtesy of Steve Shook.)

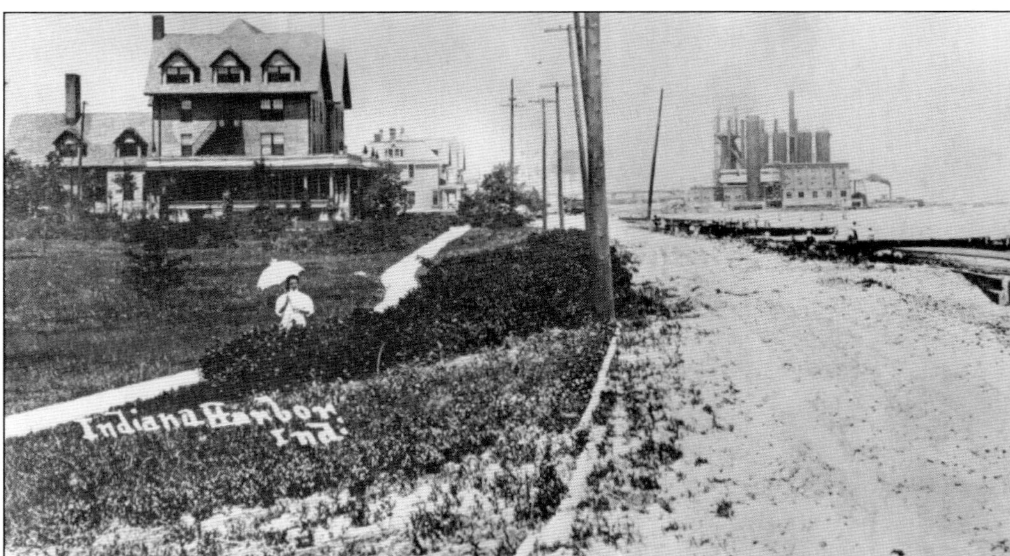

The South Bay Hotel, nestled on a cove of Lake Michigan, was at one time managed by Bertha K. Chittenden, described by newspapers of the time as a widow of wealth and refinement. Chittenden was given a three-year lease on the hotel and was able to build a sophisticated clientele. The hotel was soon known as the Western Newport. (Courtesy of the Calumet Regional Archives, Indiana University.)

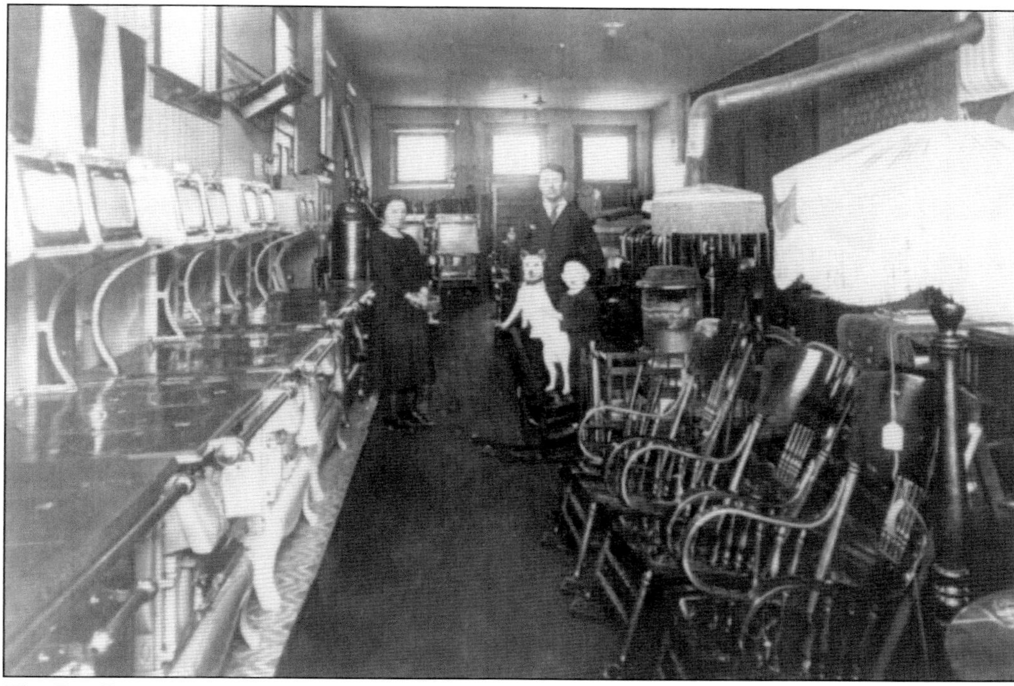

The Fair Department, one of the earliest stores in Twin City, was noted for selling a plethora of items for the home. Its interior is pictured here. (Courtesy of the Lake County Public Library.)

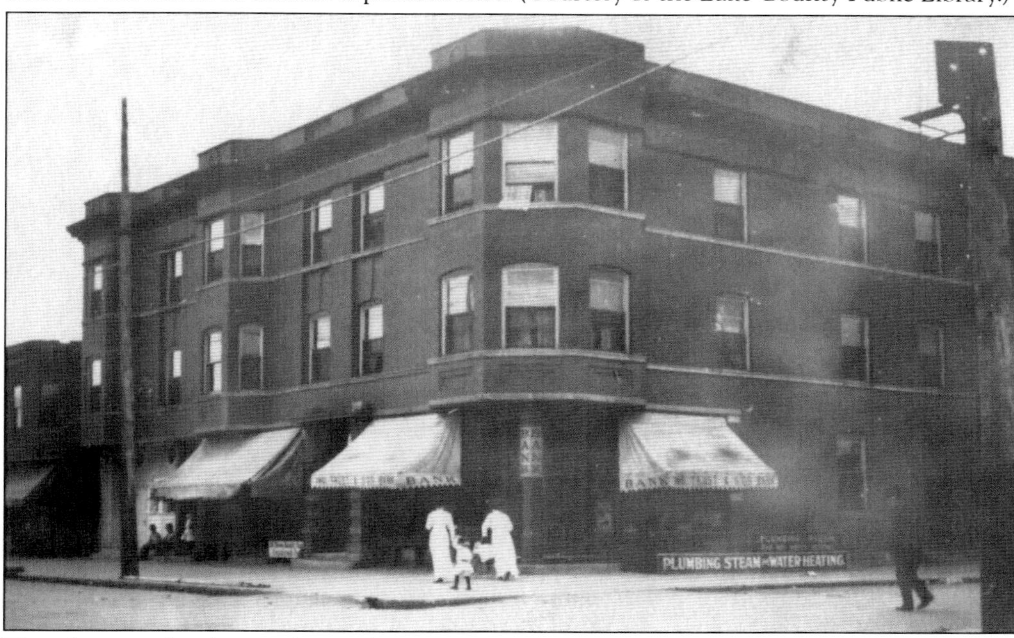

This photograph taken at the southwest corner of Michigan and Pennsylvania Avenues in 1903 shows a prosperous scene of fine, solid brick buildings and well dressed residents. Known as the O'Brien block, Indiana Harbor's first movie house was located here and was operated by Louis Greenfield, who would later become a Hollywood tycoon during the silent film era. (Courtesy of the Calumet Regional Archives, Indiana University.)

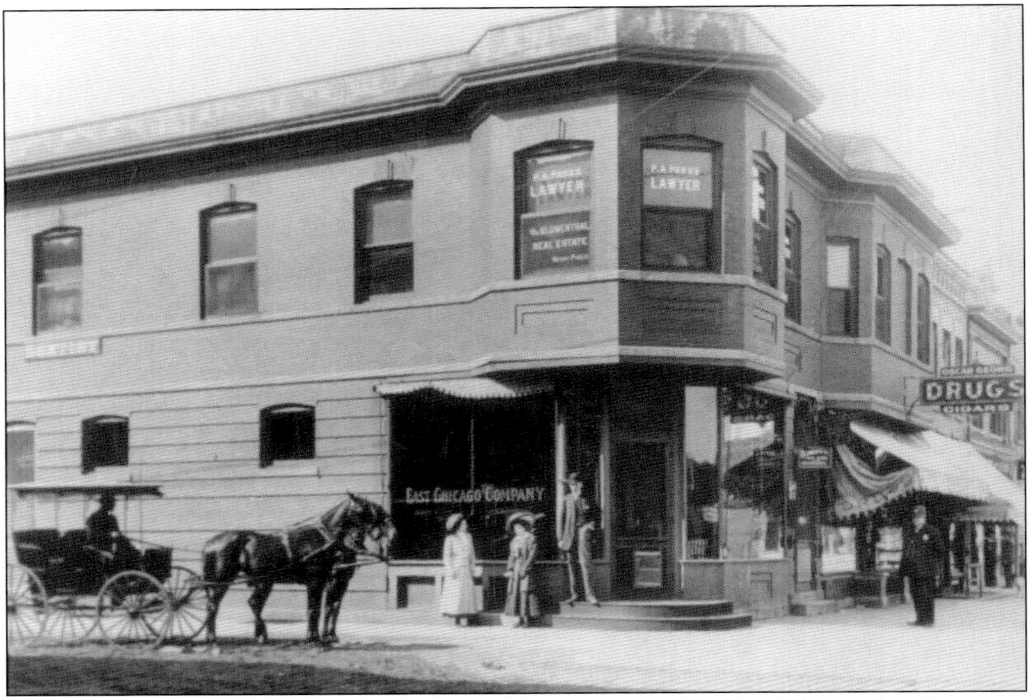

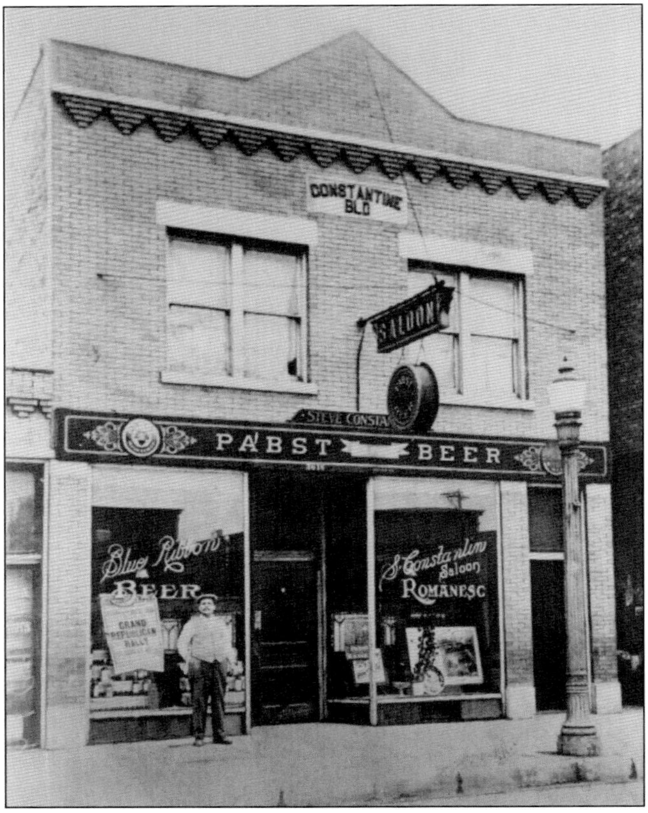

The East Chicago Land Company, located at 3336 Michigan Avenue, helped fuel the boom in property sales. Starting around 1900, salespeople from Chicago would take the train to the East Chicago Land Company's Indiana Harbor office in the morning and return home at night. (Courtesy of the Calumet Regional Archives, Indiana University.)

With all the hardworking industrial employees, the bar business boomed, to the chagrin of many mothers whose husbands stopped for drinks on payday, sometimes spending much-needed family money. (Courtesy of the Lake County Public Library.)

The Constantine Building on Main Street in Indiana Harbor housed many businesses over the years. It is pictured as a five-and-dime variety store. (Courtesy of the Lake County Public Library.)

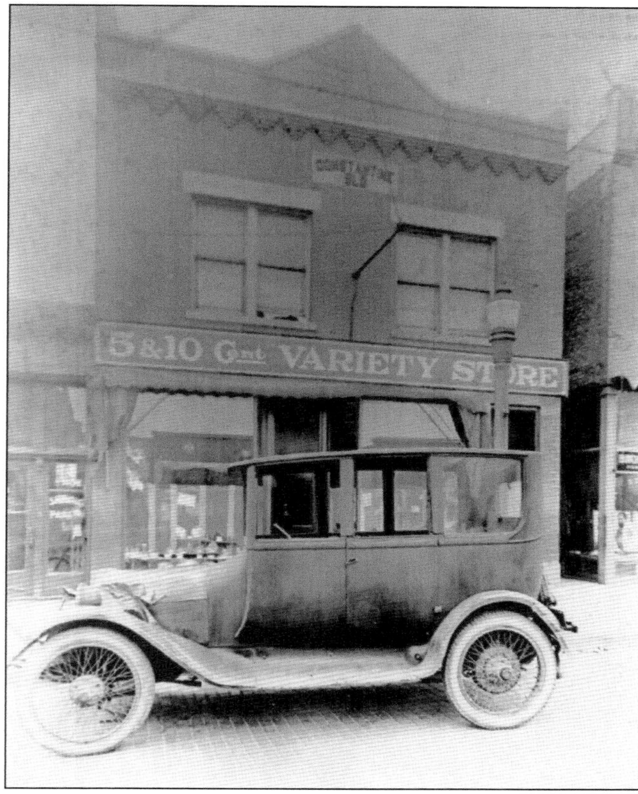

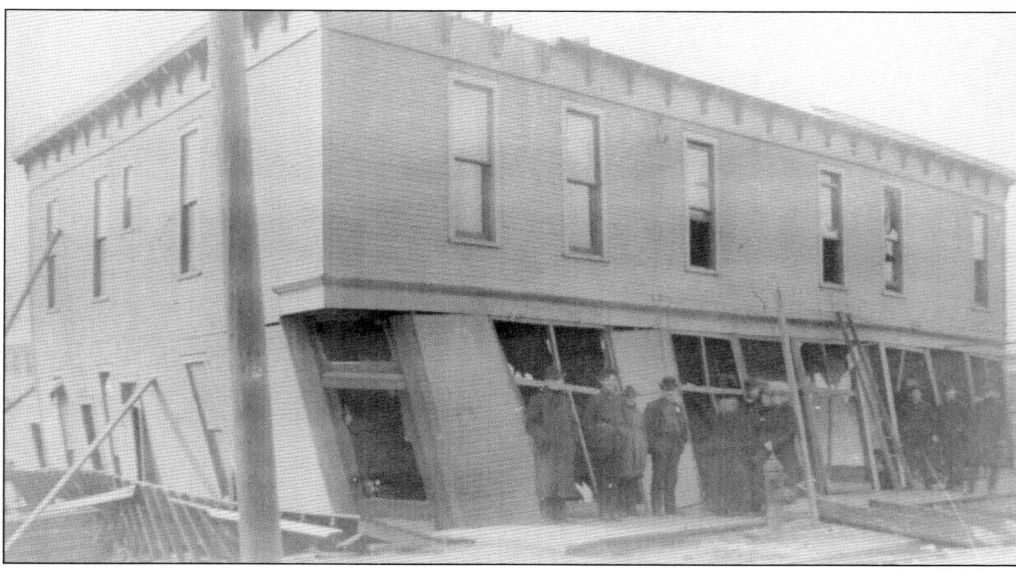

On March 30, 1904, newspapers across the state reported that a cyclone killed and injured many people and demolished property, including Republic's steel mills at East Chicago. The storm also brought streetcars to a standstill and wrecked telephone and telegraph systems in Indiana Harbor, Hammond, East Chicago, and neighboring cities. (Courtesy of the Calumet Regional Archives, Indiana University.)

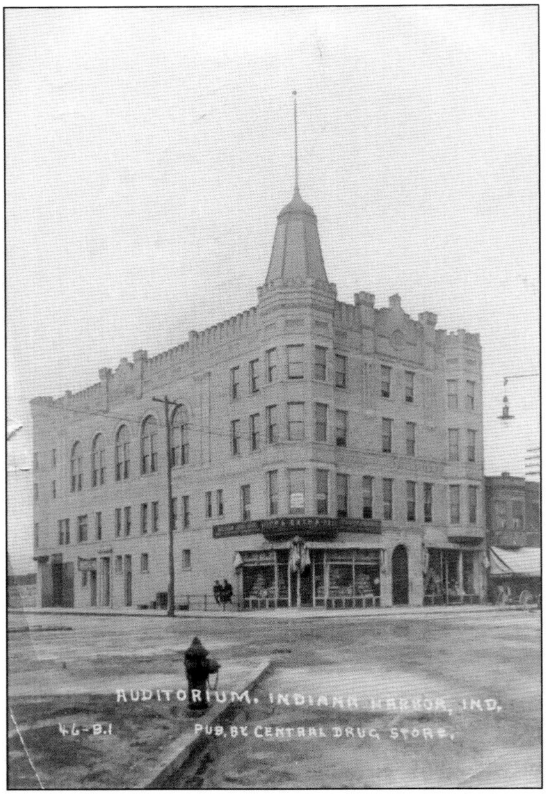

Dr. Samuel Herskovitz had physician offices in the auditorium pictured here and ran his Red Cross Drugstore on the building's first floor. An advertisement in the *Indianapolis Star* dated Saturday, April 22, 1911, read, "Druggist Wanted: good wages, one speaking Polish or Hungarian preferred. Address Dr. Herskovitz, Indiana Harbor, Ind." (Courtesy of Steve Shook.)

One of only a handful of women to graduate from Columbia University's School of Pharmacy in 1904, Nettie Sachs (later Herskovitz and then Diamond) is pictured standing next to the pharmacy counter in one of the drugstores she owned with her husband Dr. Samuel Herskovitz. (Courtesy of the Lake County Public Library.)

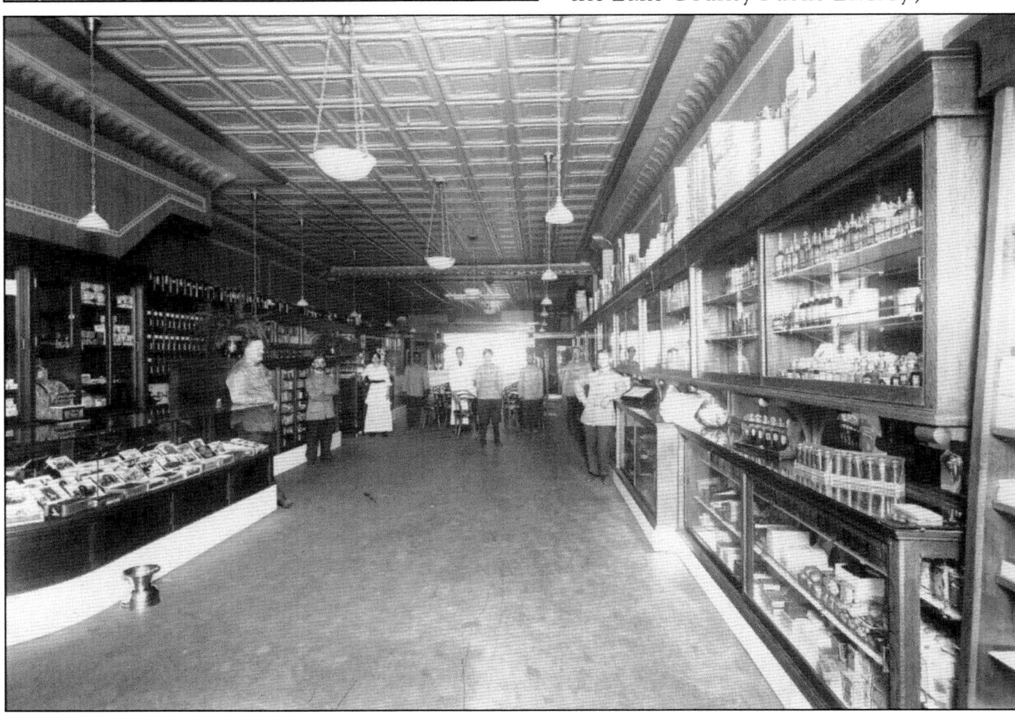

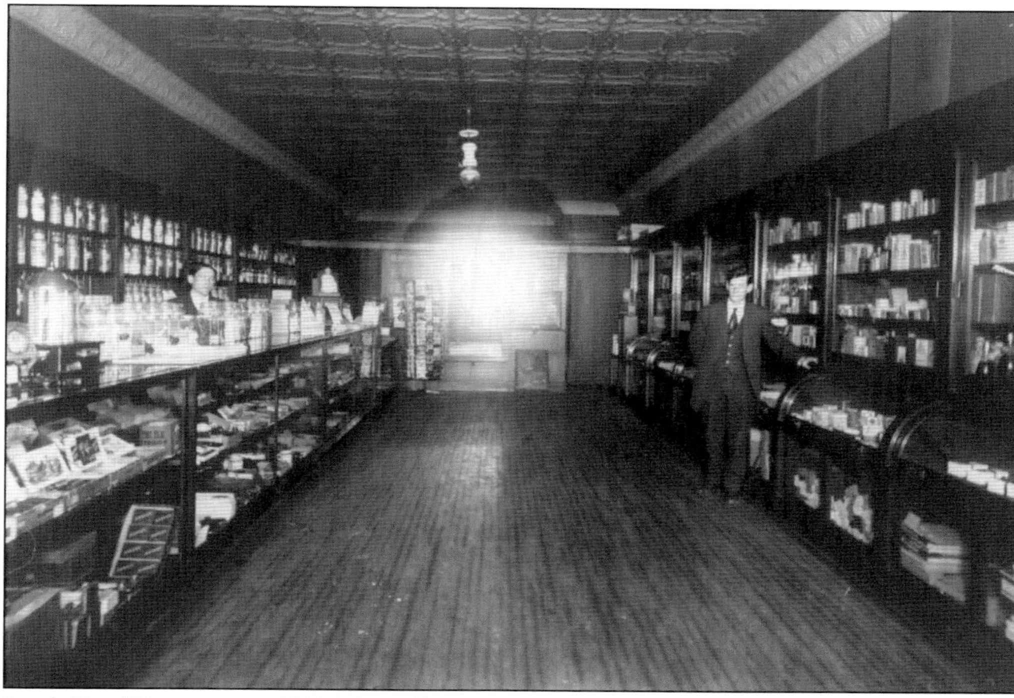

Inside Reed Drugstore in 1911, Mr. Haller is pictured at left and Mr. Earl at right. (Courtesy of the Lake County Public Library.)

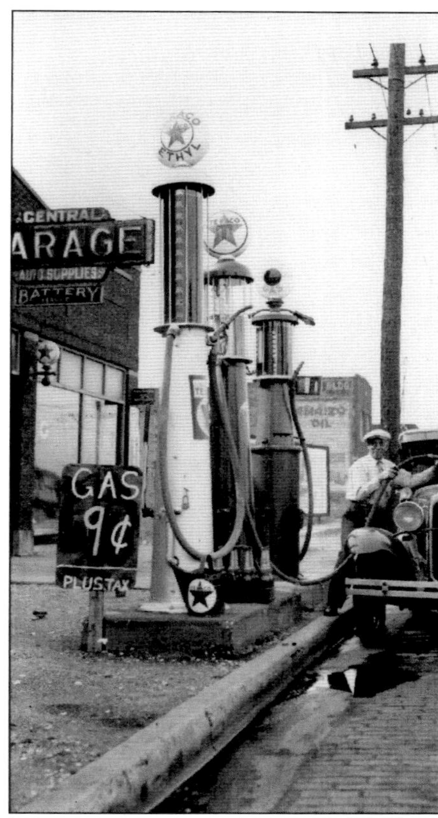

The Simbolmos brothers owned Central Gas Station, located on Magoun Avenue just off Chicago Avenue in the Calumet district between East Chicago and Indiana Harbor. (Courtesy of the Lake County Public Library.)

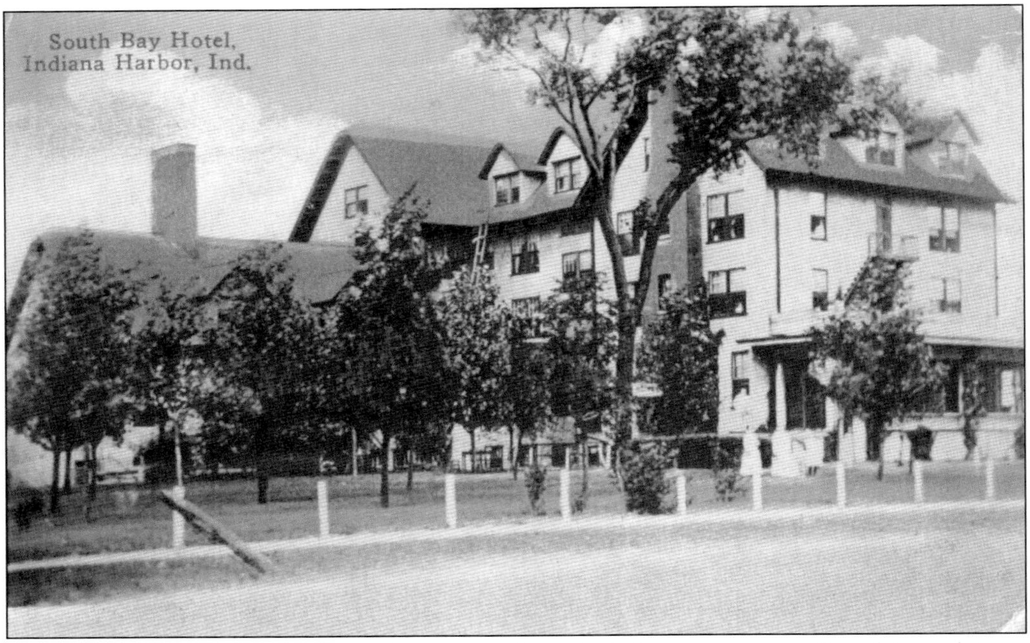

In 1910, South Bay was considered the center of social life for not only the elite of East Chicago but also those from Chicago. David Tuska, a wealthy young gambler from New York who was known to carry $30,000 in cash with him rolled up in thousand-dollar bills, kept a bachelor apartment at the hotel. (Courtesy of Steve Shook.)

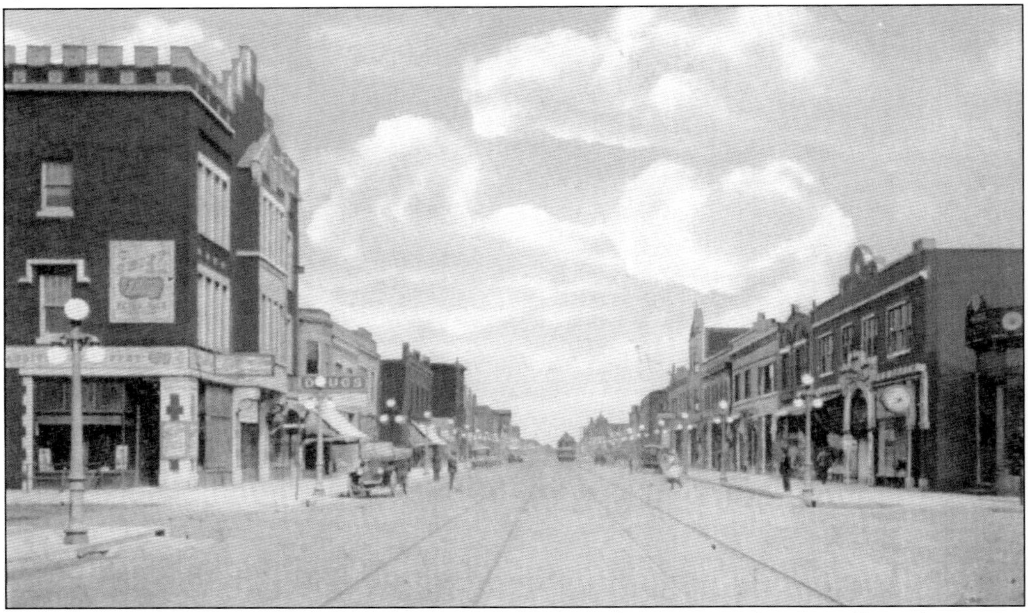

The stately Auditorium was not only home to doctors, a drugstore, and union offices, but it also had a bar and grill. On April 15, 1924, US district attorney Homer Elliott filed a suit in federal court for violation of the liquor law against the owners and operators: Morris Fishman; Mike, Cecil, Isadore, Lloyd, and Irvin Cohen; and Anna V. Cohen Fishman. Elliott asked that the place be closed for one year. (Courtesy of Andrew Prieboy.)

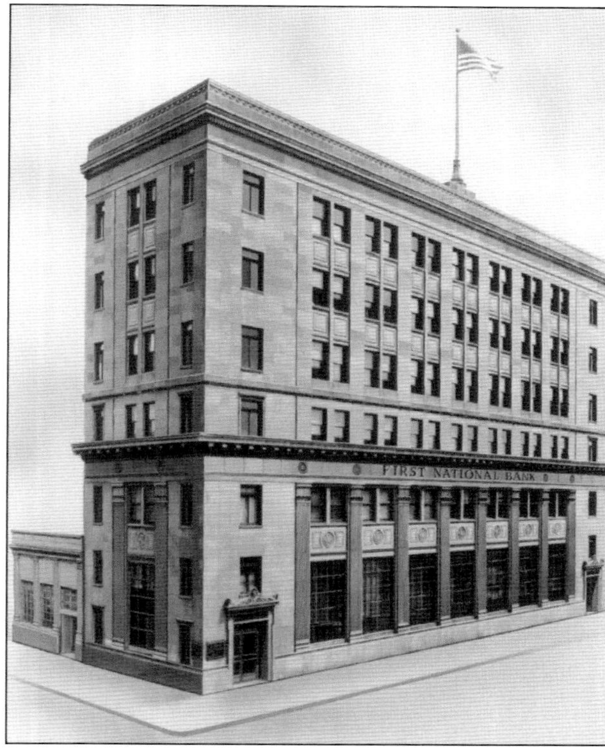

The First National Bank of East Chicago is pictured at right, and the First Calumet Trust & Savings Bank on Chicago Avenue in the Calumet area of the Twin City is pictured below. In 1918, East Chicago had eight banks and trust companies, aggregating a combined capital and surplus of $700,000 and combined deposits of $6.5 million. (Both, courtesy of the Calumet Regional Archives, Indiana University.)

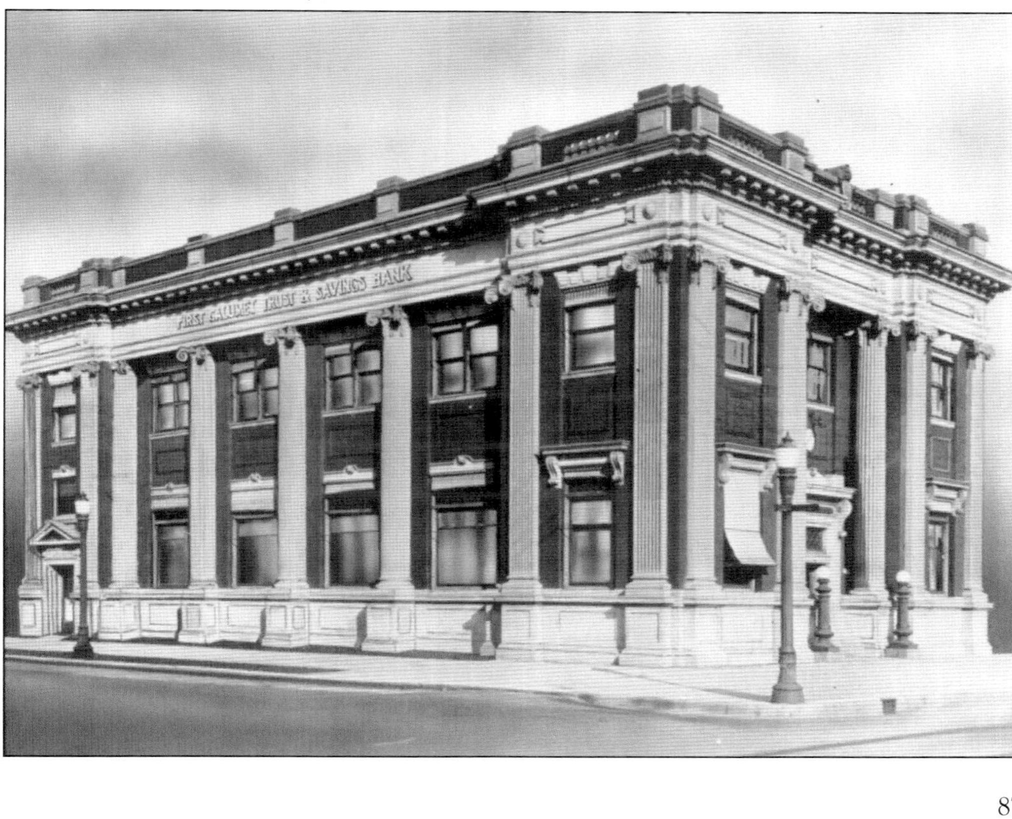

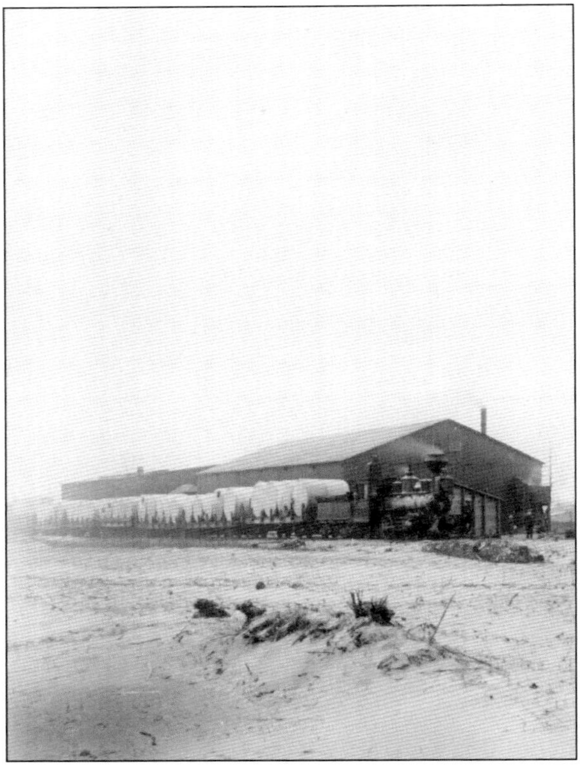

In 1888, William Graver founded Graver Tank Works, which was the first industry established in East Chicago. The company, pictured in 1913, got its start by manufacturing tanks for the Standard Oil Company refinery and was also a pioneer in the making of large steel tanks for grain elevators and oil and gas storage. (Courtesy of the Calumet Regional Archives, Indiana University.)

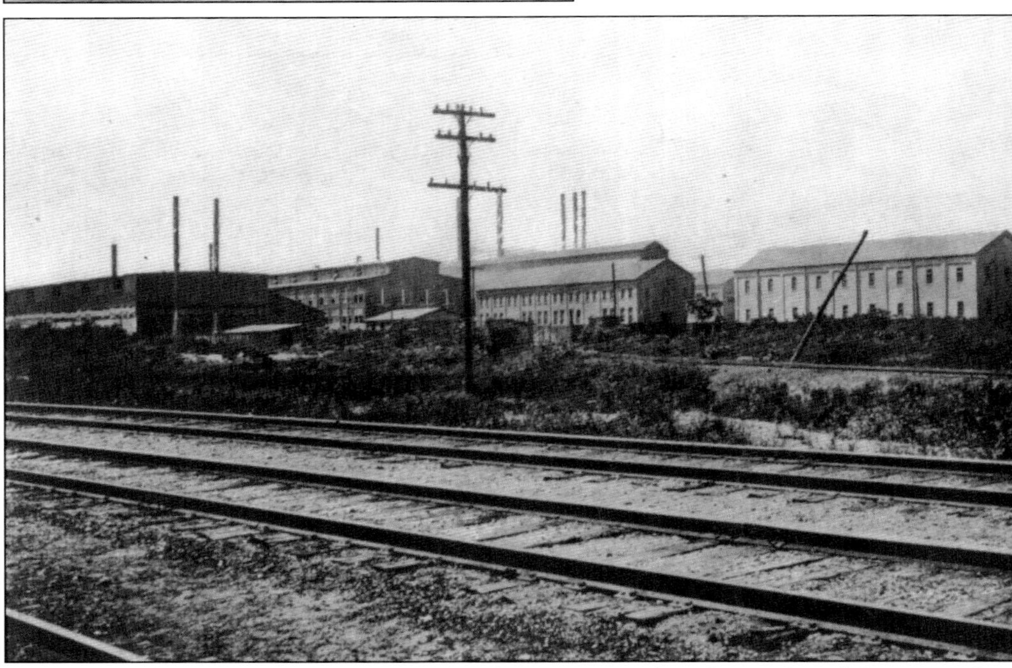

Created by the merger of eight separate foundries in 1902, the Chicago-based American Steel Foundries operated large plants in northwest Indiana, including East Chicago. (Courtesy of the Calumet Regional Archives, Indiana University.)

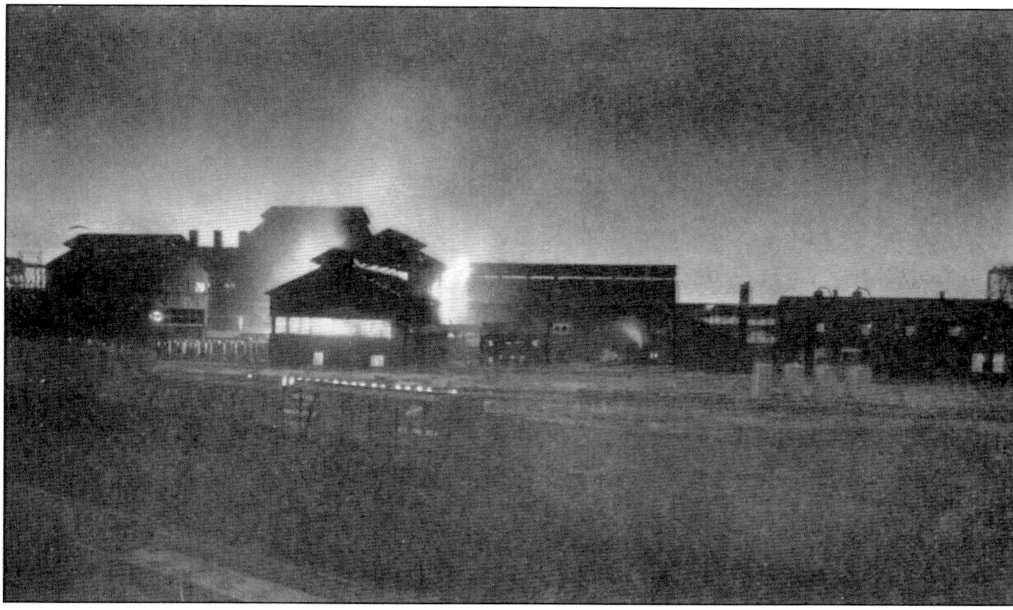

By 1923, through the purchase of steel mill assets throughout the country, the Youngstown Sheet & Tube Company became the fifth largest steelmaker in the United States. (Courtesy of the Calumet Regional Archives, Indiana University.)

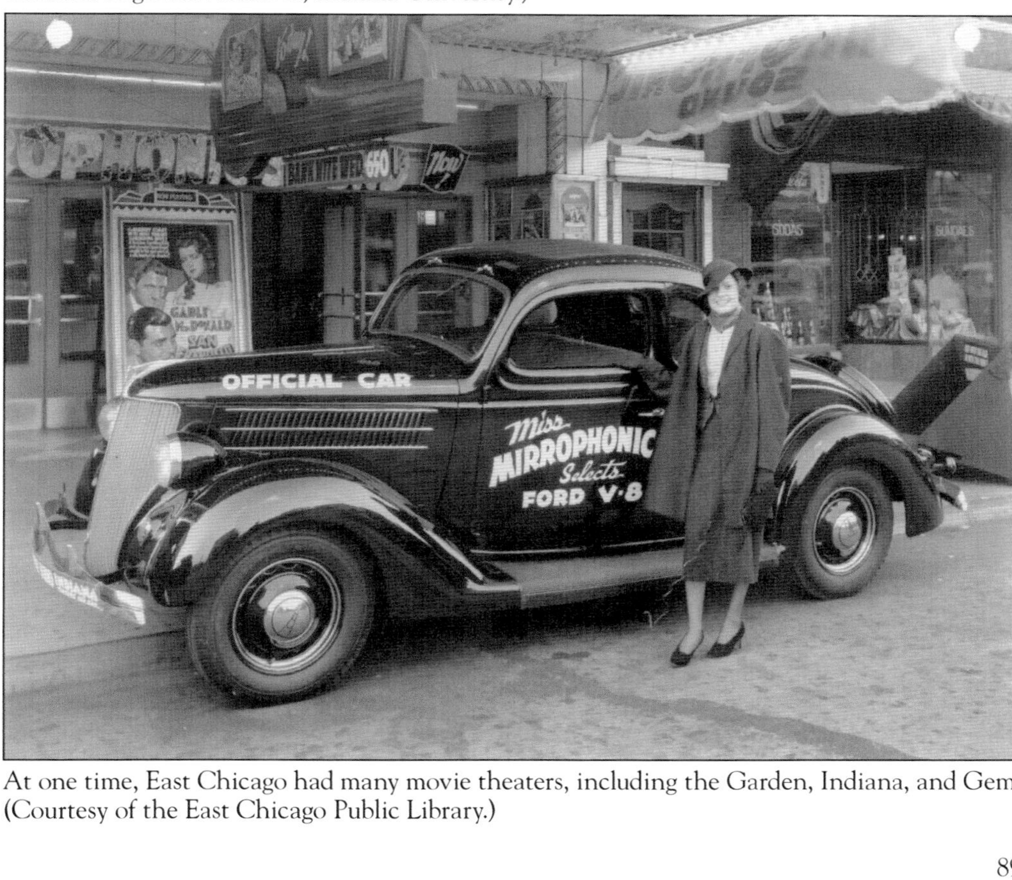

At one time, East Chicago had many movie theaters, including the Garden, Indiana, and Gem. (Courtesy of the East Chicago Public Library.)

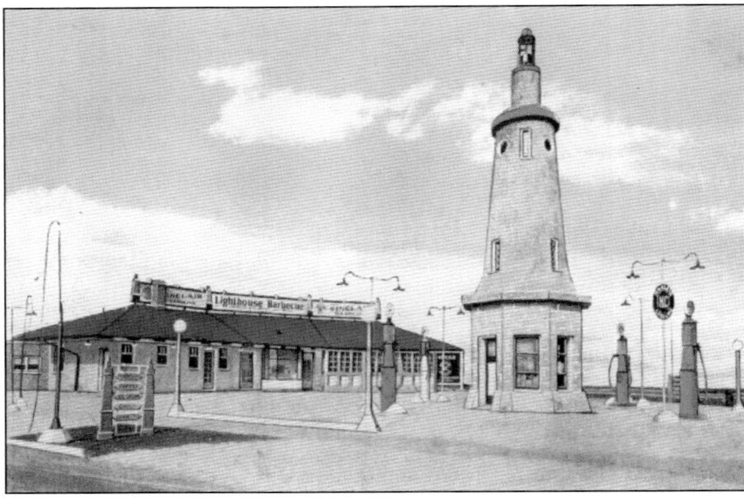

The Lighthouse Barbecue at Guthrie, Cline, and 140th Streets advertised itself as "A Real Place for Real People." (Courtesy of the East Chicago Public Library.)

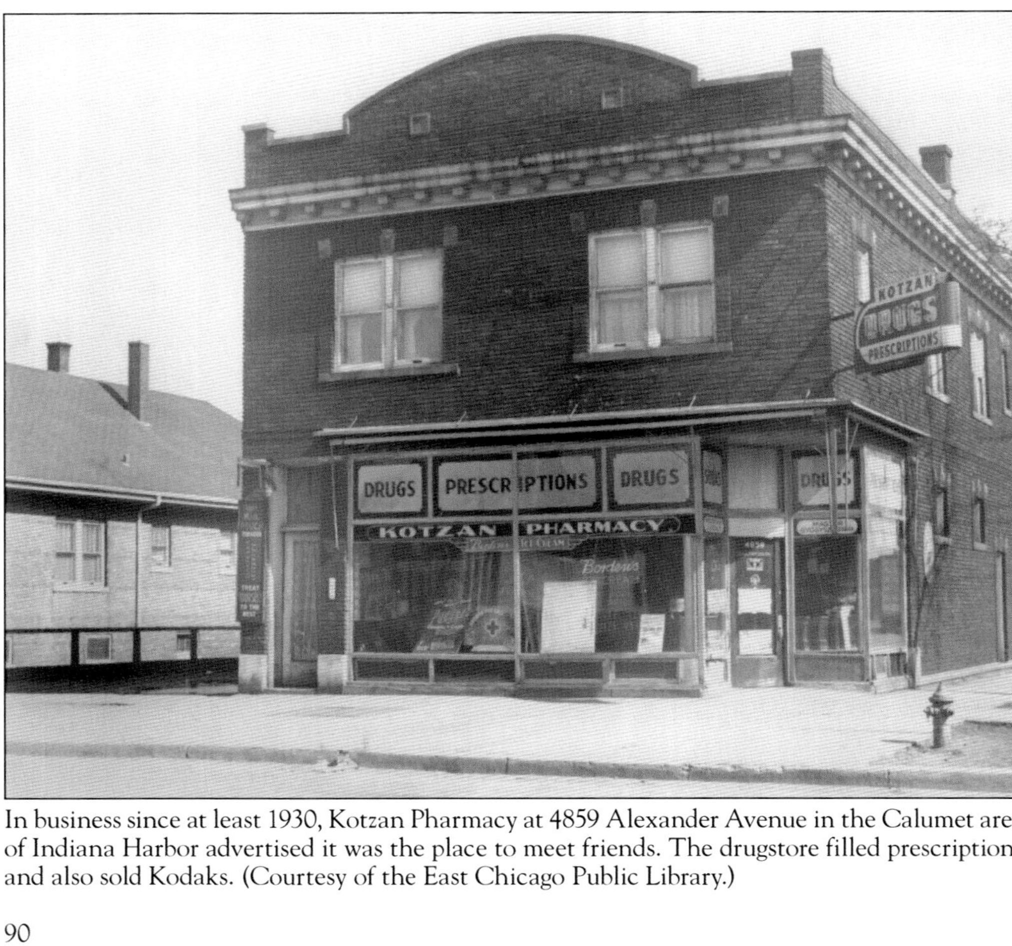

In business since at least 1930, Kotzan Pharmacy at 4859 Alexander Avenue in the Calumet area of Indiana Harbor advertised it was the place to meet friends. The drugstore filled prescriptions and also sold Kodaks. (Courtesy of the East Chicago Public Library.)

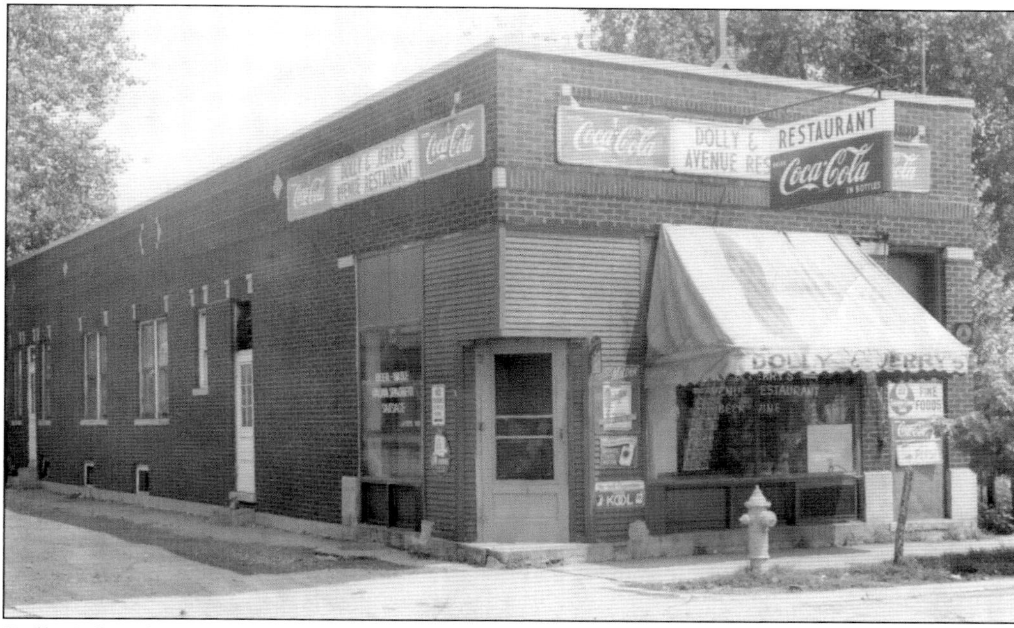

Dolly & Jerry's was a restaurant located at 4601 Euclid Avenue in Indiana Harbor. (Courtesy of the Lake County Public Library.)

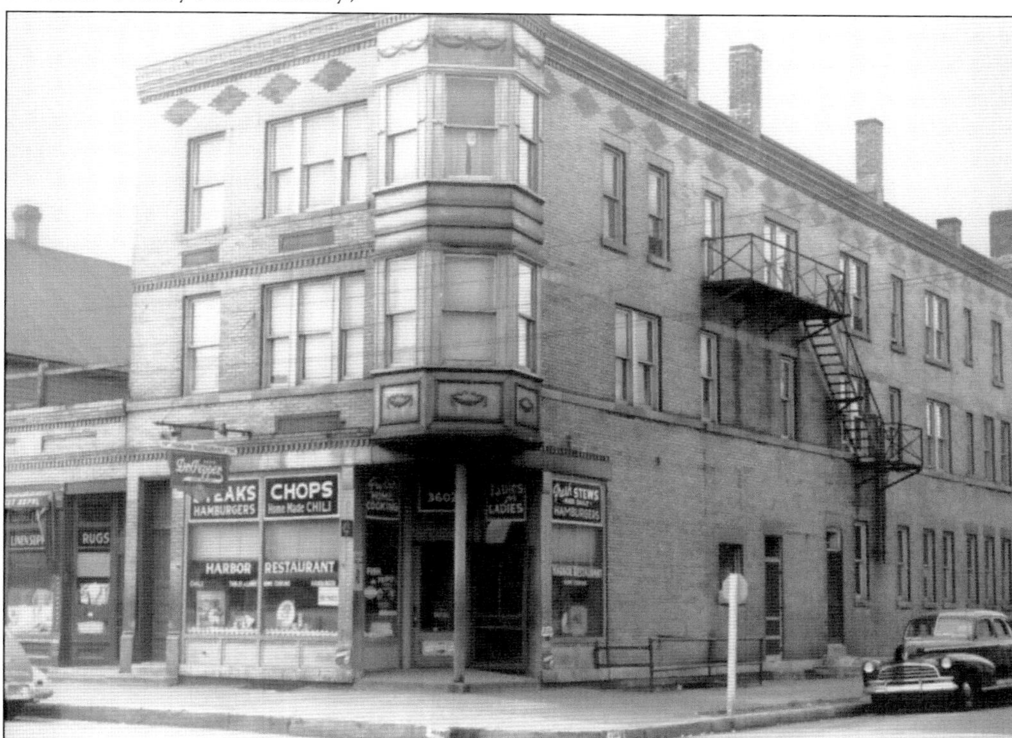

The Harbor Restaurant, a popular Indiana Harbor eatery, is shown in this classic 1940 photograph. (Courtesy of the East Chicago Public Library.)

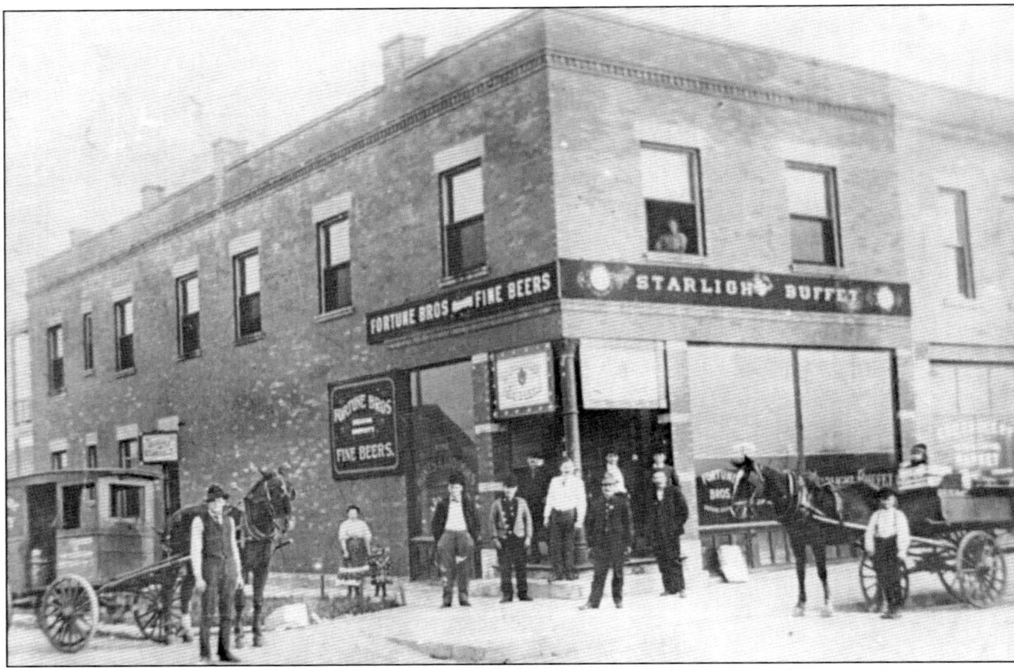

This 1920s photograph shows the Starlight Buffet in Indiana Harbor. (Courtesy of the East Chicago Public Library.)

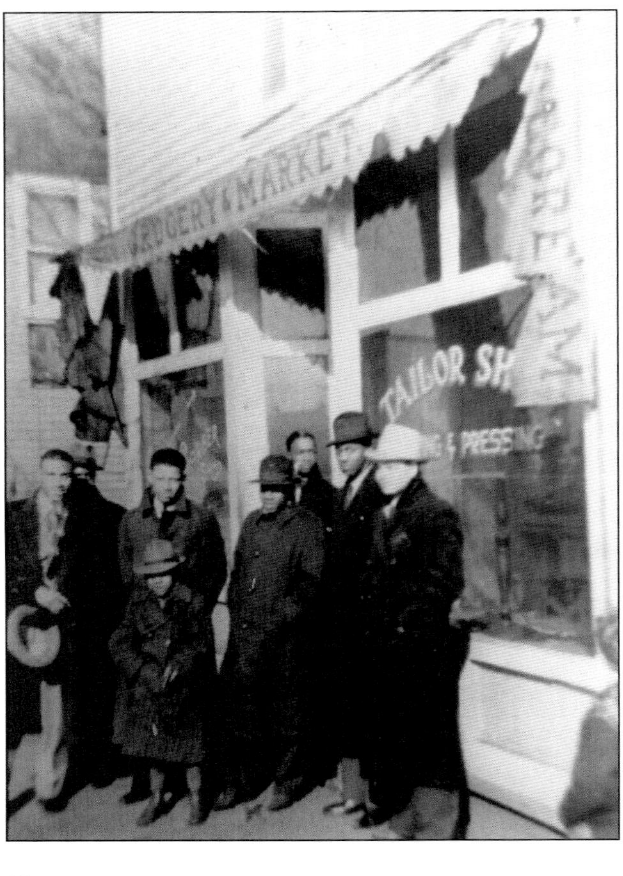

Walter Hines, William Phillips, Lenny Ruse, Spencer Allen, Wilburn Hardaway, Fred Tillotson, and Carry Hart stand in front of Edwards Barber and Tailor Shop in the Calumet area of the Twin City. Hardaway's son Thomas would become a popular art teacher at Washington High School. (Courtesy of the East Chicago Public Library.)

Eight

WHERE WE LIVED

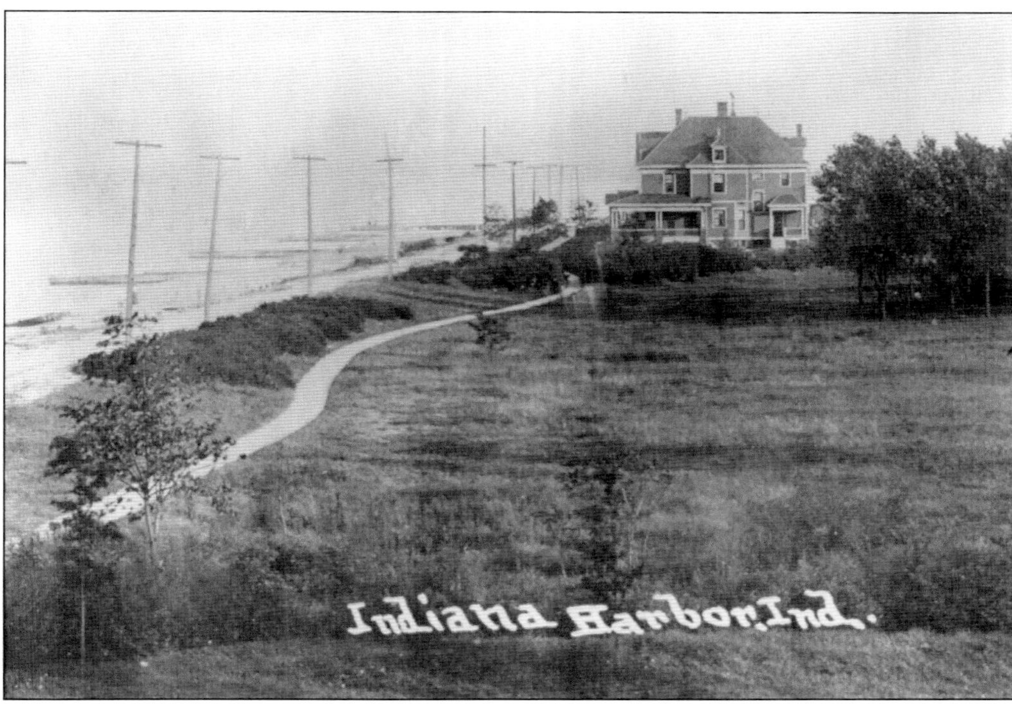

Seven homes, along with the grand South Bay Hotel, were built by Owen Aldis. One of those was the home belonging to John Stephens, the first Inland Steel superintendent. It remained in the family until the 1950s. (Courtesy of the Calumet Regional Archives, Indiana University.)

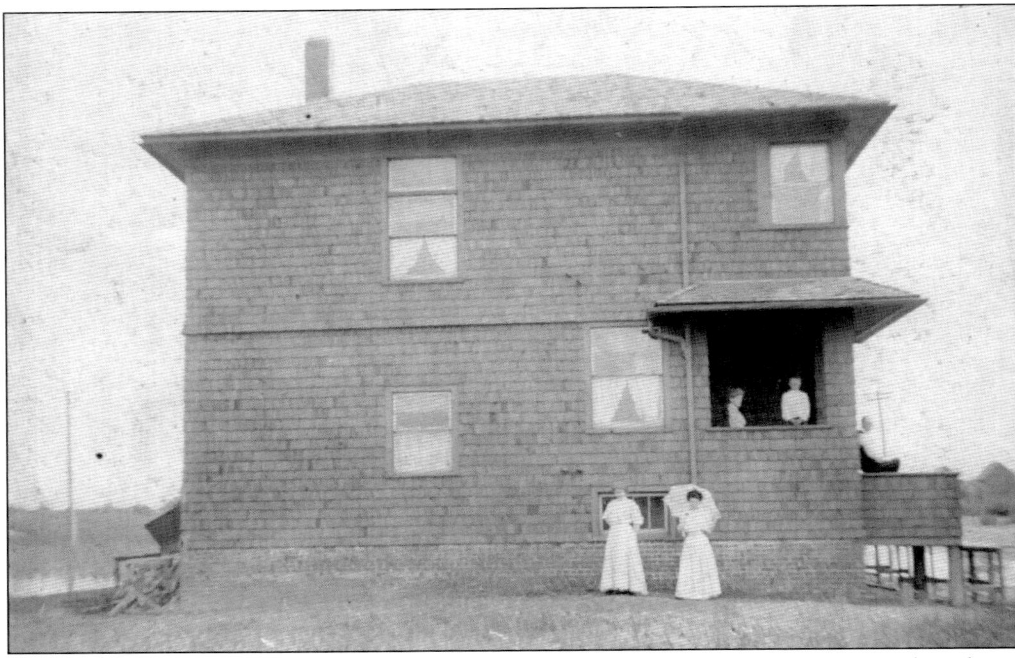

This house at 4111 Parish Avenue was one of the earliest homes built in Indiana Harbor, dating to the late 1800s. (Courtesy of Robert Grove.)

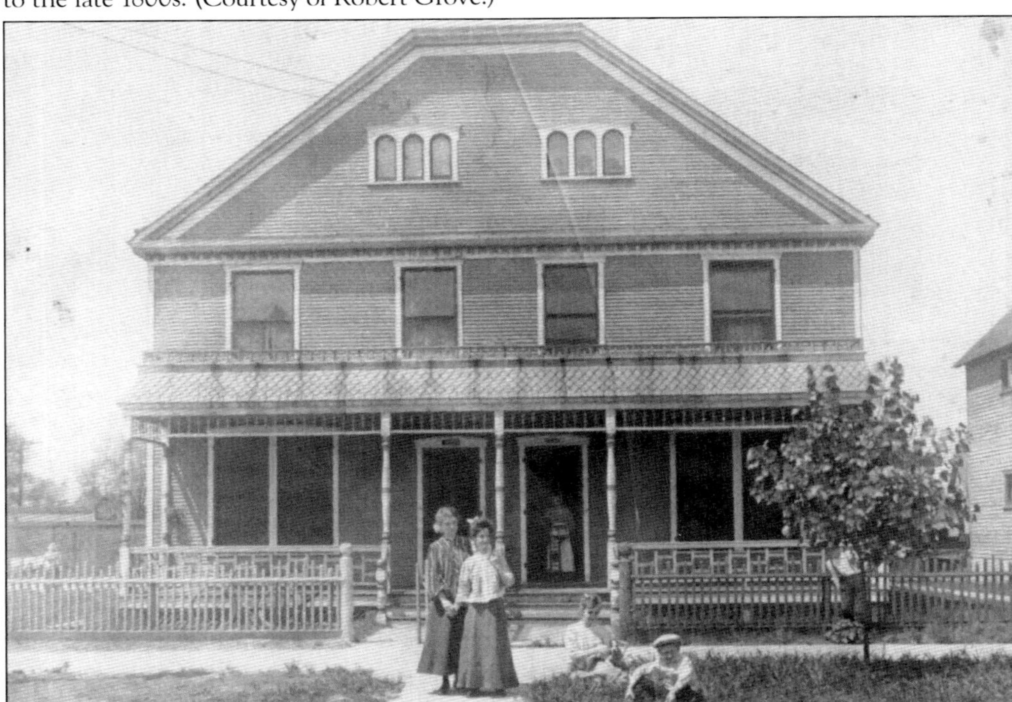

Pictured from left to right are Edith Wickey, Mae Lewis, Mrs. Lewis, Zilah Ineley, Wesley Wickey, Charley Haight, Mabel Wickey, and Trix the family dog in front of the Wickey home at 4508–4509 Magoun Avenue. (Courtesy of the East Chicago Public Library.)

Early homeowners, such as Mrs. Reese W. Williams pictured in front of her home at 4726 Baring Avenue in 1898, had to contend with difficult terrain and housing built on sand. Though just miles from Chicago, it was a desolate area, and keeping homes clean was difficult, to say the least, as residents had to contend not only with blowing sand and muddy streets but also the smoke of the mills. For a while, Lake Michigan waters were pristine enough to drink without filtration, but that did not last long as industrialization continued. (Courtesy of the East Chicago Public Library.)

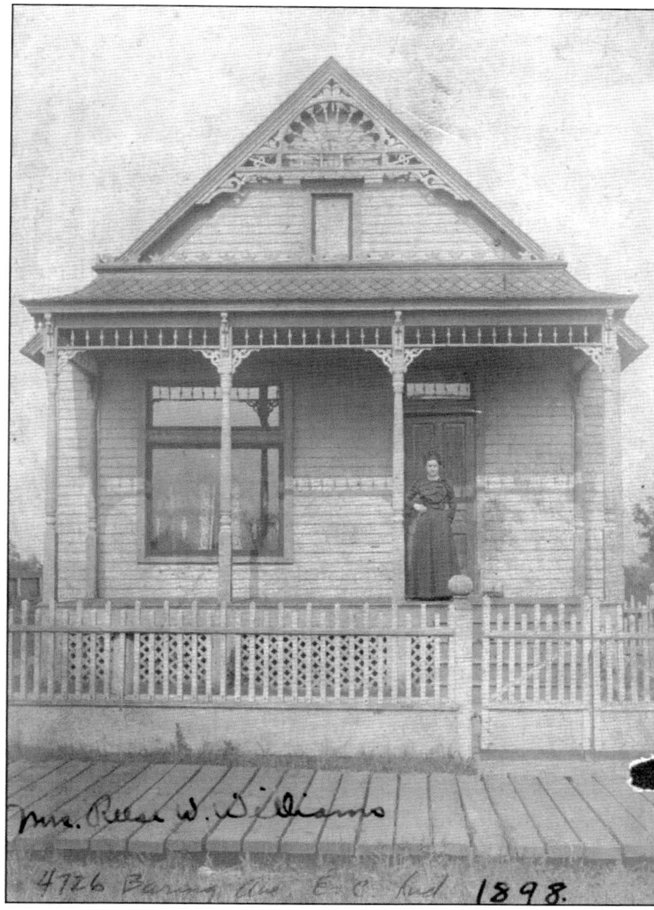

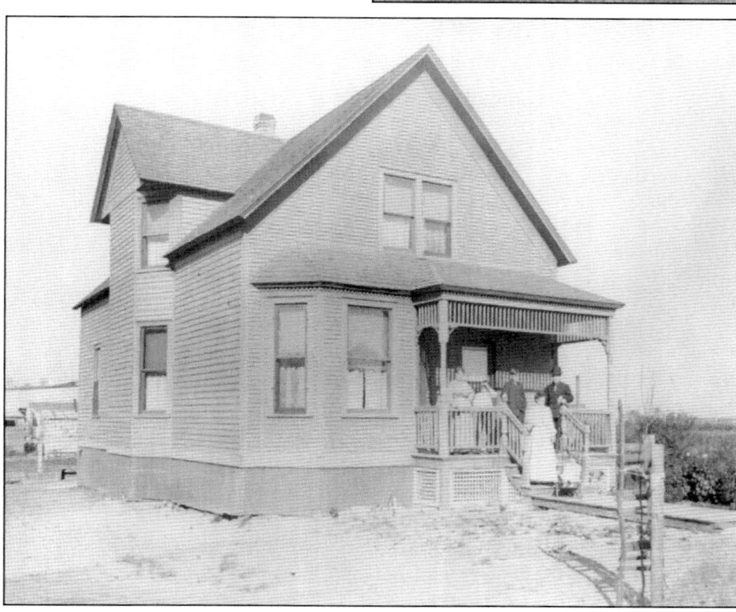

In this 1902 photograph taken in front of the John P. Anderson residence at 3506 Grapevine Street is Mrs. Anderson with her three sons—Walter, William, and Arthur—along with an out-of-town relative and unidentified baby. (Courtesy of the Calumet Regional Archives, Indiana University.)

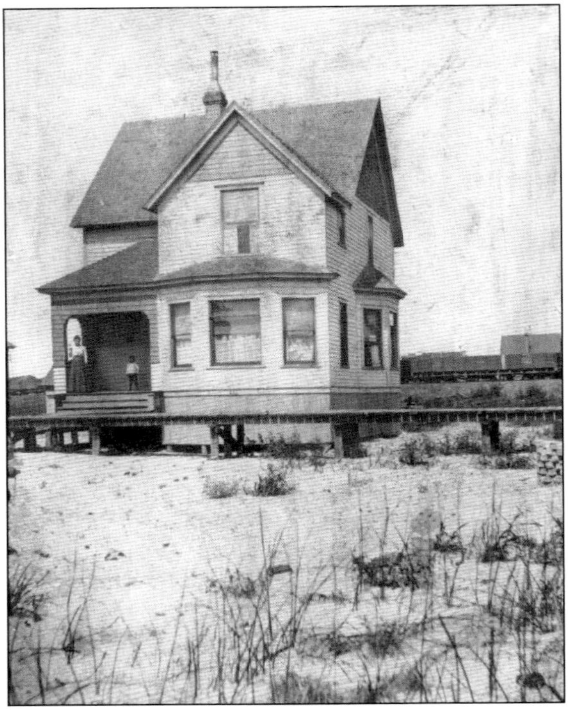

The Van Horne home was moved from Regent Street to Commonwealth Avenue in 1907, following the Baltimore & Ohio Railroad's relocation of its tracks. Many homes were put on top of flatbed trucks and rolled to other locations. (Courtesy of the Calumet Regional Archives, Indiana University.)

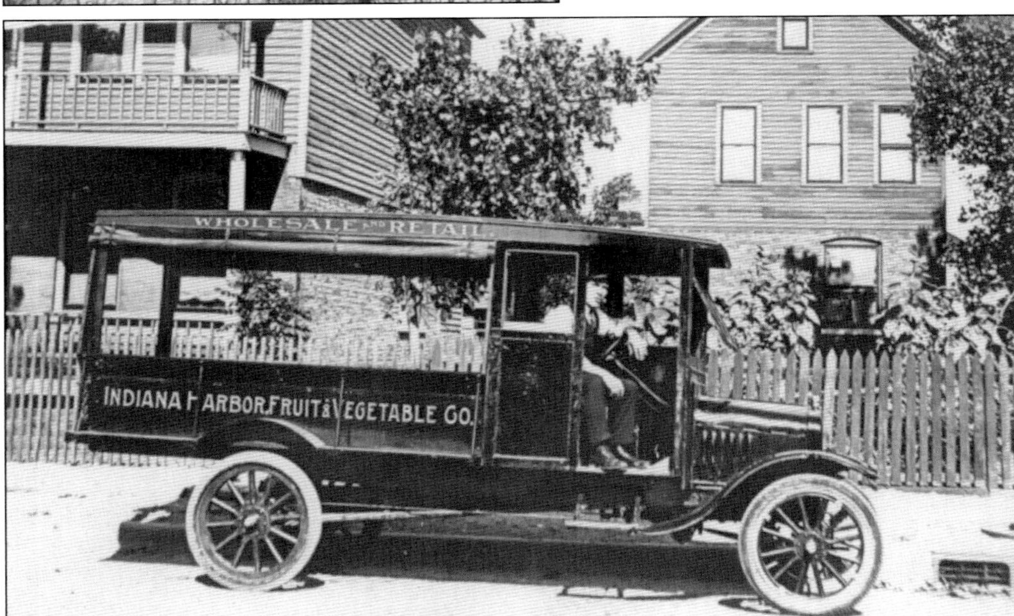

Home delivery services were provided by many local stores, including the Indiana Harbor Fruit and Vegetable Company, which distributed groceries to most of the city's neighborhoods. In the early days, home delivery often meant getting as far as the beginning of a street and then filling up a wheelbarrow with the goods and trundling across sand, mud, or muck to the home. But by the late 1910s, dirt roads morphed into paved streets complete with storm drains, making it much easier for both homeowners and deliverymen. (Courtesy of Steve Shook.)

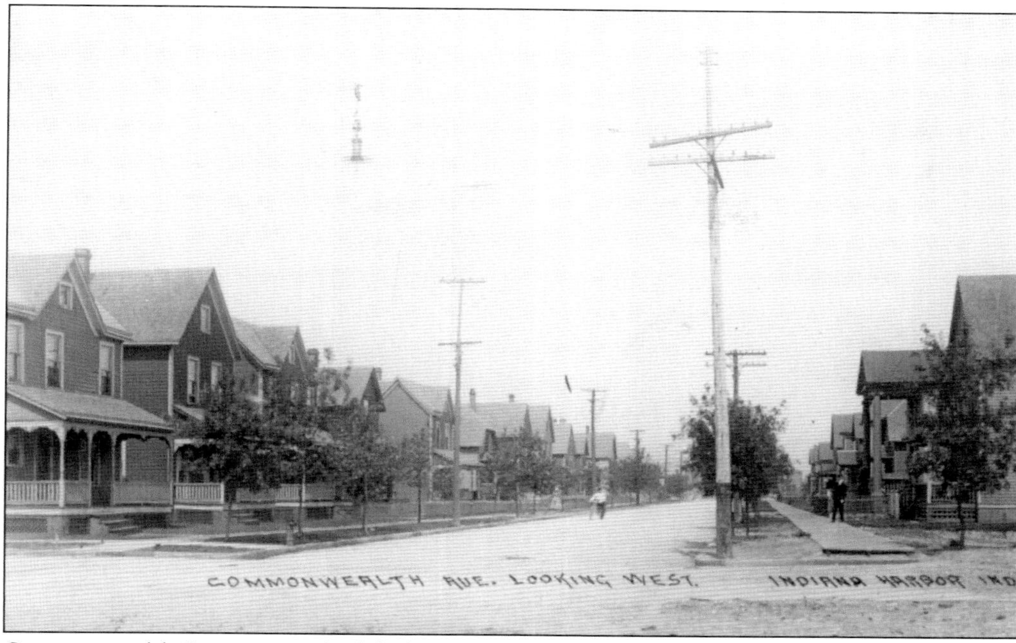

Commonwealth Street, near the lakefront, was a picturesque route lined with the homes of the city's elite. (Courtesy of the Calumet Regional Archives, Indiana University.)

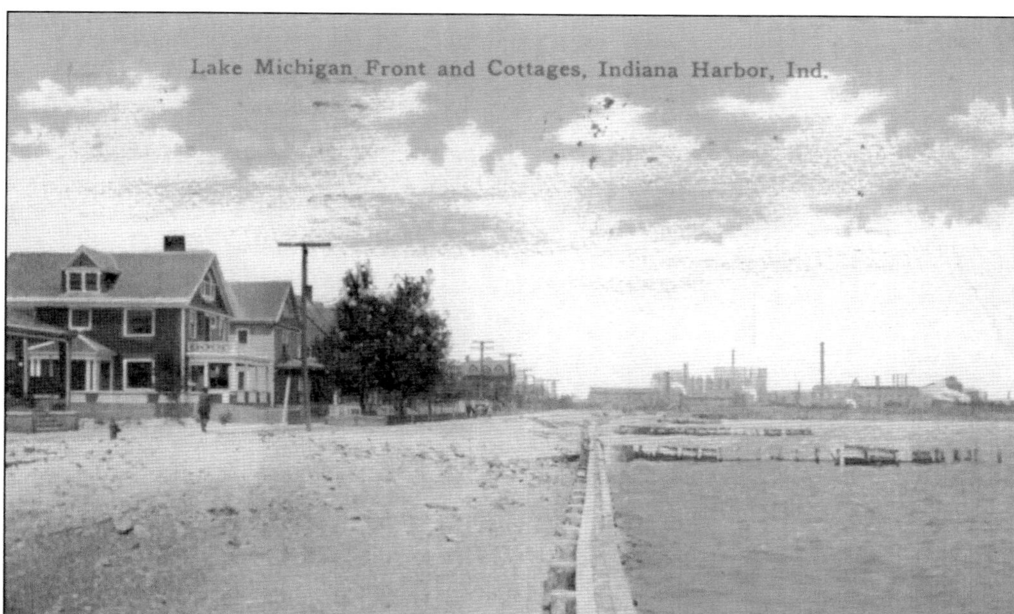

Despite the growth of the steel mills, the lakefront continued to be the place of choice for stately homes. (Courtesy of the Calumet Regional Archives, Indiana University.)

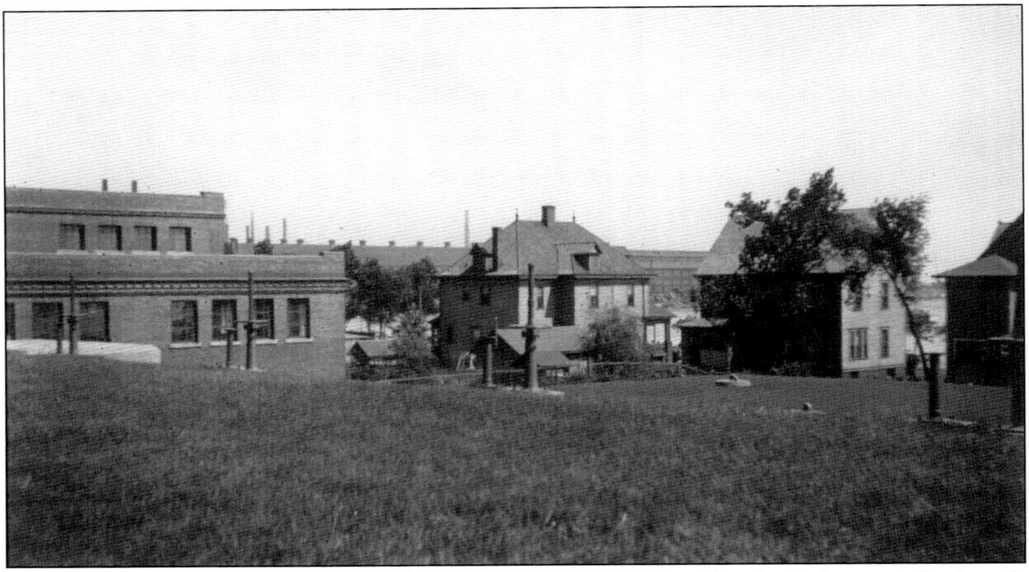

The lake and the steel mills are in the background of this photograph, which shows the backyards of homes lining the shore. Despite being a steel city, East Chicago–Indiana Harbor had nice neighborhoods with large yards and proximity to parks. (Courtesy of Archibald McKinlay.)

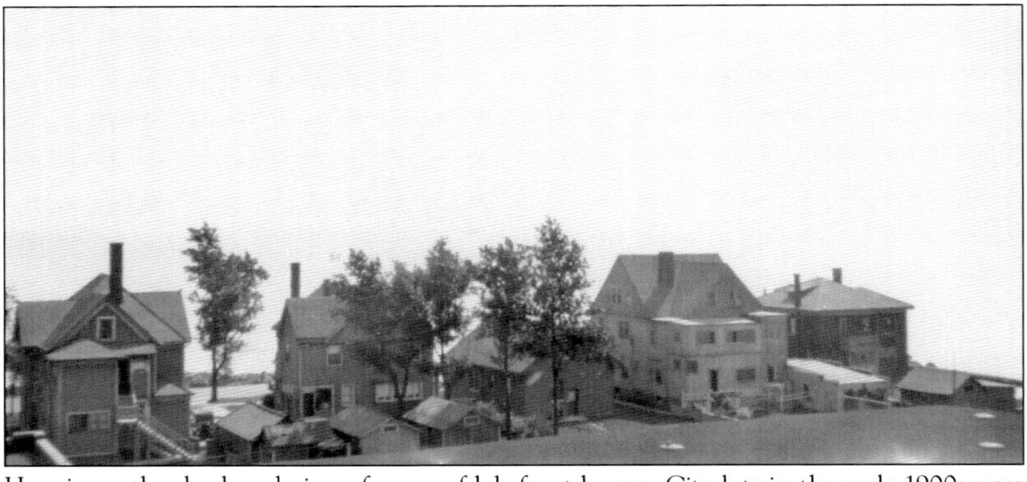

Here is another backyard view of a row of lakefront homes. City lots in the early 1900s were selling at a starting price of $225, though those closer to the lake were much more expensive. (Courtesy of Archibald McKinlay.)

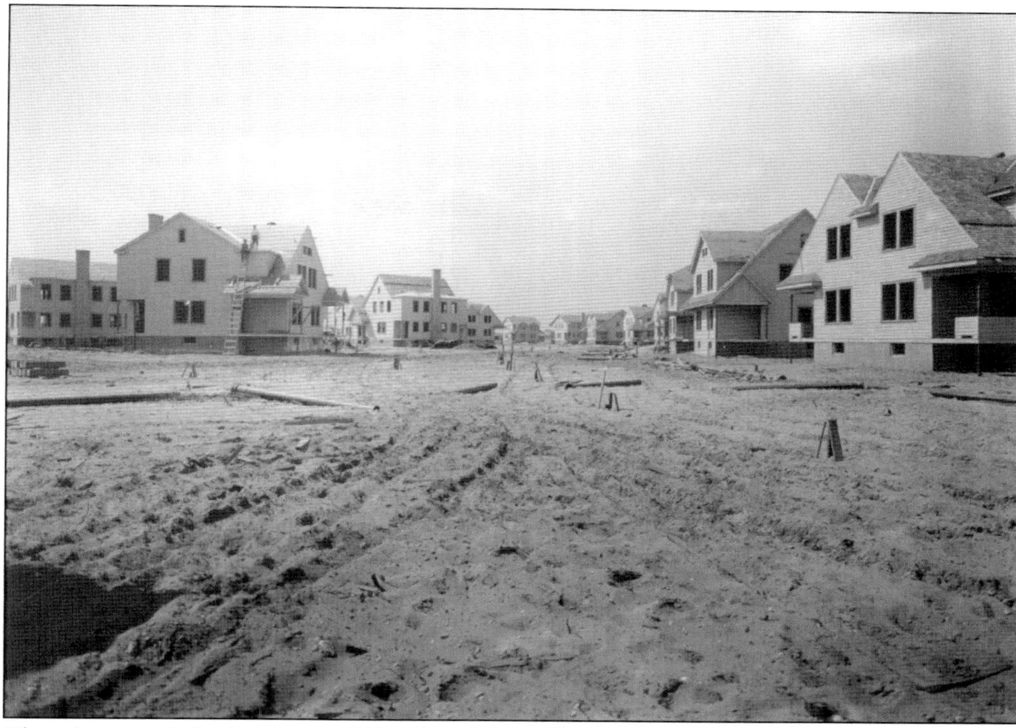

This photograph looks west on 141st Street from Short Street on September 14, 1920, as new homes go up. The boom was in full swing in the Twin City. (Courtesy of the Calumet Regional Archives, Indiana University.)

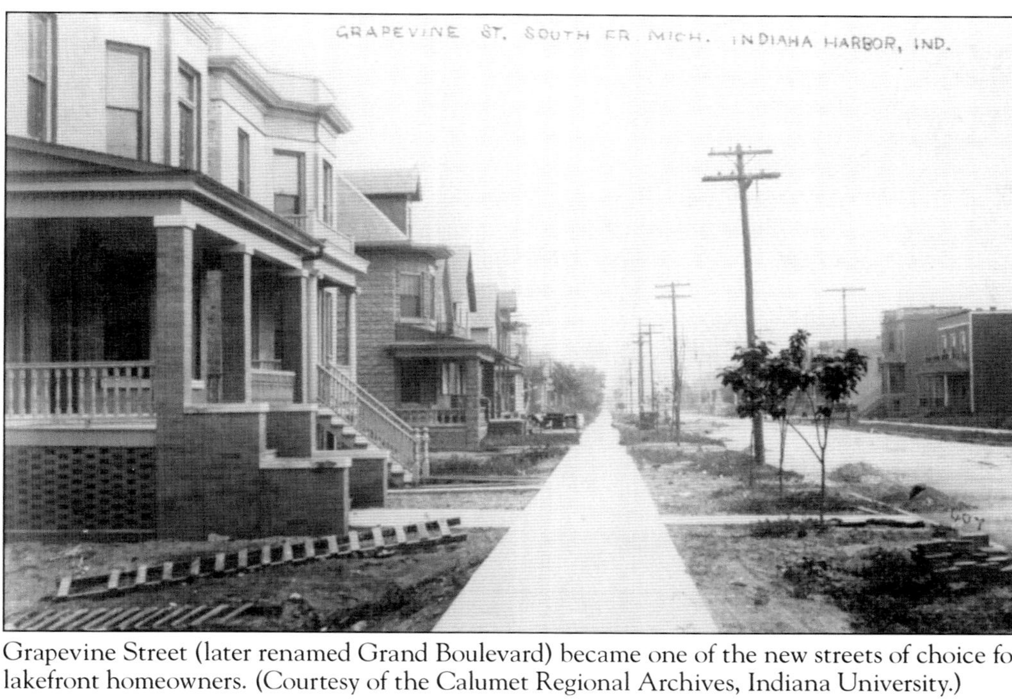

Grapevine Street (later renamed Grand Boulevard) became one of the new streets of choice for lakefront homeowners. (Courtesy of the Calumet Regional Archives, Indiana University.)

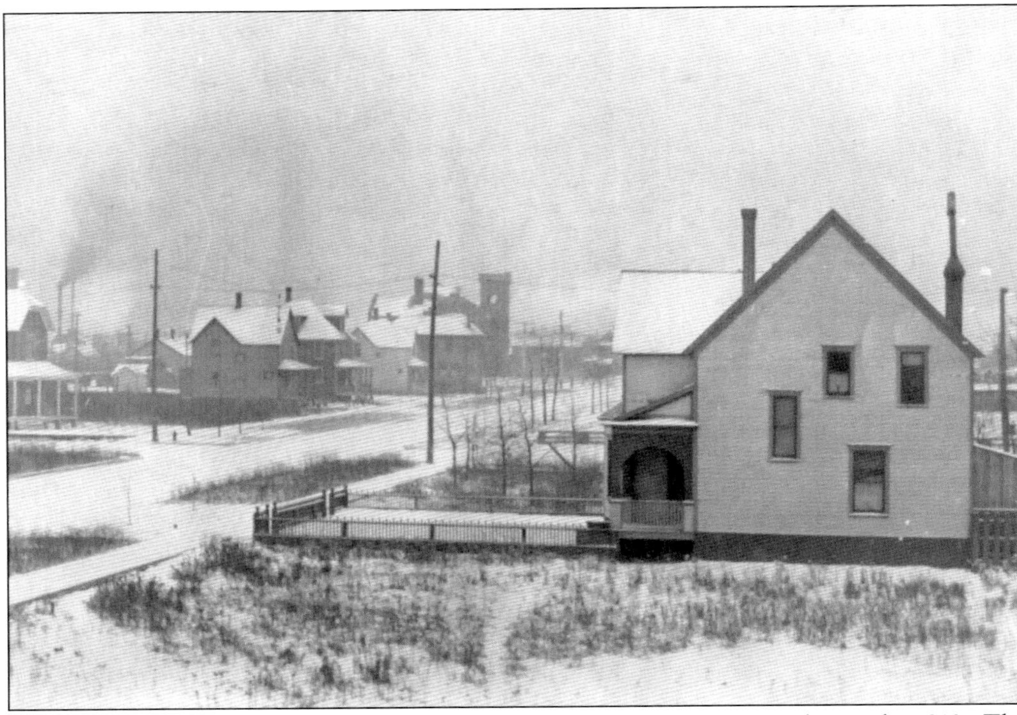

A newly built block in East Chicago is pictured here in a cozy winter scene during the 1910s. The crenelated tower in the background was part of East Chicago High School, located in a building known as North Side or Benjamin Harrison School. (Courtesy of the Briska family.)

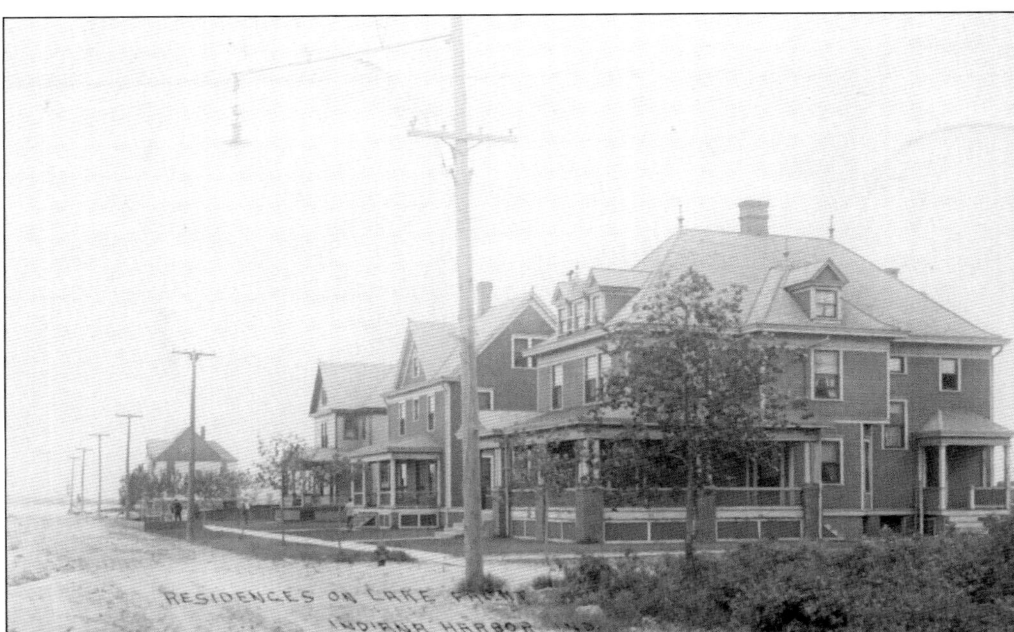

The home in the foreground is a graceful mansion belonging to the Stephens family. (Courtesy of the Calumet Regional Archives, Indiana University.)

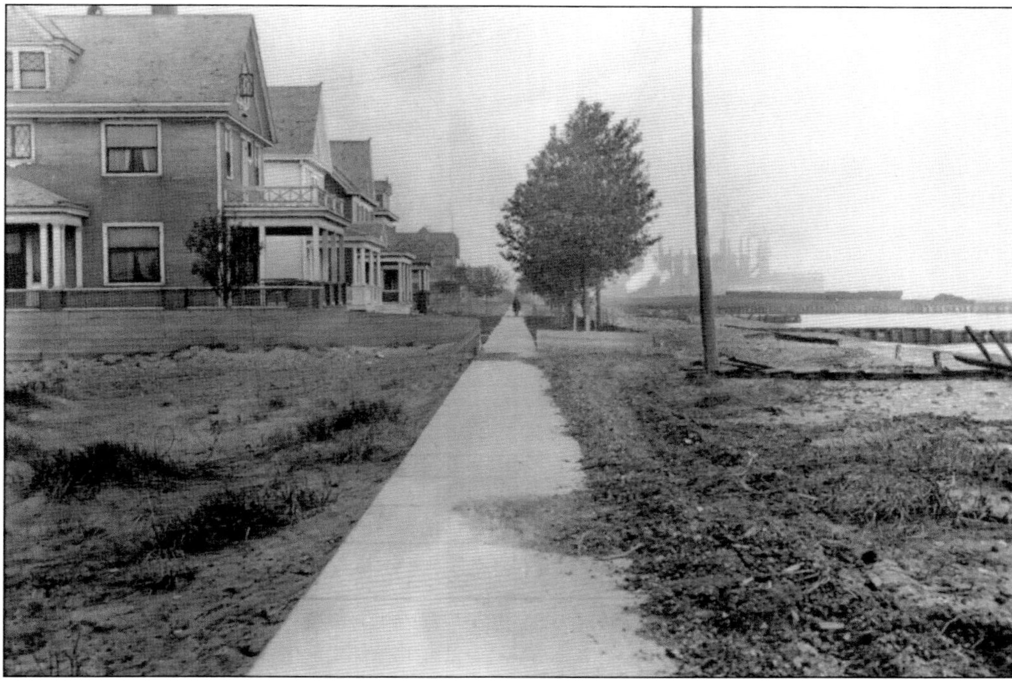

At the time these photographs were taken, Michigan Avenue, Aldis Avenue, and Charles Place bordered Lees Park, which was the city's first recreational area and also provided an appealing green space for those living on these streets. The park had a bathhouse with changing buildings for both men and women, as well as an outdoor shower. (Courtesy of the Calumet Regional Archives, Indiana University.)

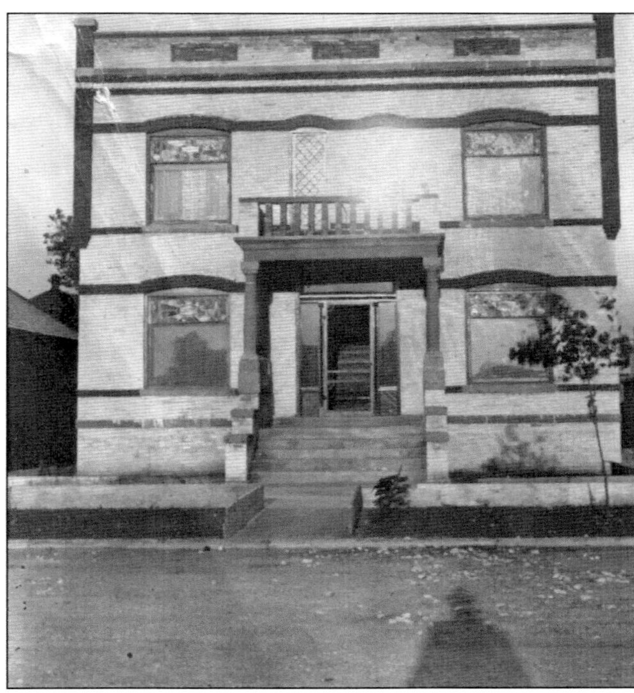

Birdie Peters, an East Chicago librarian, lived on the second floor of this apartment building at 3619 Fir Street. (Courtesy of the East Chicago Public Library.)

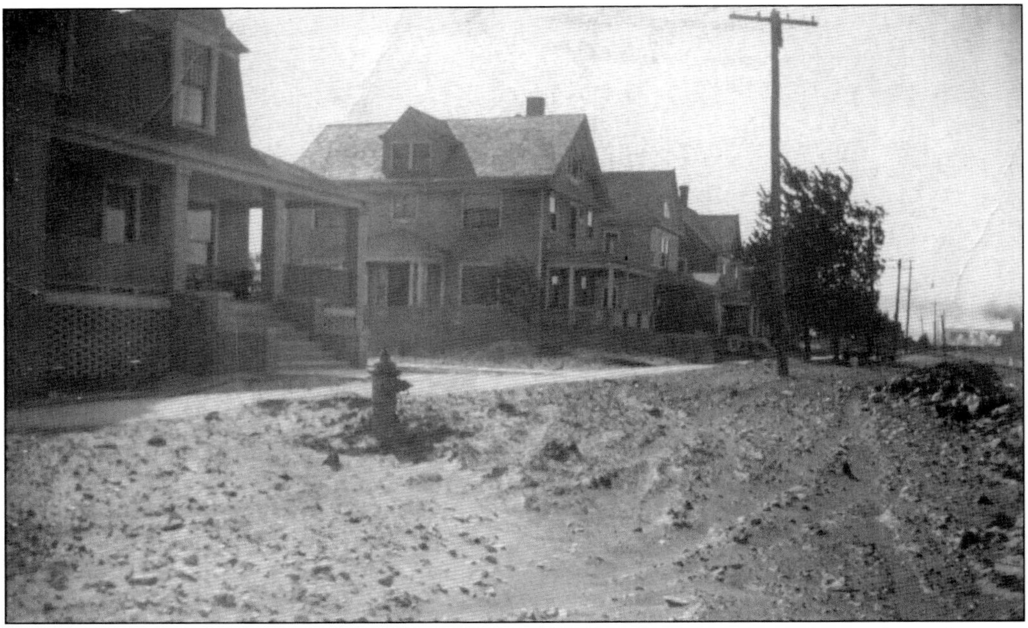

Aldis Avenue is pictured looking north around 1916. These homes belonged to such residents as the president of the Citizen's Bank and Fred Stevens of Stevens and Haywood Hardware Store. One of the most unusual buildings on Aldis and Michigan Avenues in the early 1900s was an airplane hangar belonging to George Mosny, a World War I pilot who purchased a seaplane at the end of the war. The Mosny brothers would roll the plane down the railroad tracks and float it onto the lake. (Courtesy of Archibald McKinlay.)

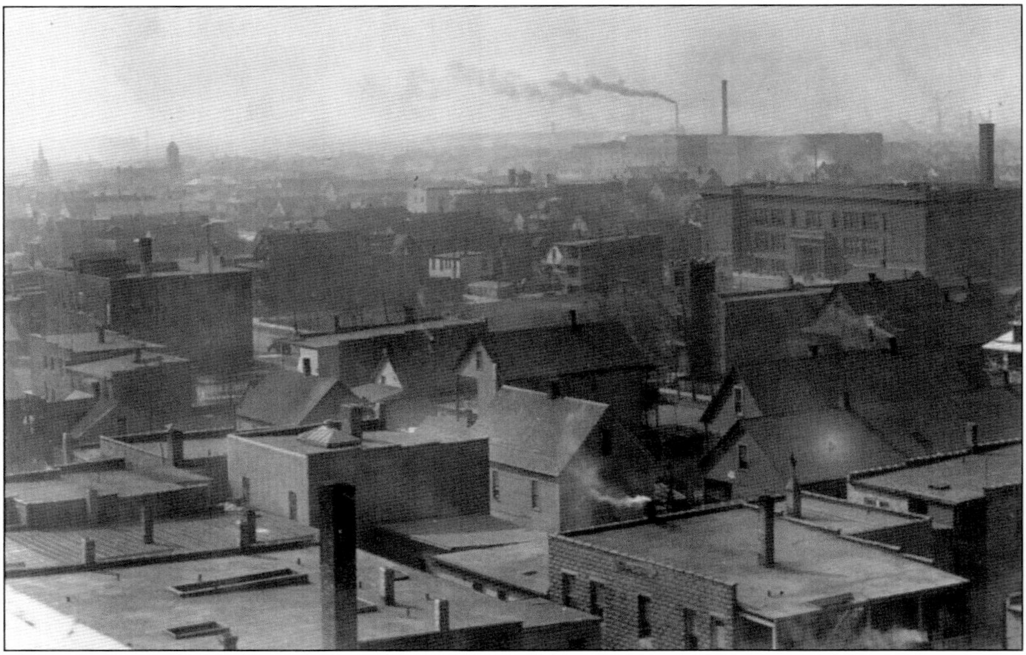

This rooftop photograph shows the homes in Indiana Harbor set amidst its many industries. (Courtesy of the East Chicago Public Library.)

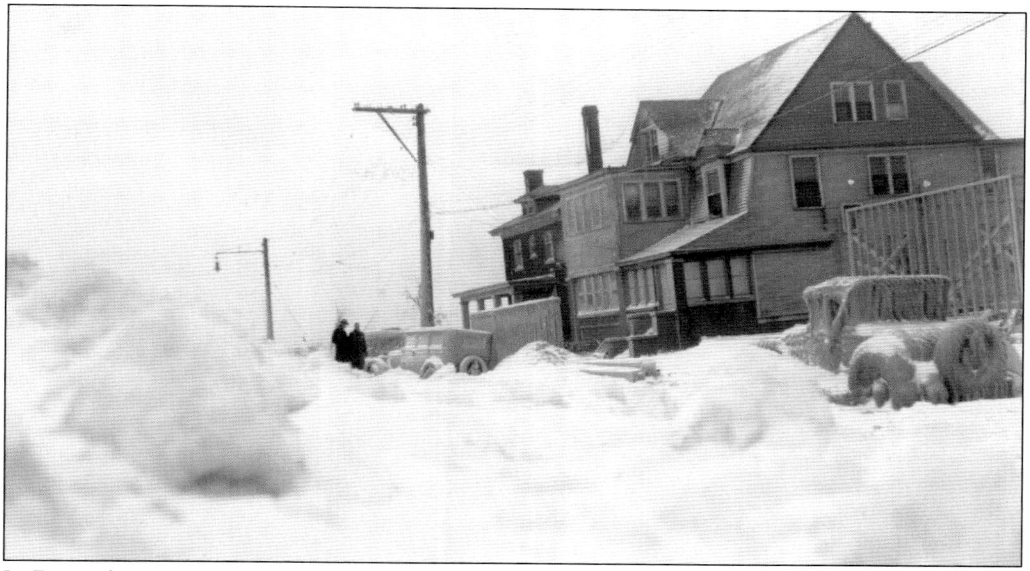

In December 1929, a huge winter storm destroyed much of the beach that ran in front of the fine homes on Aldis Avenue. Because of the ice buildup and destruction, residents had to park their cars on the sidewalk. (Courtesy of the Calumet Regional Archives, Indiana University.)

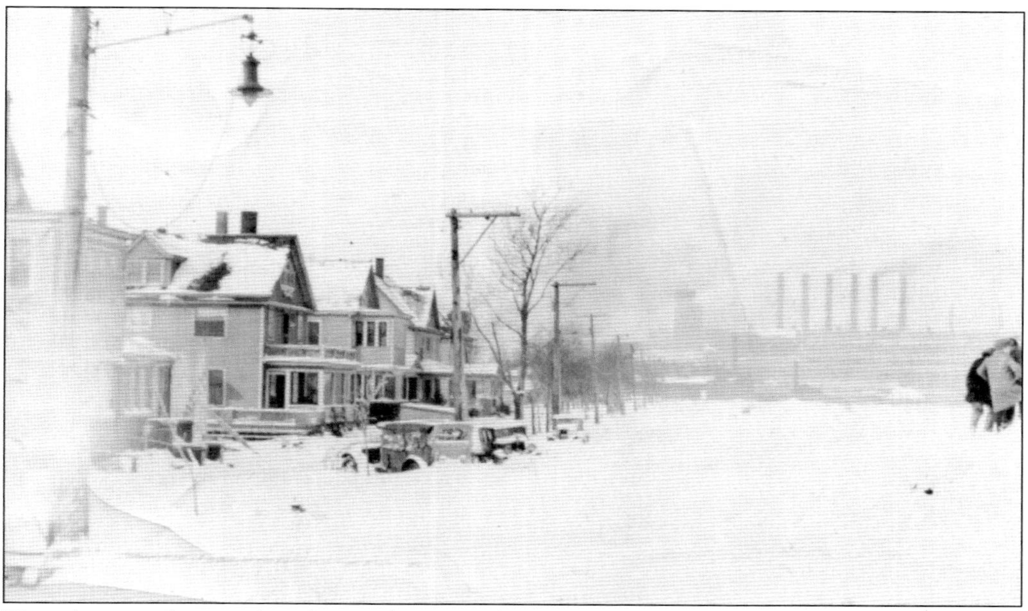

This photograph was taken during the December 1929 blizzard. People stand at far right on the iced-over lake. As rail lines and factories occupied much of the beachfront, the wealthier families who had lived there moved inland to wide, tree-lined streets bordered by Colonial, Prairie, and Tudor-style homes. They had broad, landscaped lawns, and the interiors boasted parlors, formal dining rooms, large foyers, and living rooms. (Courtesy of the Calumet Regional Archives, Indiana University.)

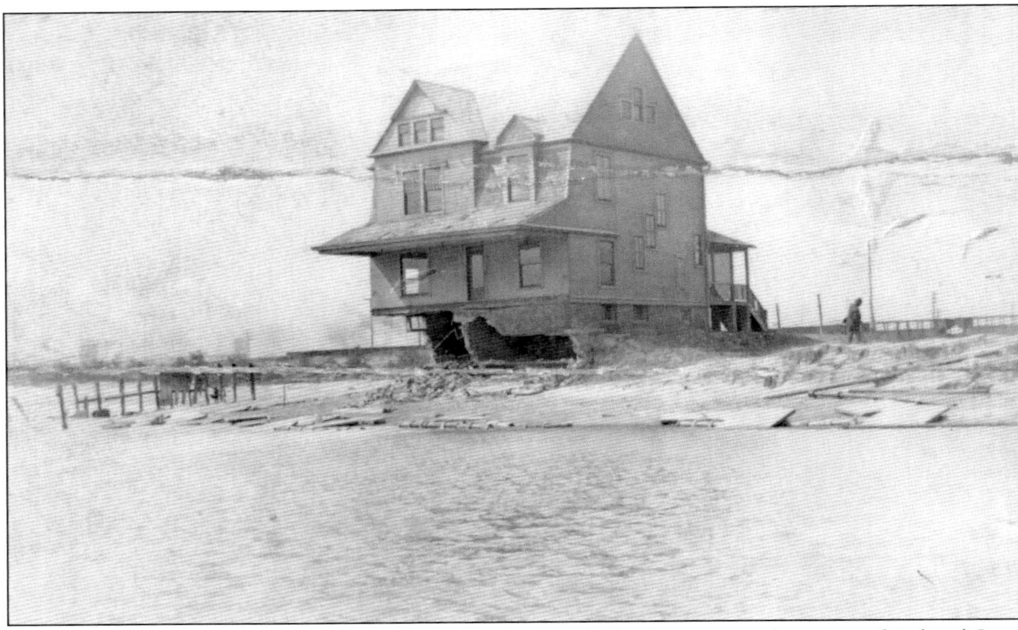

Pictured is the home of J.G. Dank, who was responsible for laying out the original Inland Steel Company. The Dank home, located at 3326 Aldis Avenue, was moved several times until it was purchased by the Howard Yant family for approximately $6,000. (Courtesy of the Calumet Regional Archives, Indiana University.)

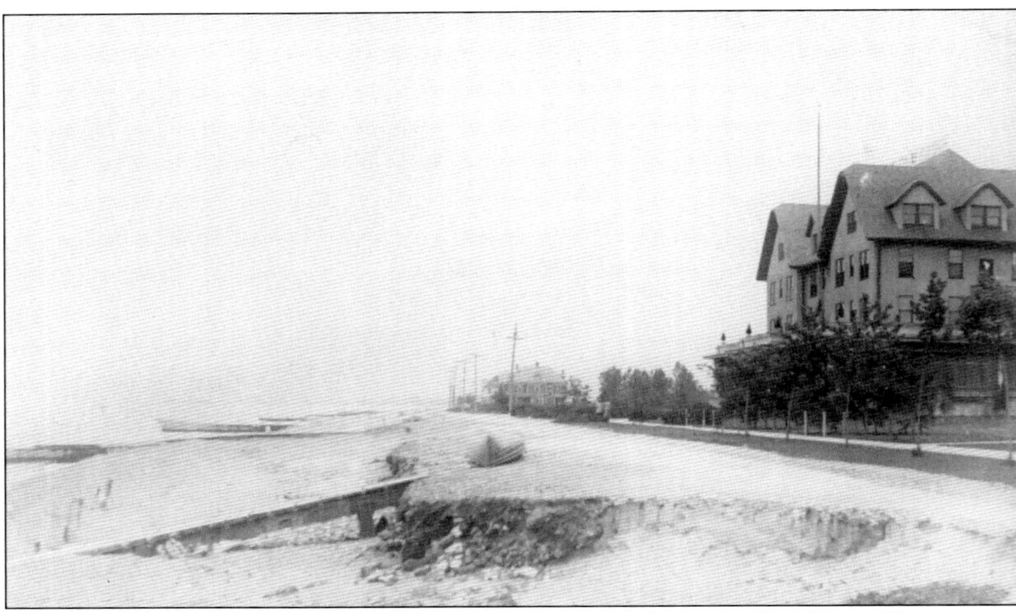

The South Bay Hotel, with the John Stephens house in the background and a small boat on the shoreline, represents the wonder of life on Lake Michigan in Indiana Harbor before the railroad line was rerouted and a bill was passed by the state that let property owners build into the lake. This allowed Inland Steel to expand and caused many homeowners to move inland. (Courtesy of the Calumet Regional Archives, Indiana University.)

Nine

How We Had Fun

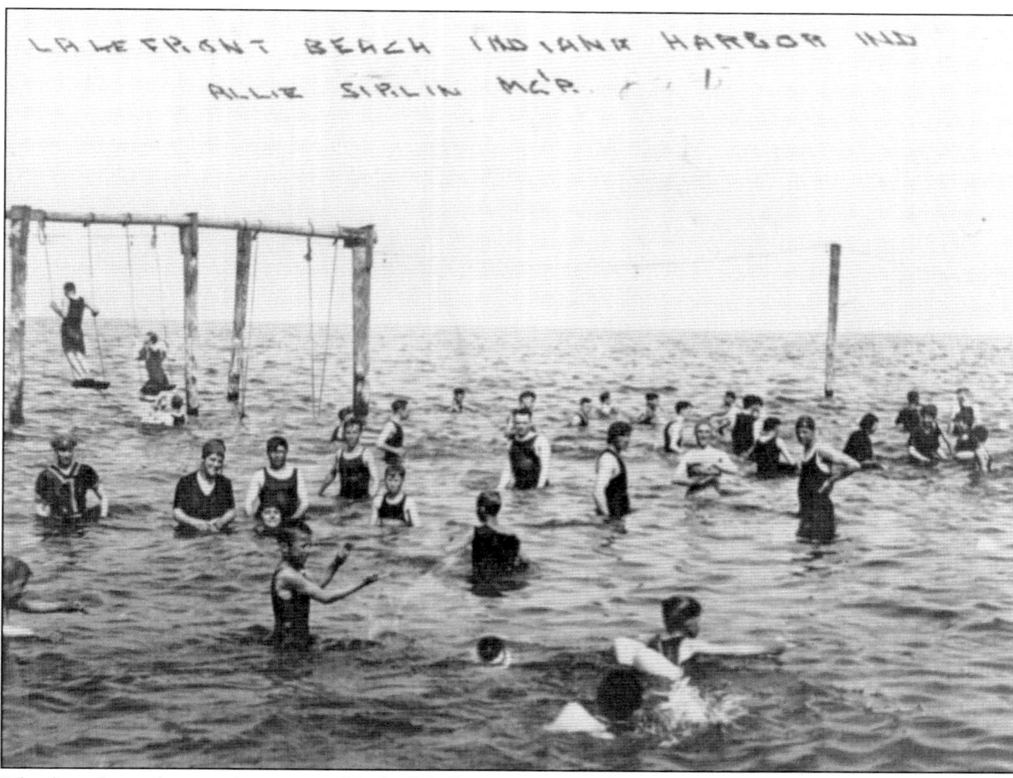

The beach at the southern tip of Lake Michigan was used as stagecoach road until around 1834. In 1908, Lees Park opened as the first public beach in East Chicago. It was named for John W. Lees, Inland Steel's second general superintendent. (Courtesy of the Calumet Regional Archives, Indiana University.)

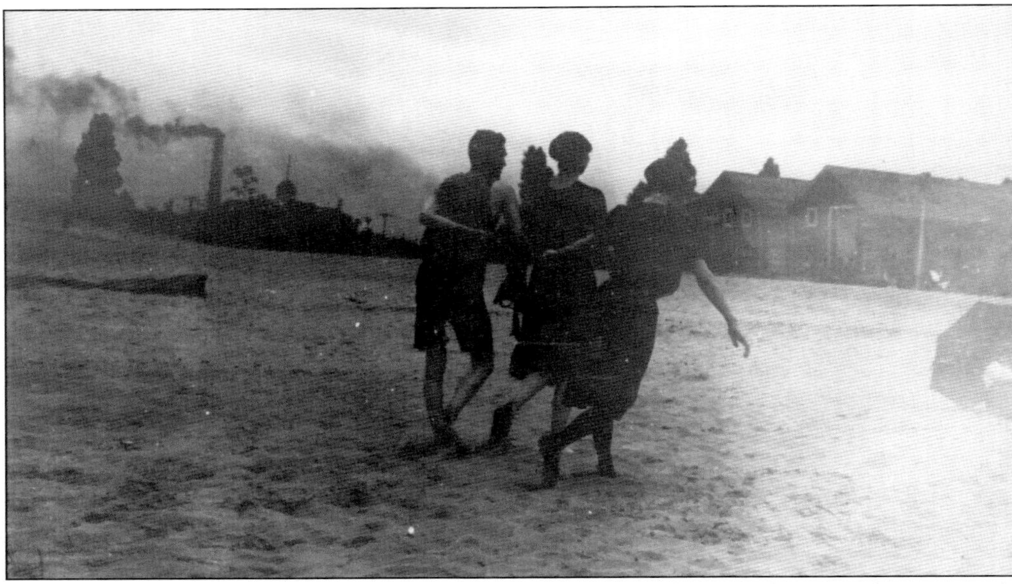

At the time this photograph was taken, George Mosny housed his seaplane in a hangar nearby and would ride it down a railroad track to the water for takeoff. As a child growing up in the 1960s, Andrew Prieboy remembers going to this beach located near Buffington Harbor and seeing the rails partially buried in the shore, leading down into the water—a remnant of long ago. The rooftops of the lakefront homes are just visible beyond the breakwater on the left. (Courtesy of the East Chicago Public Library.)

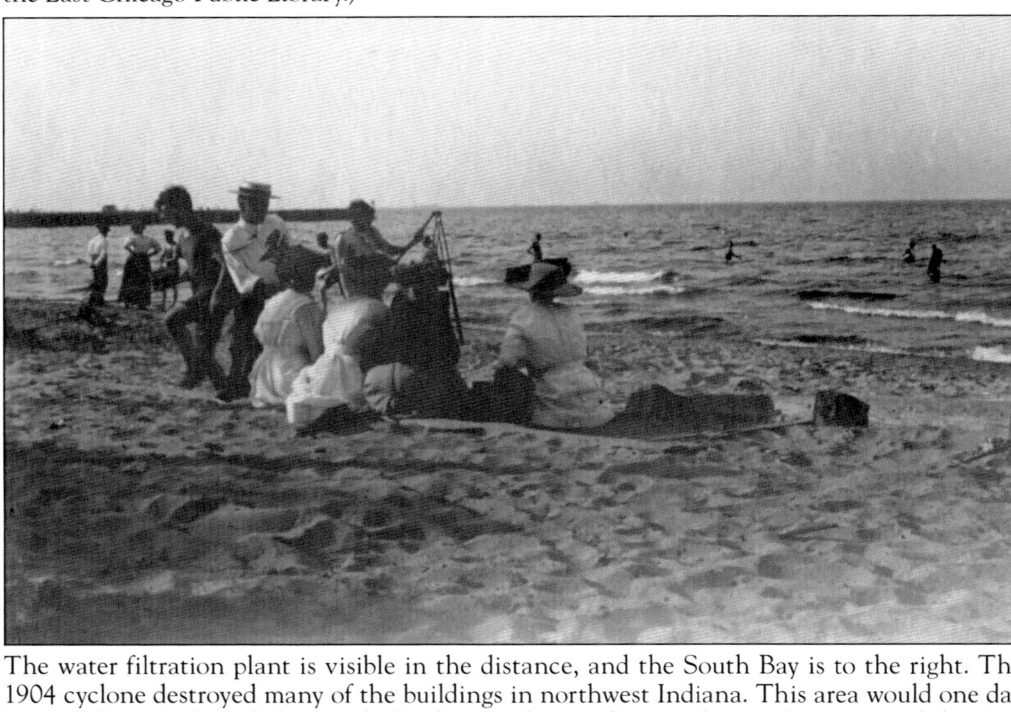

The water filtration plant is visible in the distance, and the South Bay is to the right. The 1904 cyclone destroyed many of the buildings in northwest Indiana. This area would one day become Lees Park and the beach shacks rebuilt as a dressing house. (Courtesy of the East Chicago Public Library.)

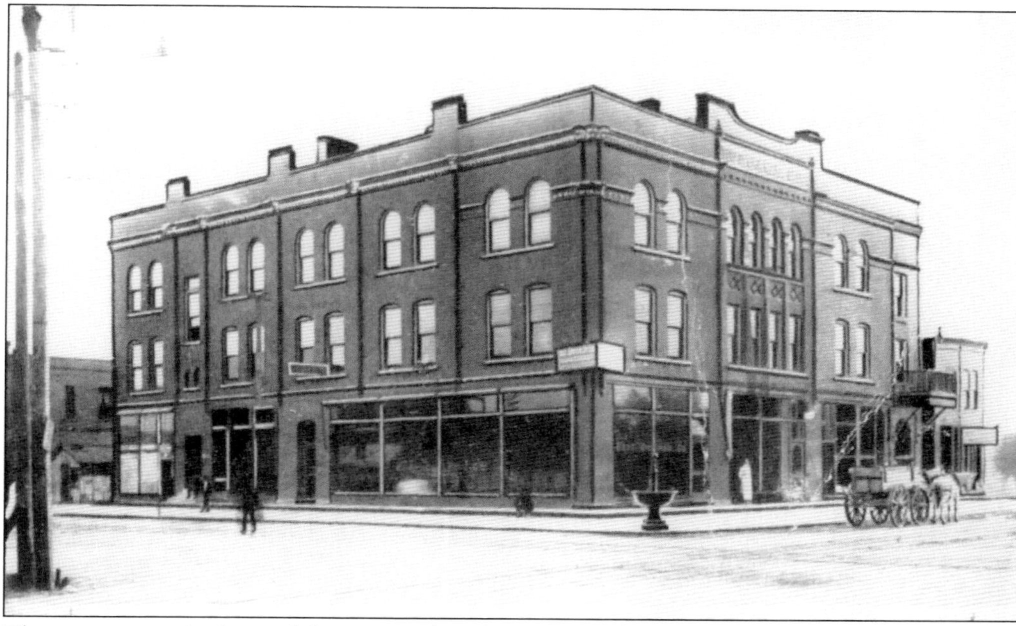

The message on the front of this postcard reads, in part, "This building was burned to the ground last Sunday morning." Given that the card was postmarked March 12, 1907, the opera house located on the corner of Forsyth (now Indianapolis Boulevard) and Chicago Avenues burned down on Sunday, March 10, 1907, following a stag party. The opera house had been built in 1890. (Courtesy of the Calumet Regional Archives, Indiana University.)

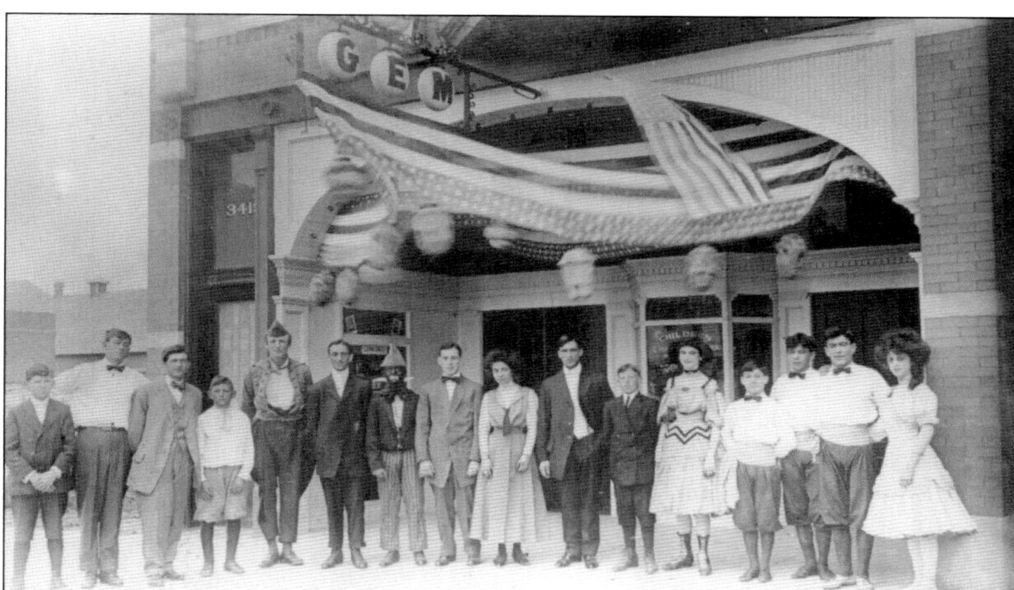

Vaudeville actors pose in front the Gem Theater in 1911. Located at 3419 Guthrie Street in Indiana Harbor, the Gem was one of several movie theaters owned and operated by Julius Nassau. (Courtesy of the Calumet Regional Archives, Indiana University.)

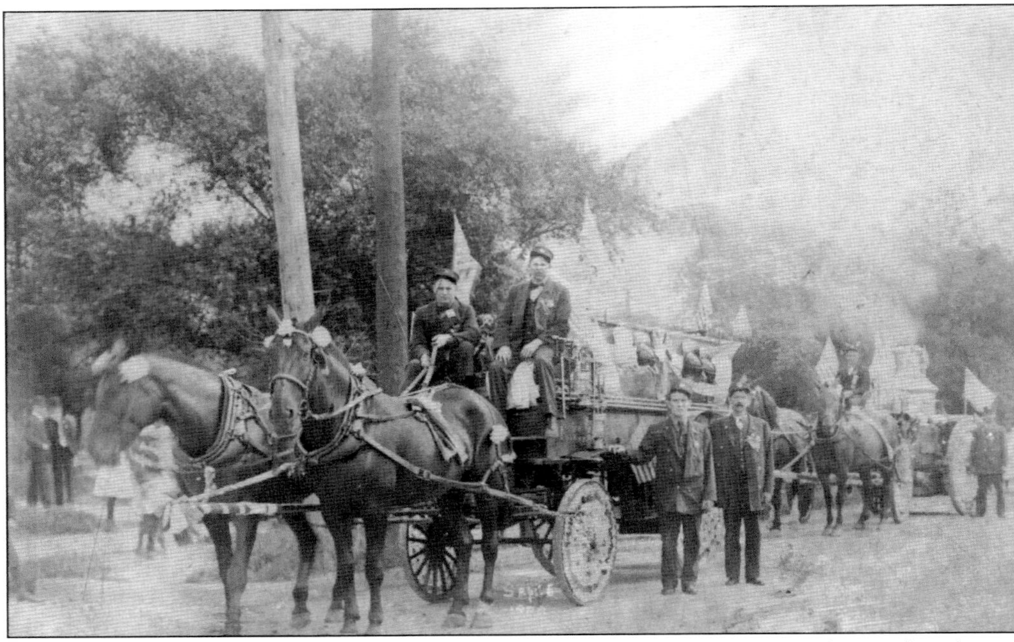

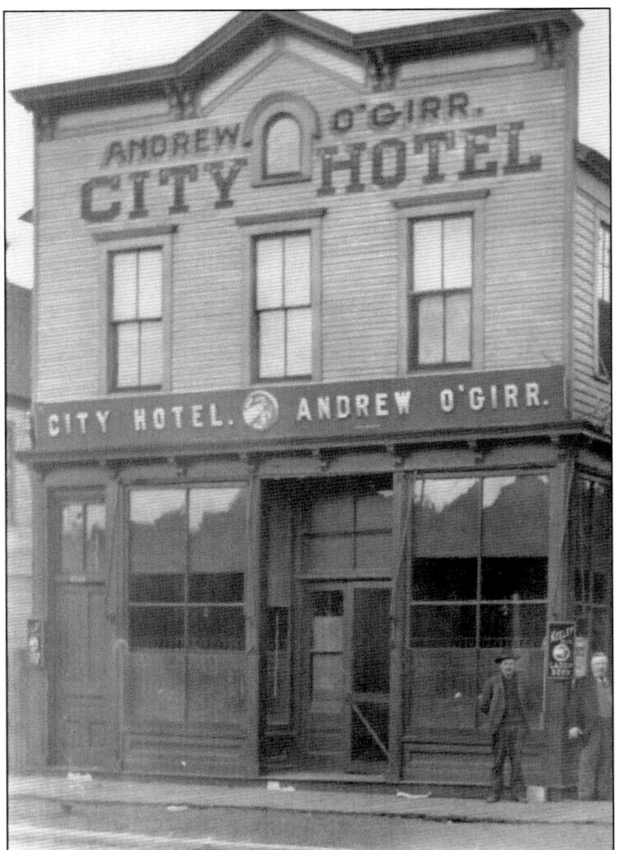

A firemen's parade marches down the street in Indiana Harbor. Holding the reins is Dan Davis, and next to him is Fred Flack. Standing from front to back are Tom Ryder and Howie Locke. (Courtesy of the Calumet Regional Archives, Indiana University.)

Andrew O'Girr's City Hotel was one of many such establishments for employed men, many of whom had moved to East Chicago to work at the mills so they could earn enough money to send for their families. (Courtesy of the Briska family.)

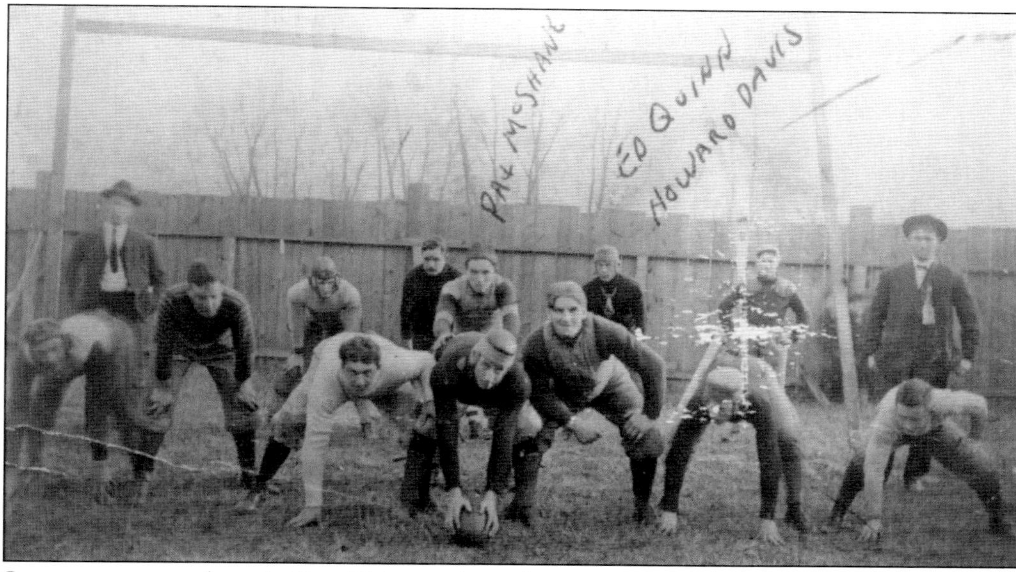

Sports teams were huge in East Chicago. According to notes on this photograph taken at Saw Mill Park in 1905, Pat McShank was in the quarterback position with Ed Quinn to the right and Howard Davis in front of him. (Courtesy of the East Chicago Public Library.)

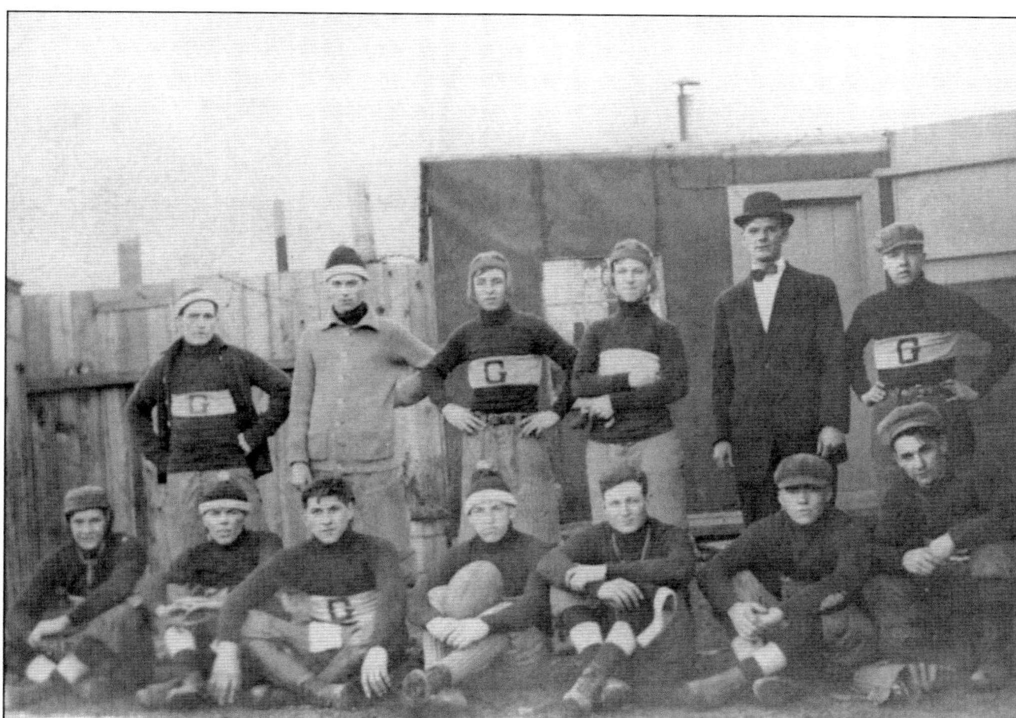

The Indiana Gophers, shown here at Saw Mill Park in 1910, were a pro team that played such competitors as the Chicago Bears in Indiana Harbor. Of course, that was a very long time ago. (Courtesy of the Calumet Regional Archives, Indiana University.)

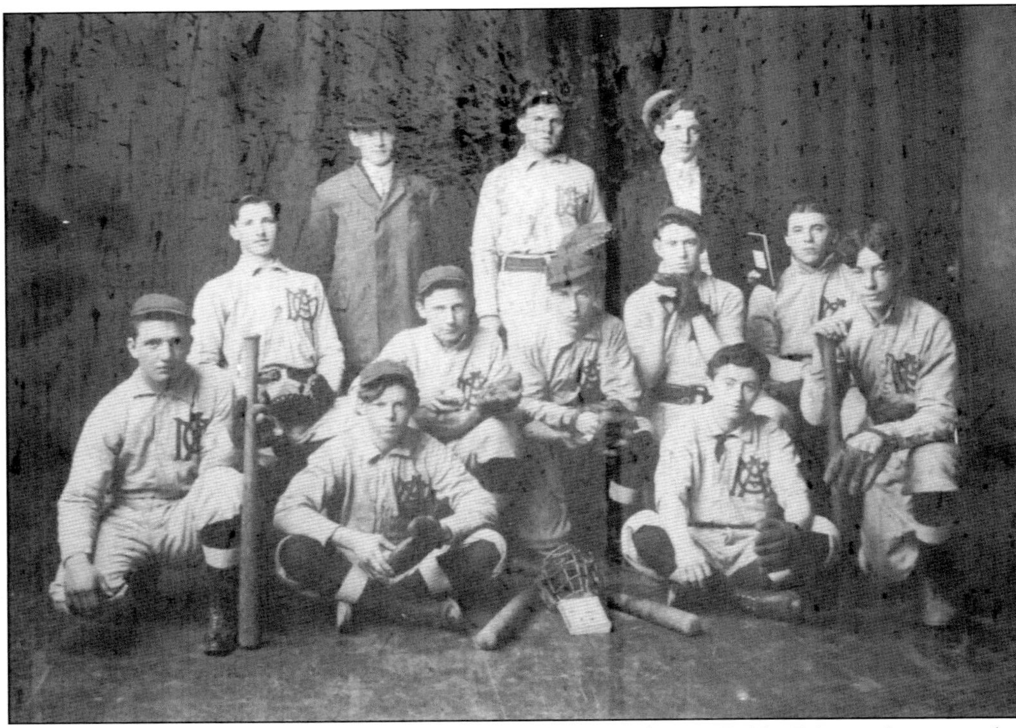

This 1914 photograph from a calendar hanging at the East Chicago Public Library shows another Twin City baseball team. Famed for its sports teams, East Chicago–Indiana Harbor ranked high in the state for storied exploits. (Courtesy of the East Chicago Public Library.)

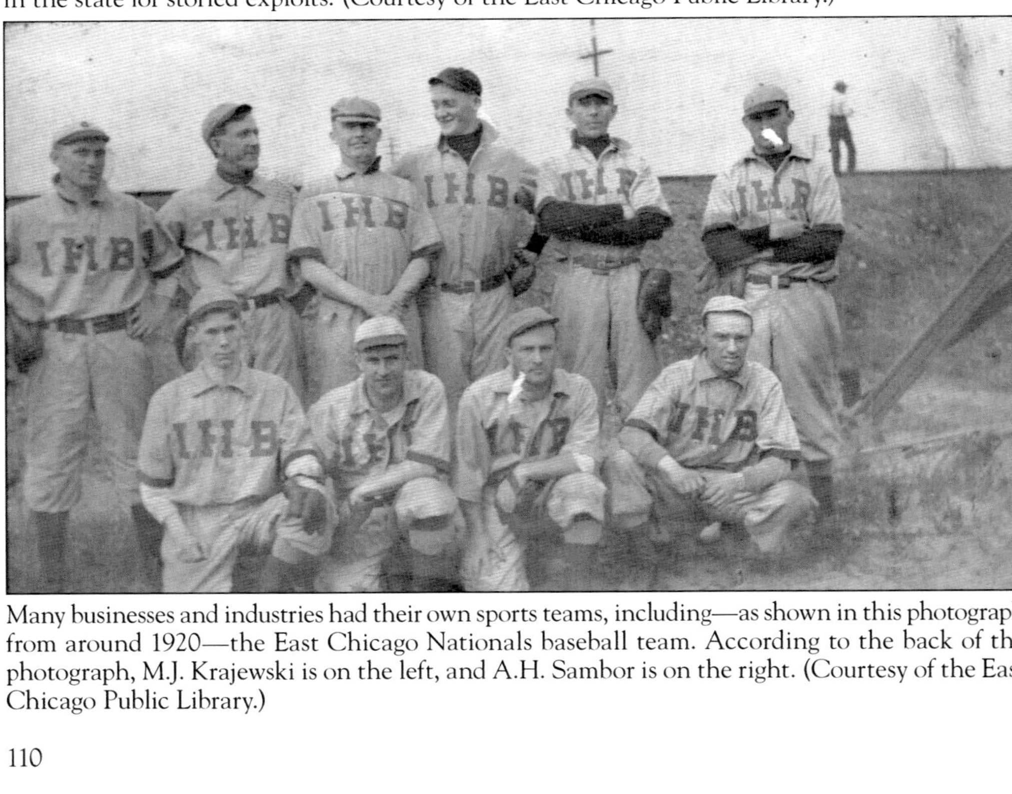

Many businesses and industries had their own sports teams, including—as shown in this photograph from around 1920—the East Chicago Nationals baseball team. According to the back of the photograph, M.J. Krajewski is on the left, and A.H. Sambor is on the right. (Courtesy of the East Chicago Public Library.)

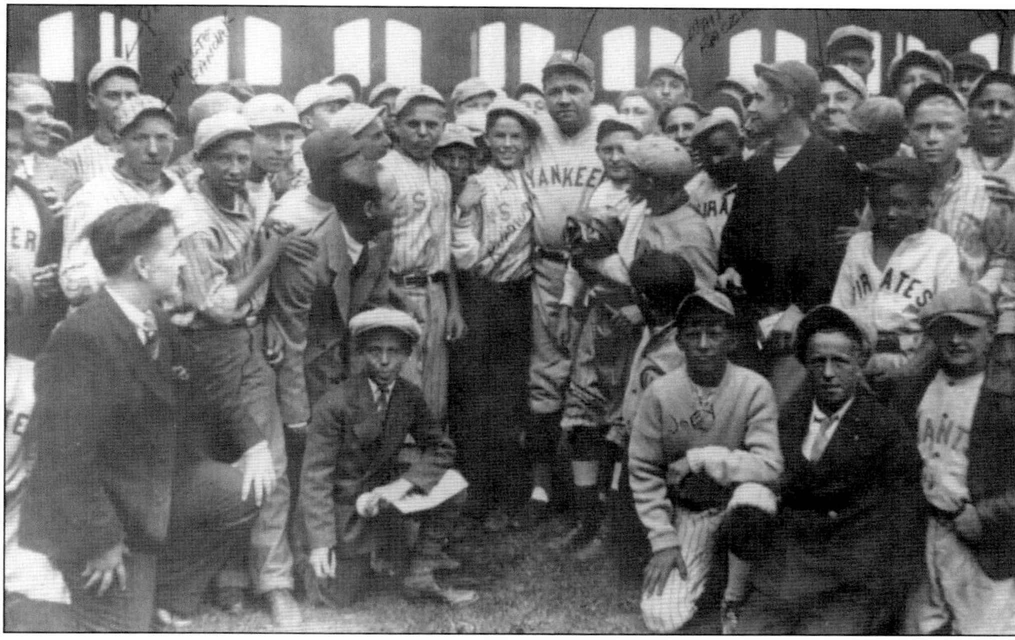

On September 10, 1925, the Junior Kiwanis Baseball League of East Chicago traveled to Comiskey Park in nearby Chicago to see a game and meet the legendary Babe Ruth. Of those identified in this photograph, to the far left of Ruth is Peto (no first name) and Walter Pandak and to his right are Walt Raczkowski and Frank Karr. (Courtesy of the East Chicago Public Library.)

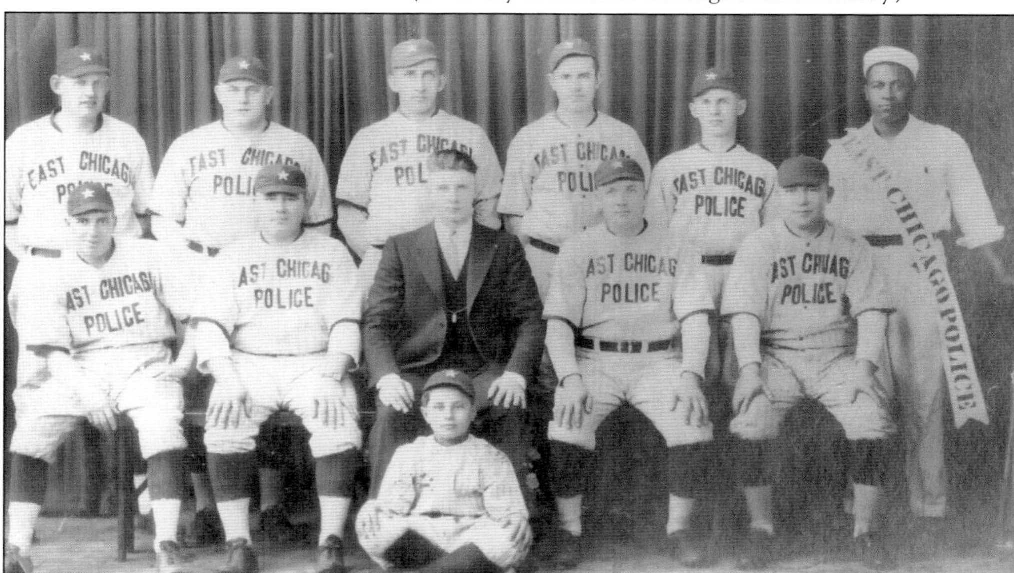

The East Chicago Police Department's baseball team is pictured around 1920. According to Peter Rucinski, former athletic director of the East Chicago Public Schools, early facilities were poor: "The football field was of equal parts cinders, clay and sand burrs. But only the visiting teams complained. Basketball benches were discarded pews from the Methodist Church. No track. No baseball diamond. Only a group of undersized boys with an oversize desire." (Courtesy of the East Chicago Public Library.)

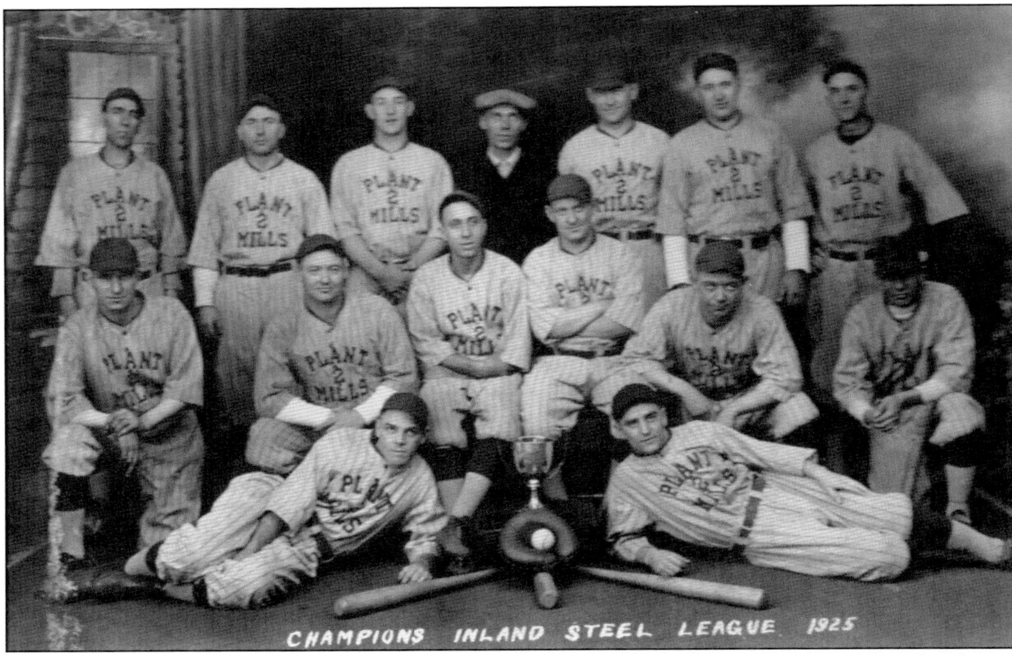

The championship Inland Steel baseball team is shown here in 1925. Peter Rucinski, former athletic director of the East Chicago Public Schools, recalled that there were no organized sports in the public schools in the fall of 1913. At his first interview, new coach Floyd Murray was told that football was not a high school sport and it should fizzle out as soon as possible. (Courtesy of the East Chicago Public Library.)

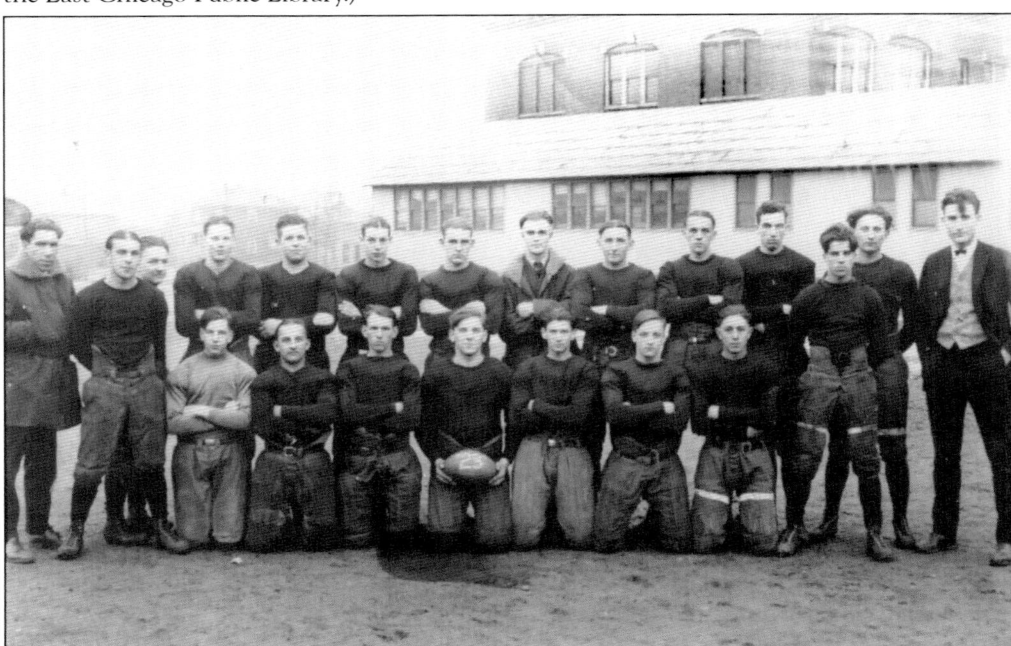

The East Chicago Washington High School football team is pictured in 1926, shortly after the school opened. (Courtesy of the Calumet Regional Archives, Indiana University.)

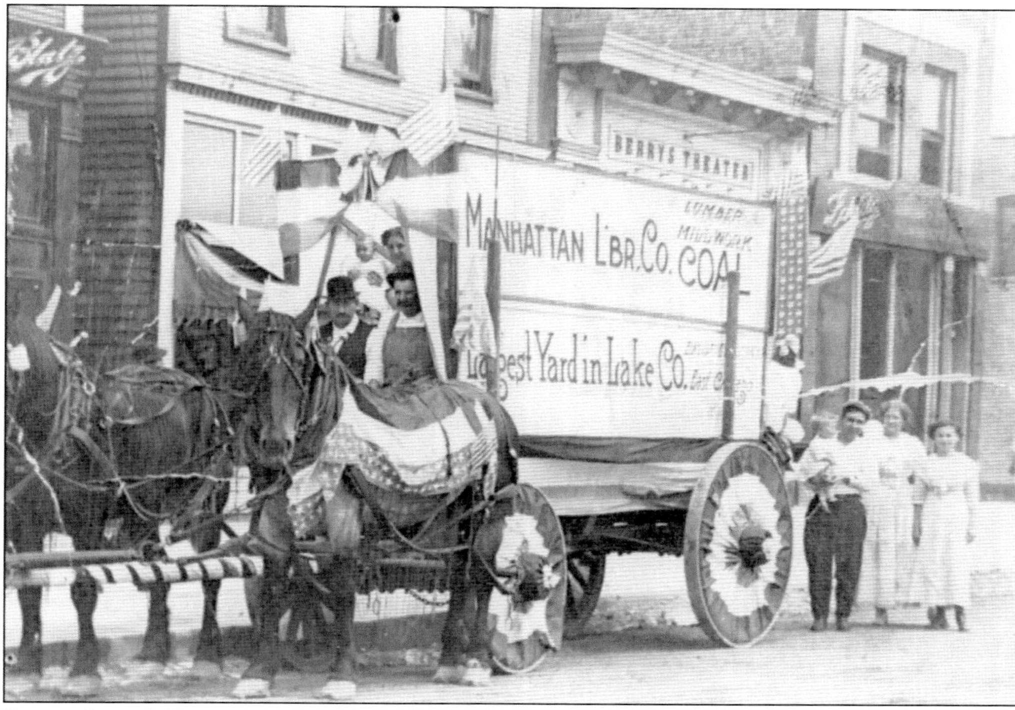

Pictured are different city parades in the early part of the 20th century. (Both, courtesy of the East Chicago Public Library.)

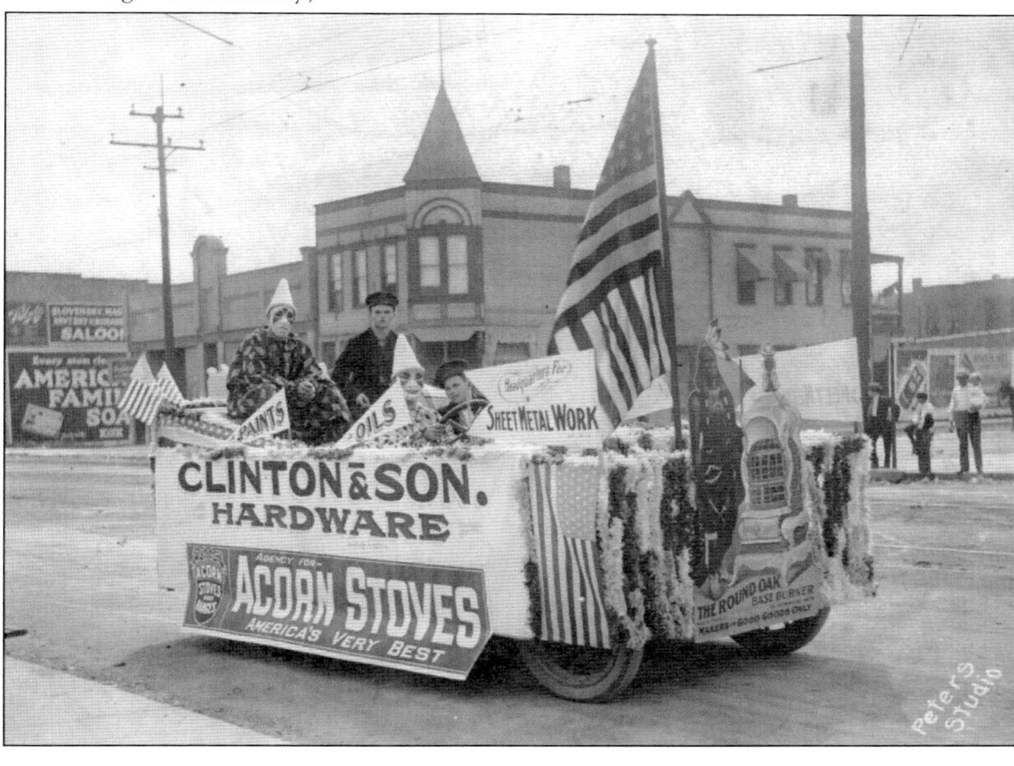

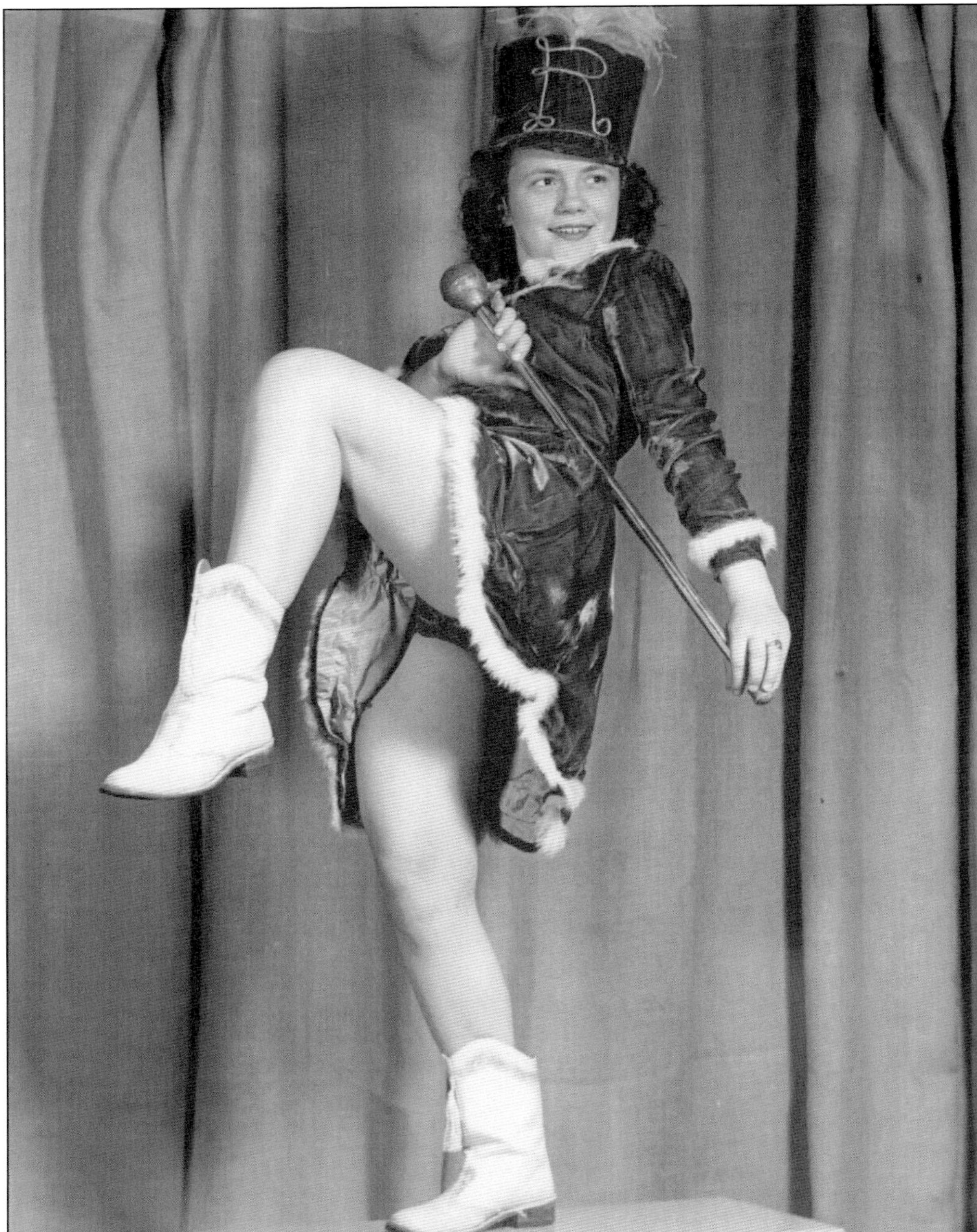

Drum majorette Rita Burell of East Chicago Roosevelt High School strikes a pose for the camera. (Courtesy of the East Chicago Public Library.)

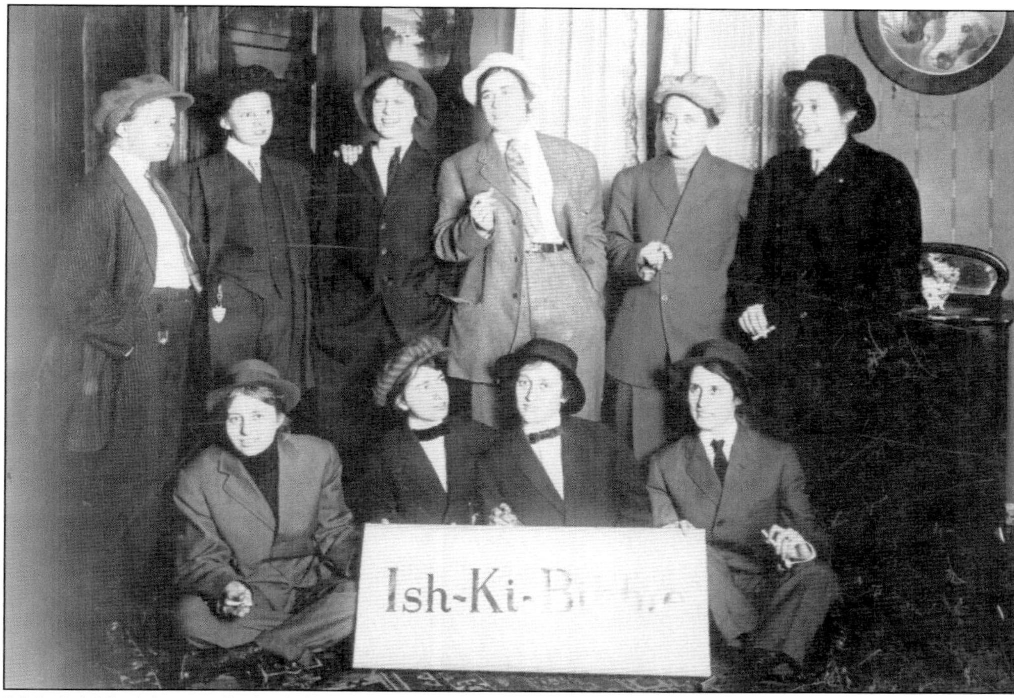

Ishkabibble (also spelled Ish ki Bibble, as well as several other ways) became a popular slang term meaning "I should care," equivalent to the current "don't worry" or "I could care less." Where it came from is unclear, but in 1913, the term was all the rage and would continue to be for the next two decades. These women, dressed as men, were members of the Ish Ki Bibble Club in East Chicago. According to the back of the photograph above, pictured from left to right in the first row are unidentified, Rose McManus, Mary Sternberg, and Ann Saunders Lewis. Jane McNab is the only name listed in the second row. (Both, courtesy of the East Chicago Public Library.)

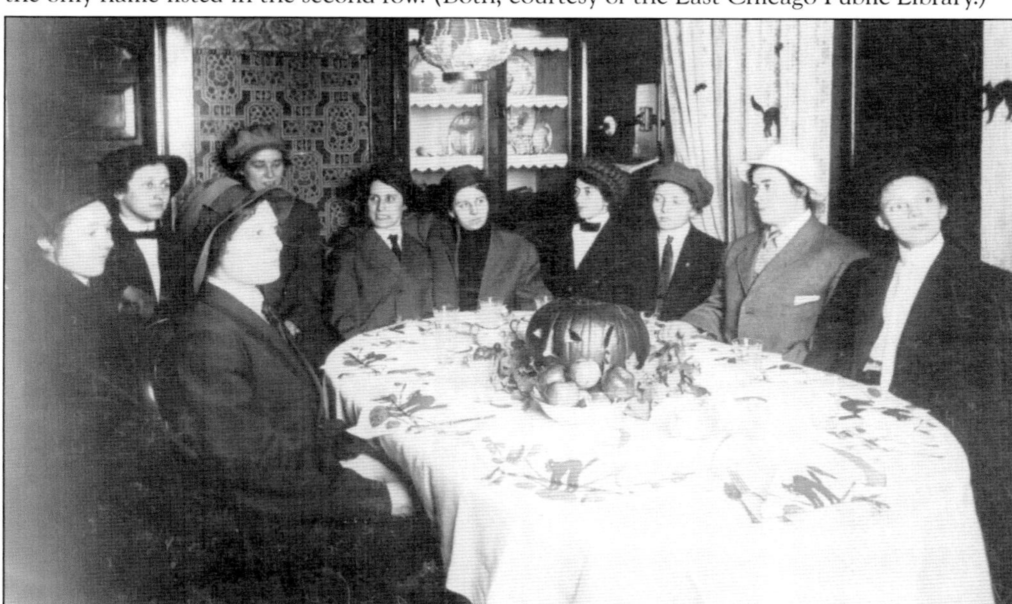

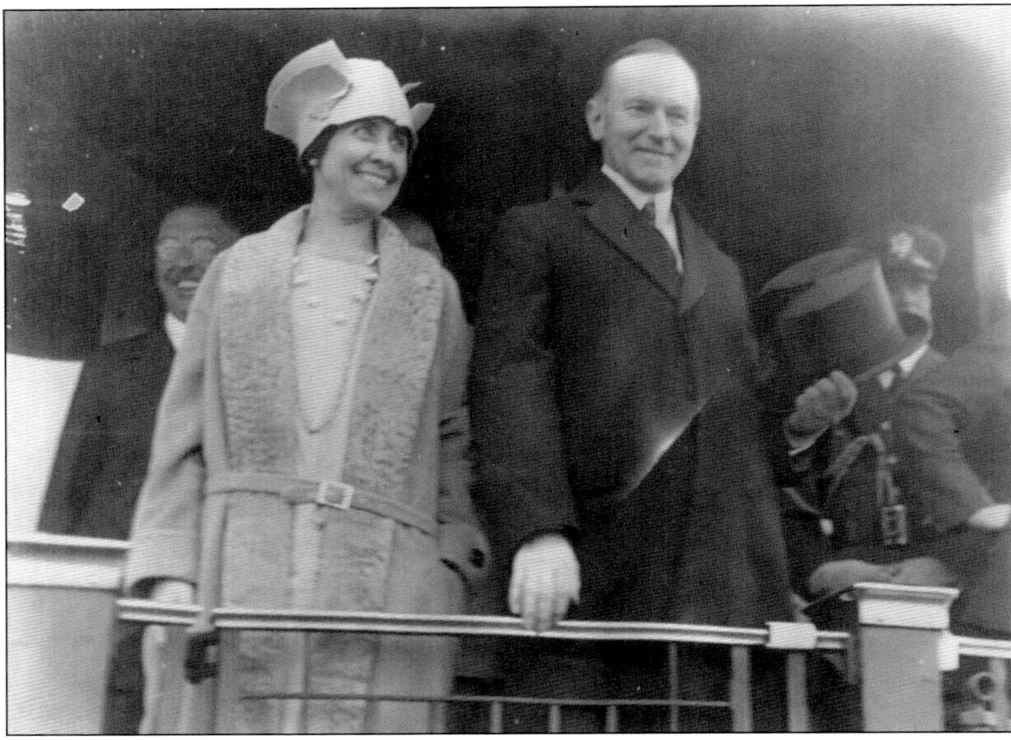

Pres. Calvin Coolidge arrived by train in East Chicago on June 14, 1927. Many other powerful national political figures visited East Chicago, including Sen. John F. Kennedy shortly before he was elected president and Pres. Lyndon B. Johnson. (Both, courtesy of the East Chicago Public Library.)

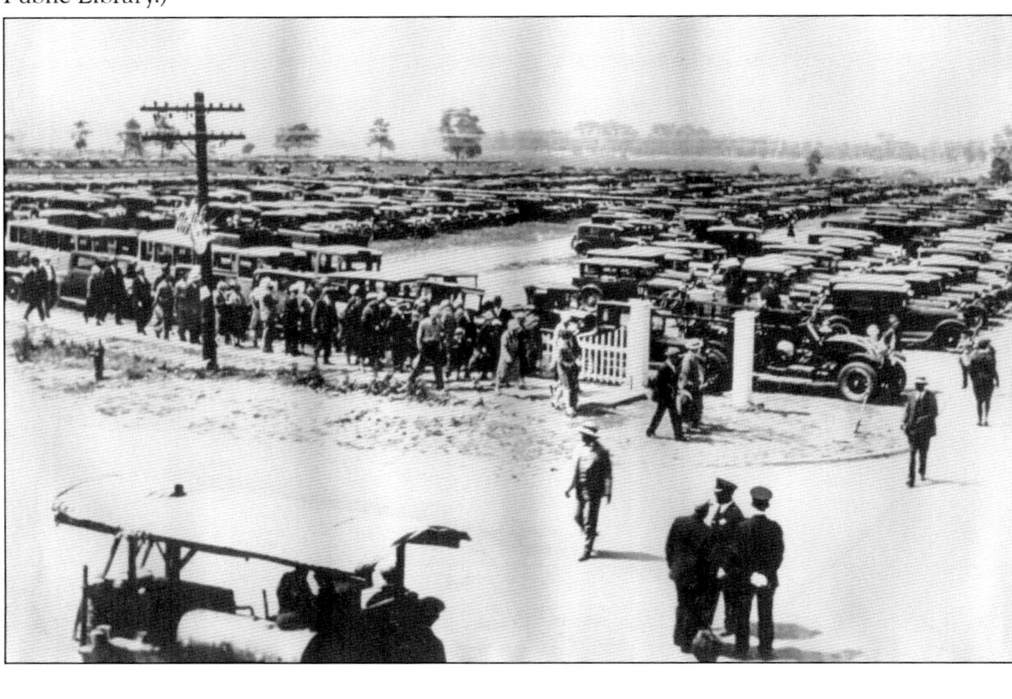

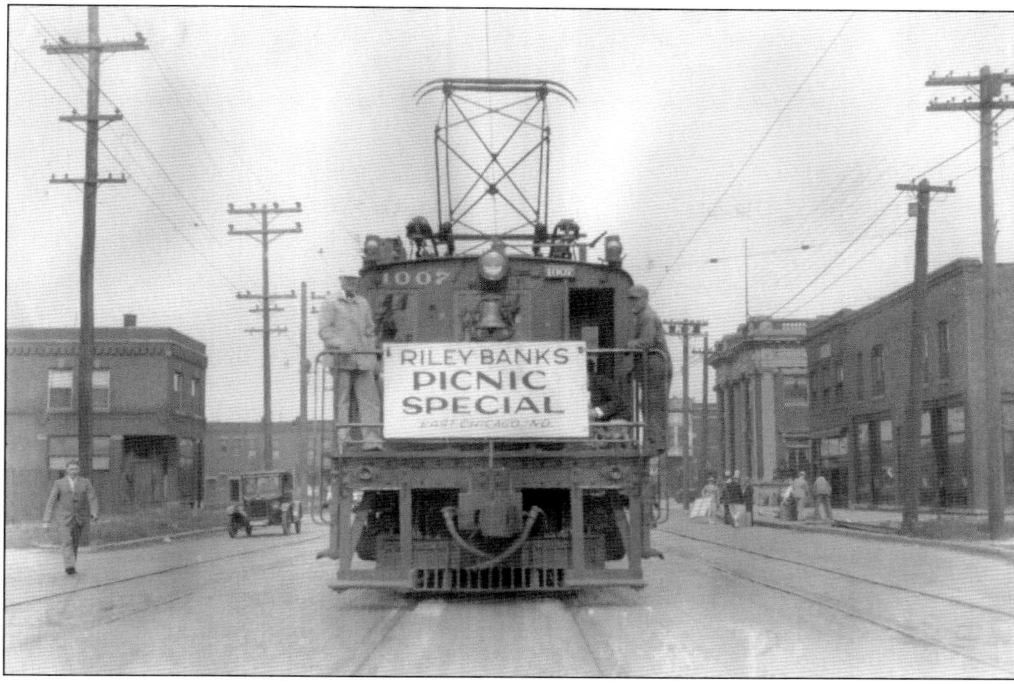

In 1928, workers at South Shore Railroad gathered for a special picnic put on by Col. Walter J. Riley, a former stagecoach driver who became a great philanthropist and the senior vice president and director of the First National Bank of East Chicago. (Both, courtesy of the East Chicago Public Library.)

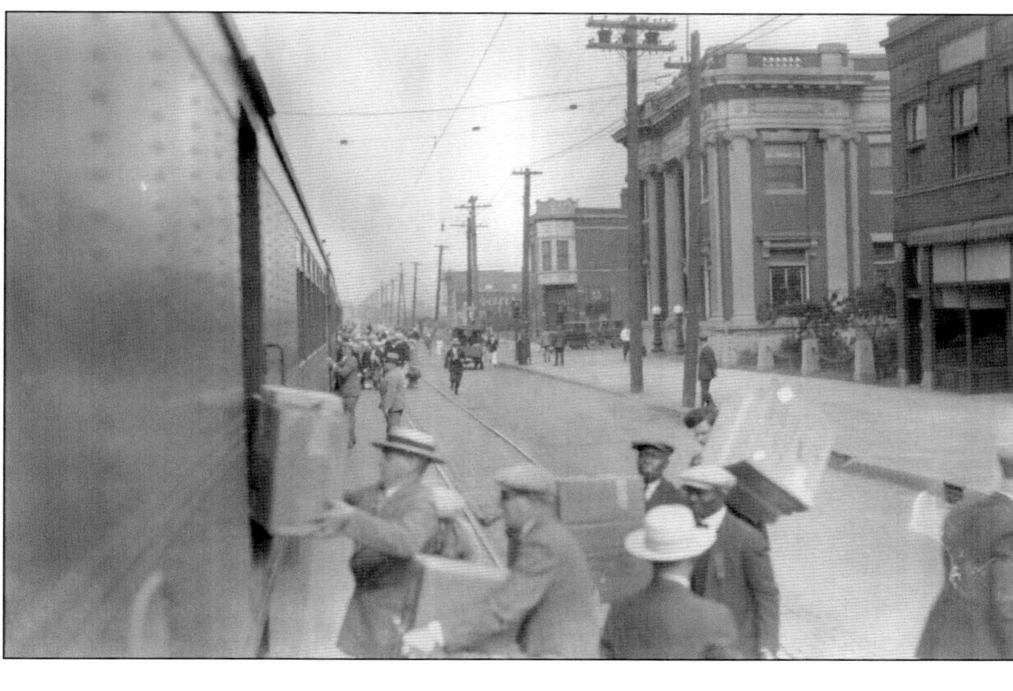

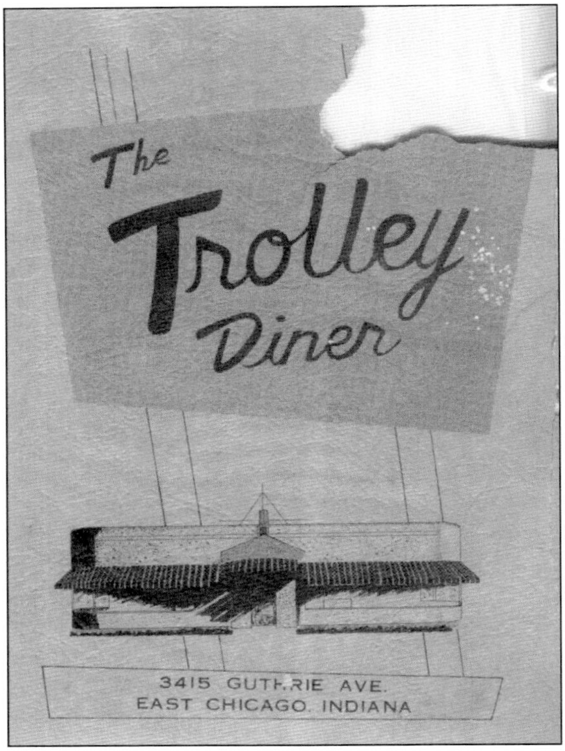

The Trolley Diner was a longtime favorite eating place in Indiana Harbor. It was housed in—you guessed it—an old trolley car. (Both, courtesy of the East Chicago Public Library.)

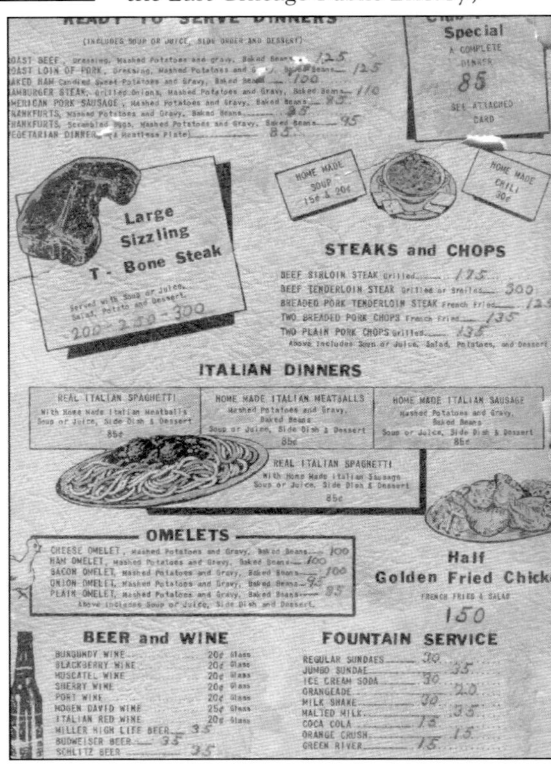

READY TO SERVE DINNERS

(INCLUDES SOUP OR JUICE, SIDE ORDER AND DESSERT)

OAST BEEF, Dressing, Mashed Potatoes and Gravy, Baked Beans ... 125
OAST LOIN OF PORK, Dressing, Mashed Potatoes and Gravy, Baked Beans ... 125
AKED HAM Candied Sweet Potatoes and Gravy, Baked Beans ... 100
AMBURGER STEAK, Grilled Onions, Mashed Potatoes and Gravy, Baked Beans ... 110
MERICAN PORK SAUSAGE, Mashed Potatoes and Gravy, Baked Beans ... 85
RANKFURTS, Mashed Potatoes and Gravy, Baked Beans ... 85
RANKFURTS, Scrambled Eggs, Mashed Potatoes and Gravy, Baked Beans ... 95
EGETARIAN DINNER (A Meatless Plate) ... 85

Special
A COMPLETE DINNER
85
SEE ATTACHED CARD

Large Sizzling T - Bone Steak
Served with Soup or Juice, Salad, Potato and Dessert
200 - 250 - 300

HOME MADE SOUP 15¢ & 20¢

HOME MADE CHILI 30¢

STEAKS and CHOPS

BEEF SIRLOIN STEAK Grilled ... 175
BEEF TENDERLOIN STEAK Grilled or Broiled ... 300
BREADED PORK TENDERLOIN STEAK French Fried ... 125
TWO BREADED PORK CHOPS French Fried ... 135
TWO PLAIN PORK CHOPS Grilled ... 135
Above Includes Soup or Juice, Salad, Potatoes, and Dessert

ITALIAN DINNERS

REAL ITALIAN SPAGHETTI	HOME MADE ITALIAN MEATBALLS	HOME MADE ITALIAN SAUSAGE
With Home Made Italian Meatballs Soup or Juice, Side Dish & Dessert 85¢	Mashed Potatoes and Gravy, Baked Beans Soup or Juice, Side Dish & Dessert 85¢	Mashed Potatoes and Gravy, Baked Beans Soup or Juice, Side Dish & Dessert 85¢

REAL ITALIAN SPAGHETTI
With Home Made Italian Sausage
Soup or Juice, Side Dish & Dessert
85¢

OMELETS

CHEESE OMELET, Mashed Potatoes and Gravy, Baked Beans ... 100
HAM OMELET, Mashed Potatoes and Gravy, Baked Beans ... 100
BACON OMELET, Mashed Potatoes and Gravy, Baked Beans ... 100
ONION OMELET, Mashed Potatoes and Gravy, Baked Beans ... 95
PLAIN OMELET, Mashed Potatoes and Gravy, Baked Beans ... 85
Above Includes Soup or Juice, Side Dish and Dessert.

Half Golden Fried Chicke
FRENCH FRIES & SALAD
150

BEER and WINE

BURGUNDY WINE	20¢ Glass
BLACKBERRY WINE	20¢ Glass
MUSCATEL WINE	20¢ Glass
SHERRY WINE	20¢ Glass
PORT WINE	20¢ Glass
MOGEN DAVID WINE	25¢ Glass
ITALIAN RED WINE	20¢ Glass
MILLER HIGH LIFE BEER	35
BUDWEISER BEER	35
SCHLITZ BEER	35

FOUNTAIN SERVICE

REGULAR SUNDAES	30
JUMBO SUNDAE	35
ICE CREAM SODA	30
ORANGEADE	20
MILK SHAKE	30
MALTED MILK	35
COCA COLA	15
ORANGE CRUSH	15
GREEN RIVER	15

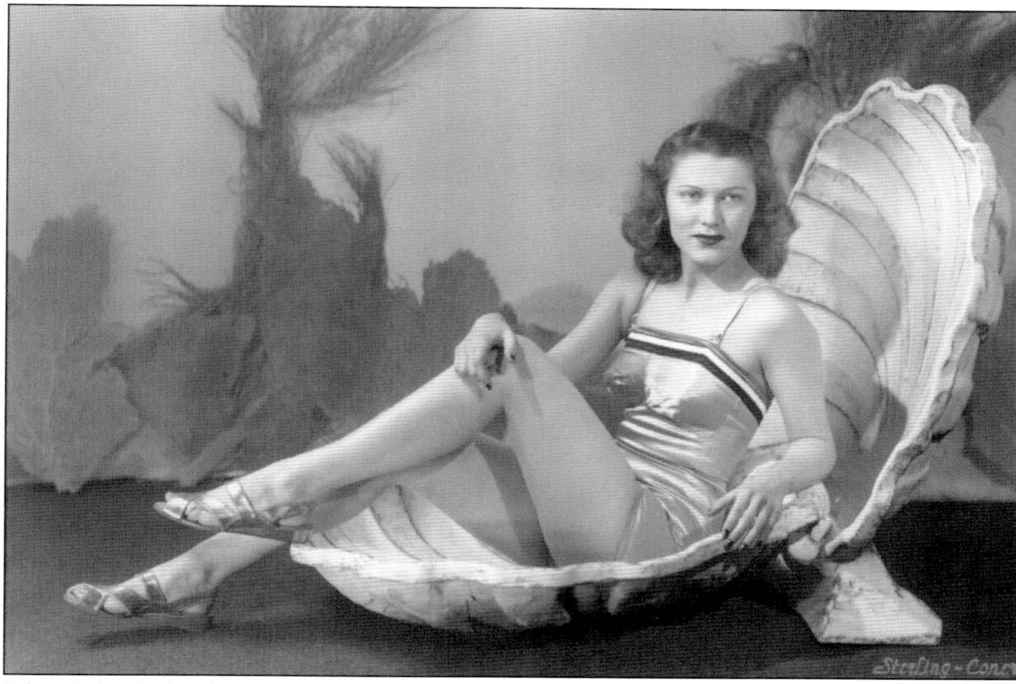

Silvia Pelei Godocik, a Romanian girl from Indiana Harbor, glamorously poses in a clamshell in this 1946 photograph. (Courtesy of the East Chicago Public Library.)

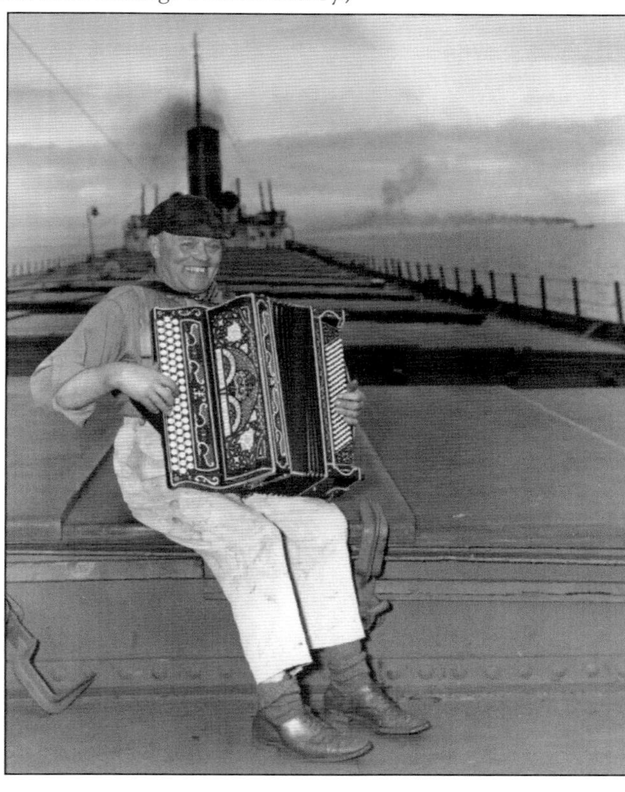

In 1968, the Indiana Harbor and Ship Canal was the busiest harbor on Lake Michigan, with incoming and outgoing shipments estimated at between 15 and 30 million tons a year. Here, a crew member of the *Phillip D. Block* ore boat takes a work break and plays his concertina in 1947. (Courtesy of the Calumet Regional Archives, Indiana University.)

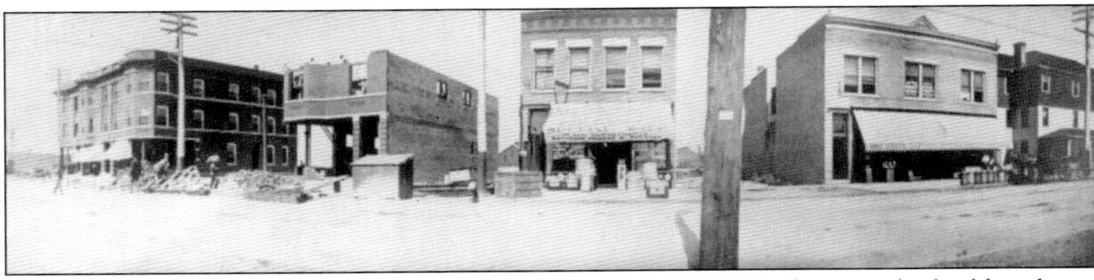

The west side of Michigan Avenue is pictured on August 27, 1904, showing the building boom. At far left is the Indiana Harbor Hotel.

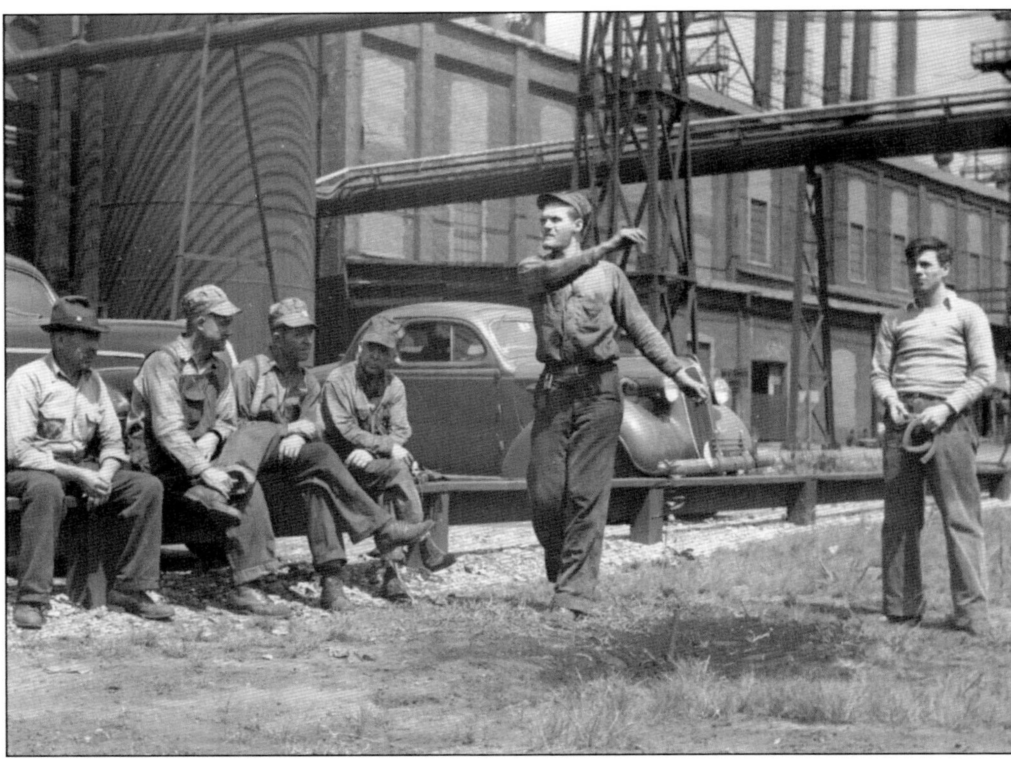

Labor unions produced a solidarity between workers who understood the need for job security. One saying was, "United we stand; divided we beg." Here, steel mill workers show camaraderie in play—pitching horseshoes—as well as work. (Courtesy of the Calumet Regional Archives, Indiana University.)

Ten

Street Scenes

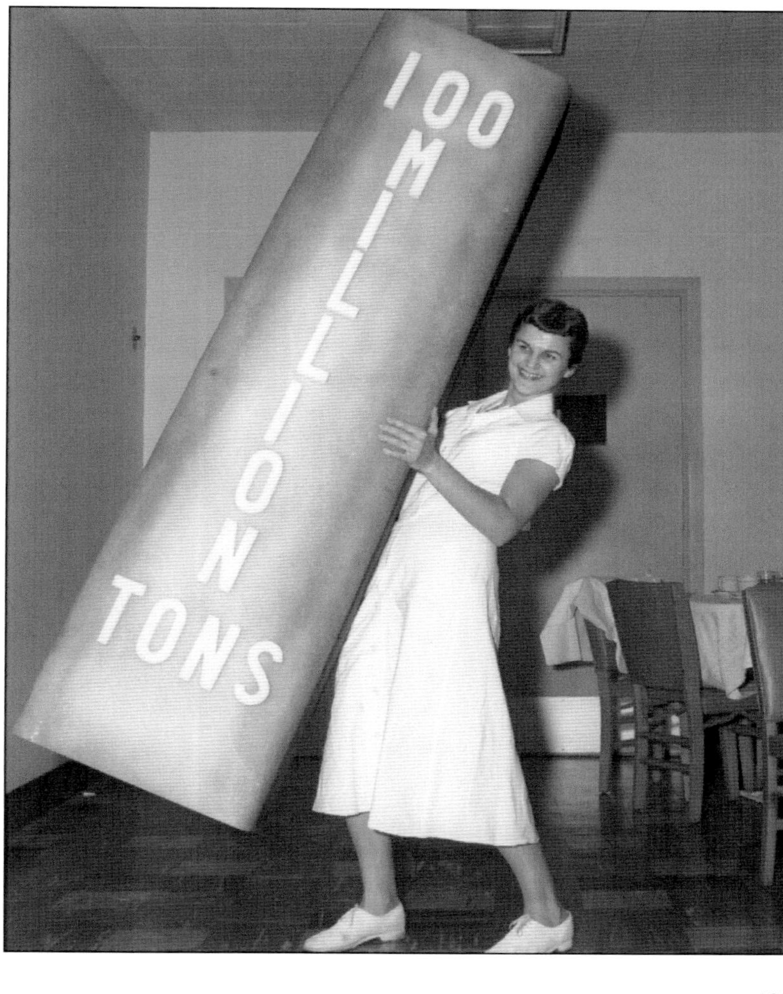

Waitress Beatrice Higuet carries a replica of ceremonial ingot at an Inland Steel gathering on March 11, 1957. (Courtesy of the Calumet Regional Archives, Indiana University.)

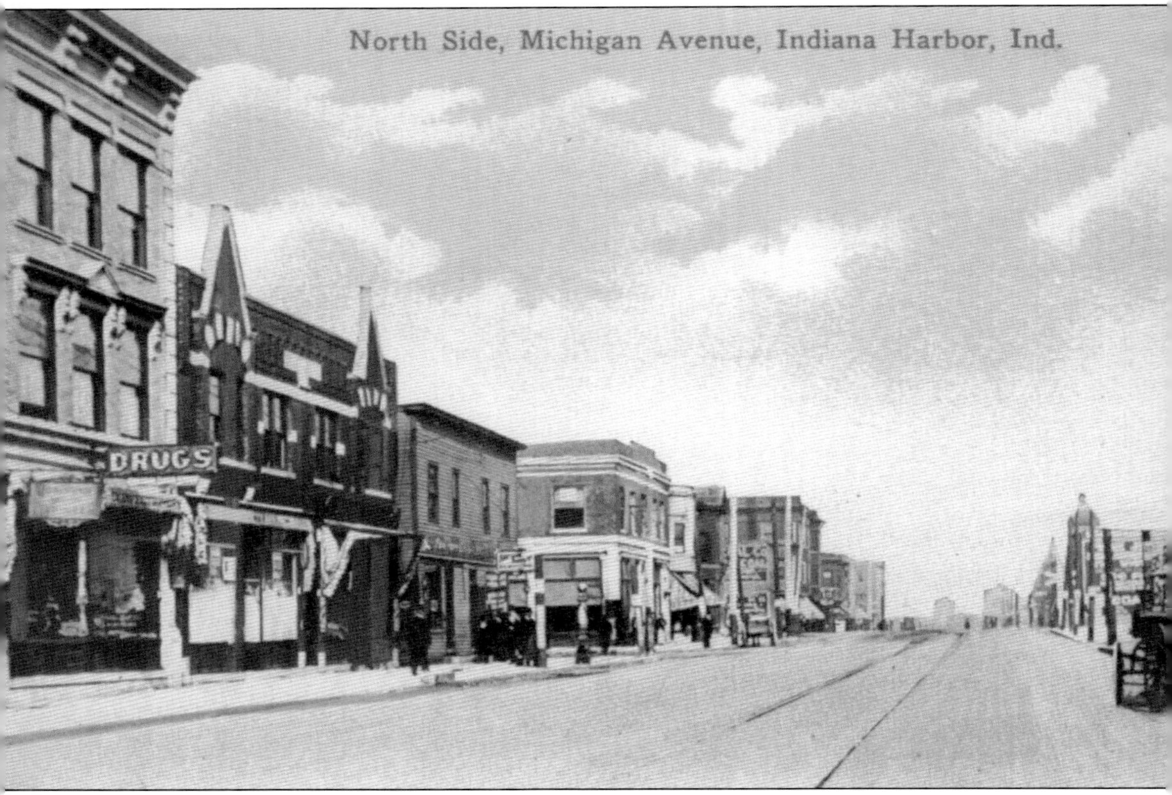

This postcard photograph of the north side of Michigan Avenue in Indiana Harbor taken before 1910 shows trolley tracks running down the center of the street. These tracks passed such businesses as Central Drugs (at left). Trolley stops let workers and shoppers jump off, make purchases, and then continue on their journey. (Courtesy of the Calumet Regional Archives, Indiana University.)

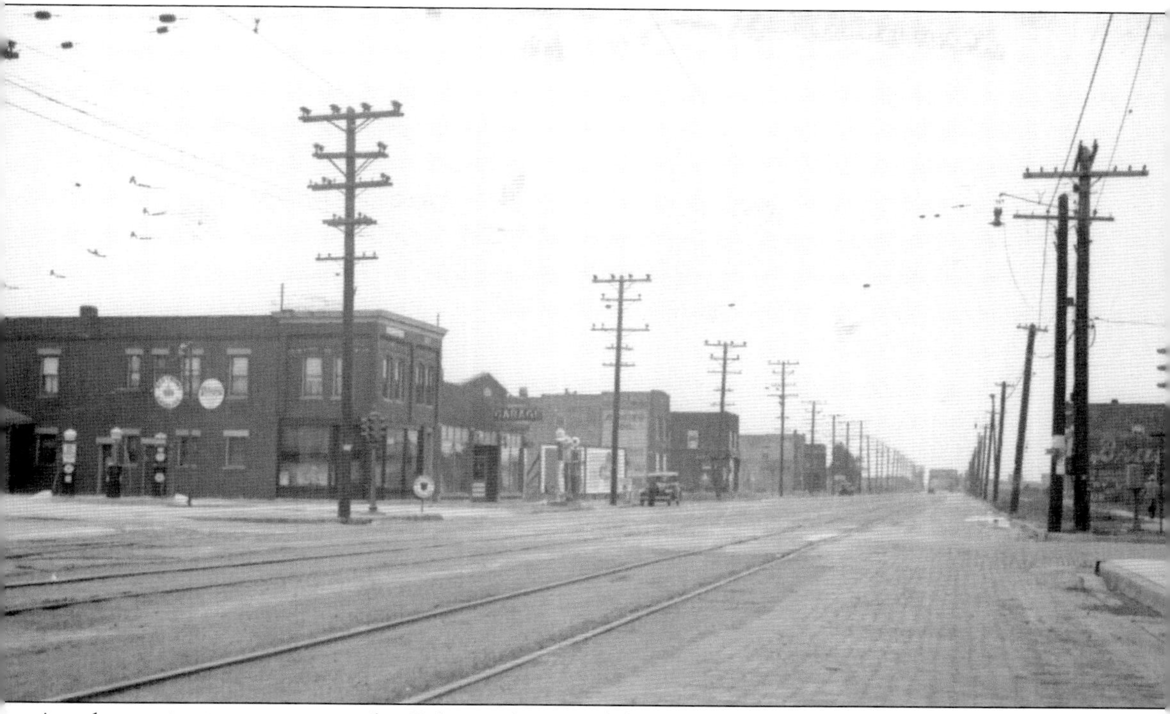

Another major intersection in the Calumet district of the Twin City was Chicago and Kennedy Avenues. Calumet extended east to Cline Avenue, west to the canal, and north to the Harbison Walker Refractory. To the south was the Grand Calumet River. (Courtesy of the Calumet Regional Archives, Indiana University.)

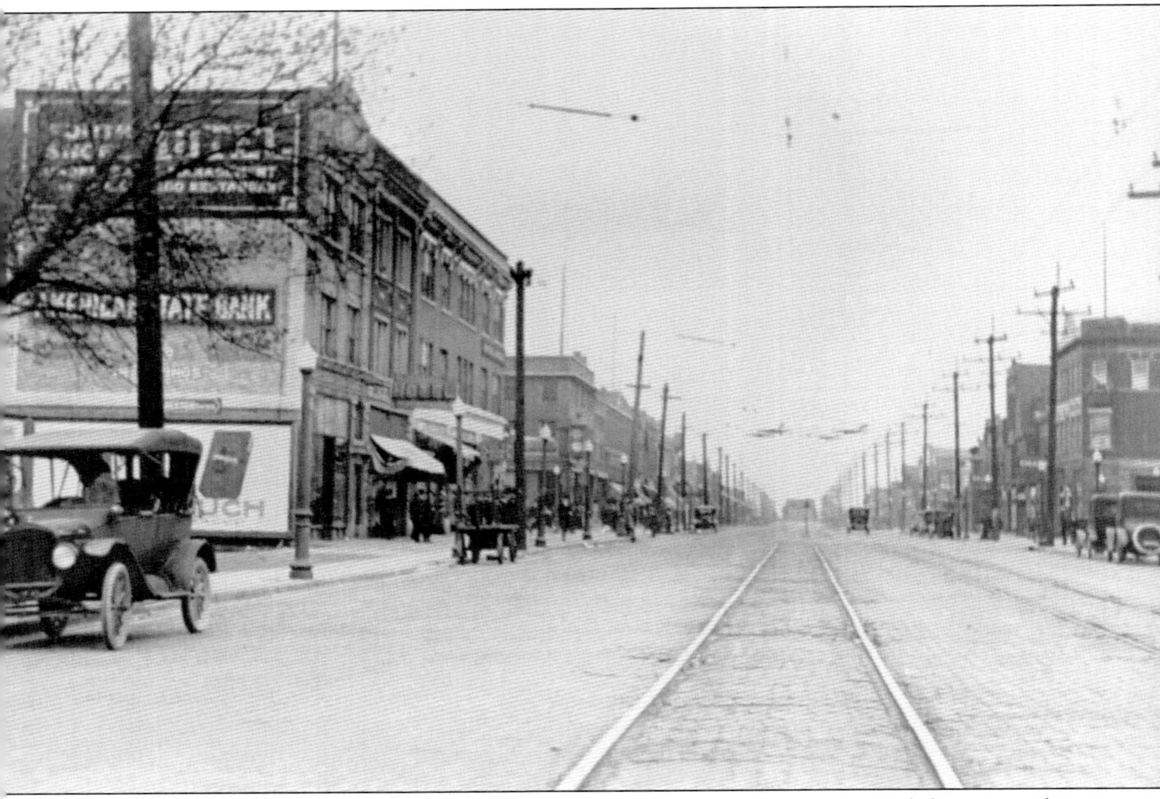

East Chicago was one of very few cities with a passenger train in a central downtown location from 1906 to 1956. This provided easy access to gambling in East Chicago for customers from Chicago, Hammond, Gary, Michigan City, and South Bend. (Courtesy of the Calumet Regional Archives, Indiana University.)

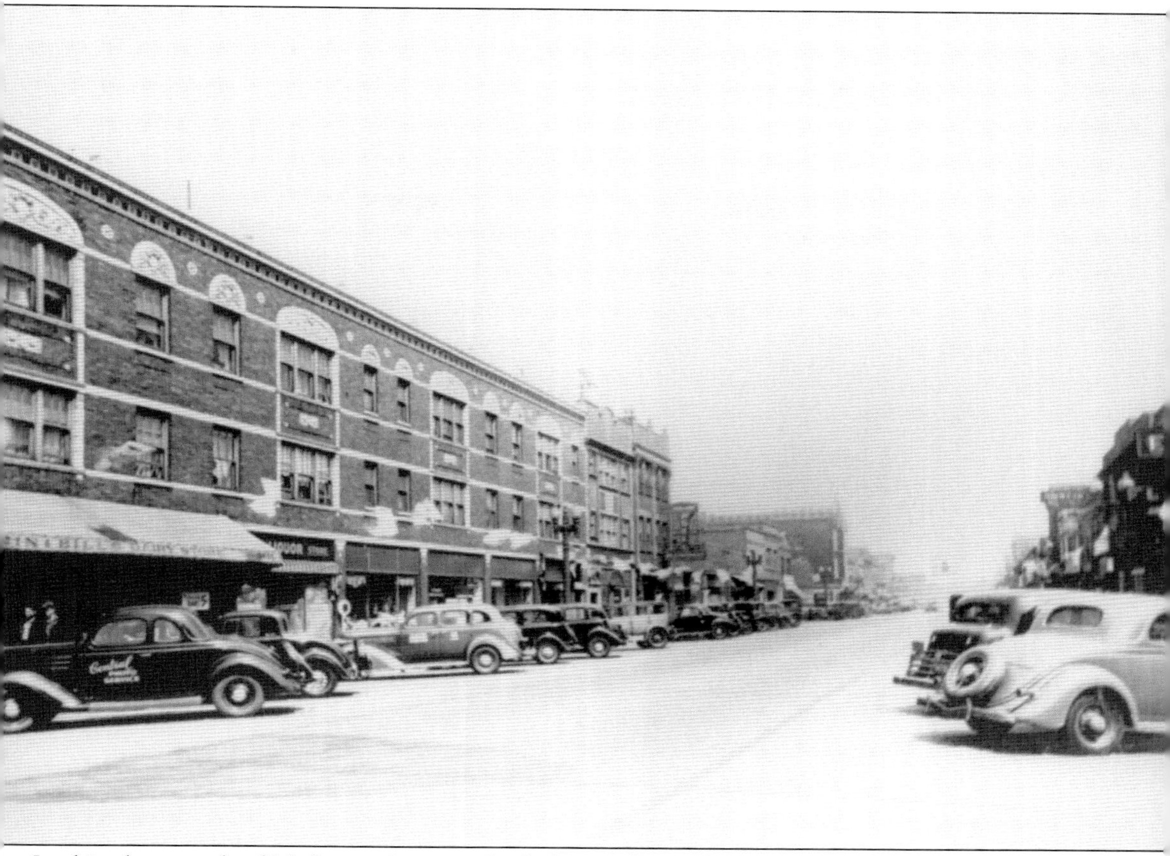

In this photograph of Michigan Avenue, the Indiana Theater building is visible on the left. A close look reveals that the name "Central Photography" is written on the black car in the left foreground. (Courtesy of the East Chicago Public Library.)

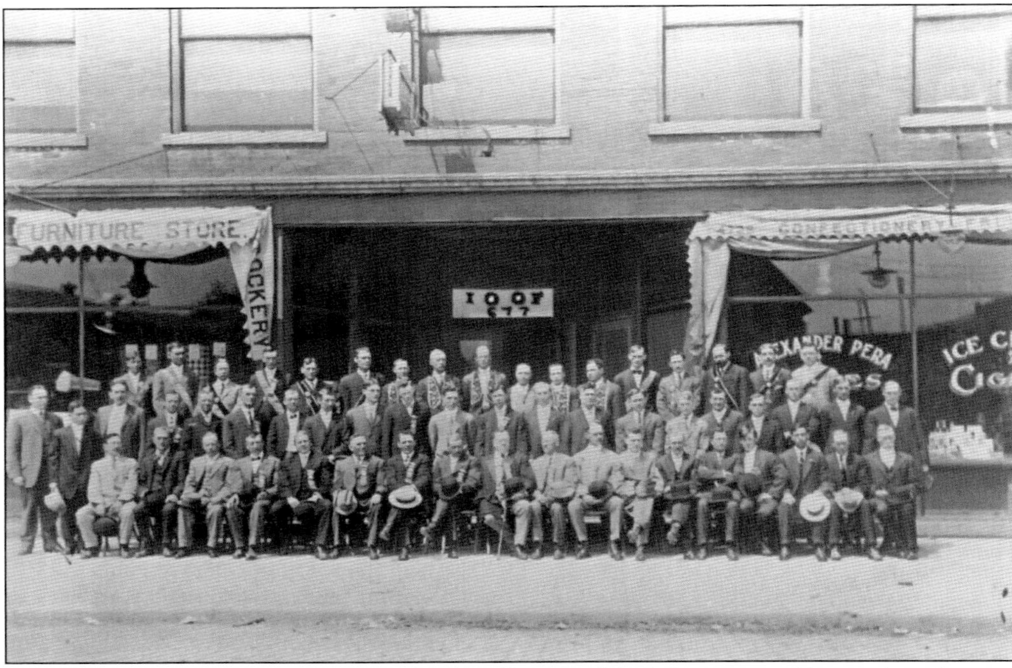

Members of the Independent Order of Odd Fellows, a global altruistic and benevolent fraternal organization, gather on Olcott Avenue in East Chicago. (Courtesy of the East Chicago Public Library.)

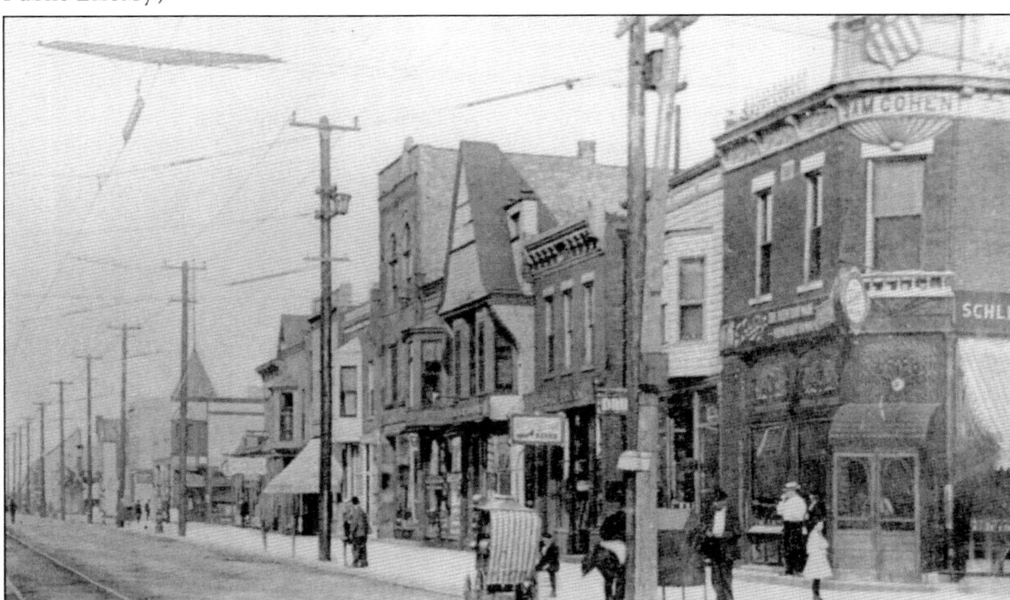

East Chicago and Indiana Harbor, divided by the Little Calumet River, were also different in terms of class. Indiana Harbor, pictured here, was the "East Side" home of Inland Steel, with a large population of working class families—many of them immigrants from other countries. East Chicago's "West Side" was where the American-born business community lived. (Courtesy of the East Chicago Public Library.)

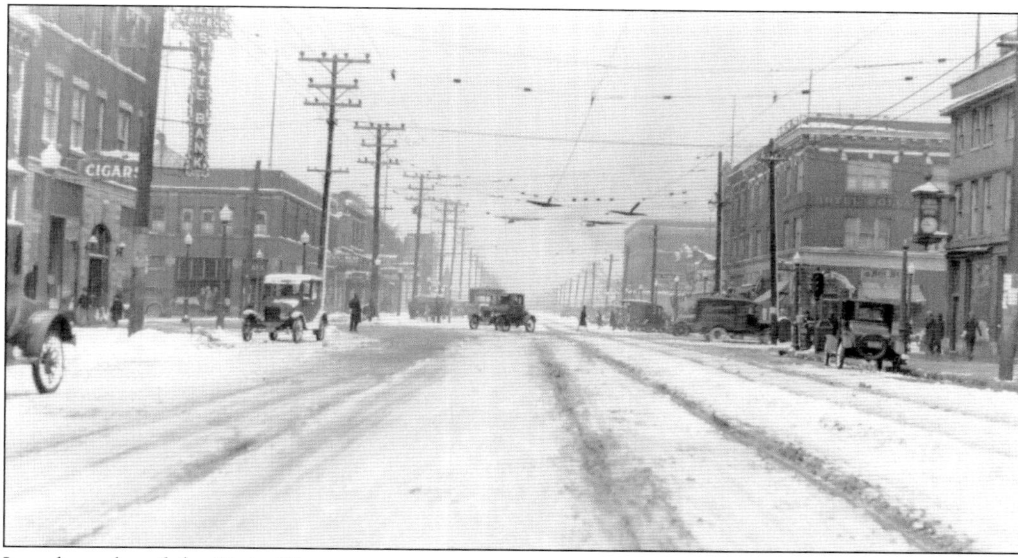

Locals spoke of the Twin City to describe spatial, residential, and class divisions at the heart of the town's identity. The intersection of Forsyth and Chicago Avenues in East Chicago, pictured here in the 1920s, was considered to boast shops catering to the more elite. (Courtesy of the East Chicago Public Library.)

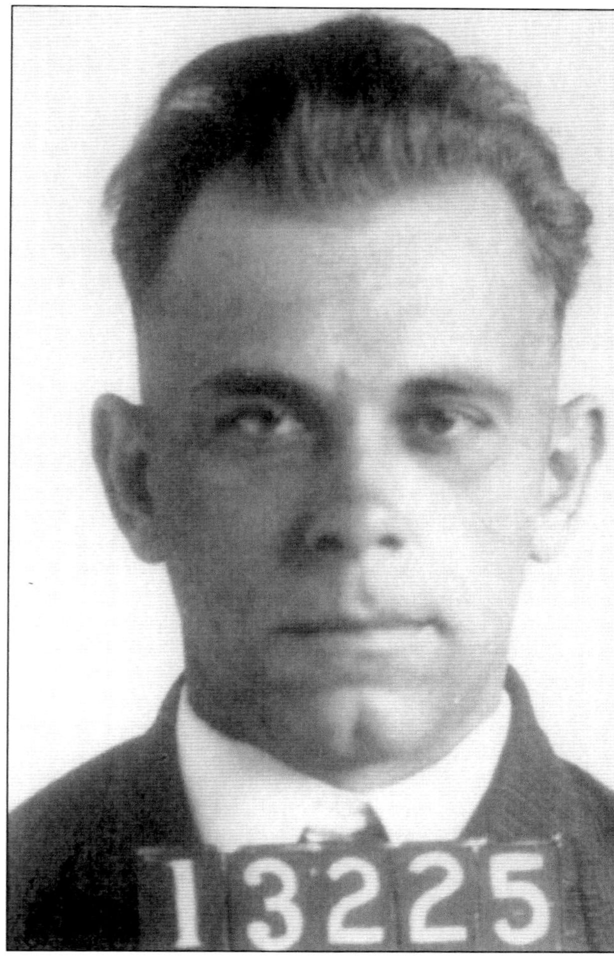

On January 15, 1934, bank robber John Dillinger held up the First National Bank on the corner of Chicago and Forsyth Avenues, getting away with $22,500 and allegedly killing police officer William O'Malley during his getaway. His trial date, set for March 12, 1934, had to be postponed, as Dillinger broke out of the Crown Point, Indiana, jail on March 3, 1934. (Courtesy of the South Shore Convention and Visitors Authority.)